THE POLITICS OF LANGUAGE CONTACT IN THE HIMALAYA

The Politics of Language Contact in the Himalaya

Edited by Selma K. Sonntag and Mark Turin

https://www.openbookpublishers.com

© 2019 Selma K. Sonntag and Mark Turin. Copyright of individual chapters is maintained by the chapters' authors.

This work is licensed under a Creative Commons Attribution 4.0 International license (CC BY 4.0). This license allows you to share, copy, distribute and transmit the text; to adapt the text and to make commercial use of the text providing attribution is made to the authors (but not in any way that suggests that they endorse you or your use of the work). Attribution should include the following information:

Selma K. Sonntag and Mark Turin (eds.), *The Politics of Language Contact in the Himalaya*. Cambridge, UK: Open Book Publishers, 2019, https://doi.org/10.11647/OBP.0169

In order to access detailed and updated information on the license, please visit, https://doi.org/10.11647/OBP.0169#copyright

Further details about CC BY licenses are available at, https://creativecommons.org/licenses/by/4.0/

All external links were active at the time of publication unless otherwise stated and have been archived via the Internet Archive Wayback Machine at https://archive.org/web

Updated digital material and resources associated with this volume are available at https://doi.org/10.11647/OBP.0169#resources

Every effort has been made to identify and contact copyright holders and any omission or error will be corrected if notification is made to the publisher.

ISBN Paperback: 978-1-78374-704-7
ISBN Hardback: 978-1-78374-705-4
ISBN Digital (PDF): 978-1-78374-706-1
ISBN Digital ebook (epub): 978-1-78374-707-8
ISBN Digital ebook (mobi): 978-1-78374-708-5
ISBN XML: 978-1-78374-709-2
DOI: 10.11647/OBP.0169

Cover image: Edward Lear, *Kinchinjunga* (1877). Yale Center for British Art, public domain, https://collections.britishart.yale.edu/vufind/Record/1670566
Cover design: Anna Gatti.

Contents

Contributors   vii
Preface   xi

Introduction: Language Politics and Language Contact   1
Selma K. Sonntag

1. Language Contact and the Politics of Recognition amongst   17
   Tibetans in the People's Republic of China:
   The rTa'u-Speaking 'Horpa' of Khams
   Tunzhi (Sonam Lhundrop), Hiroyuki Suzuki, and Gerald Roche

    Vertical and Horizontal Politics of Language Contact in Tibet   17
    The rTa'u-speaking 'Horpa': Ambiguous Origins   20
    and Shifting Polysemy
    rTa'u-speakers and Contemporary Tibetan Language Politics   30
    Conclusion   40

2. What Happened to the Ahom Language? The Politics of   49
   Language Contact in Assam
   Selma K. Sonntag

    The Mandala State   52
    The Ahom Kingdom   57
    The Colonial State   66
    The Modern State   70
    Conclusion   74

3. **Transforming Language to Script: Constructing Linguistic Authority through Language Contact in Schools in Nepal**   79
Uma Pradhan

    Linguistic Authority Through Language Contact   81
    Writing Language, Claiming "Authenticity"   85
    Language, Dialect, and Making "Corrections"   93
    Language, Script, and Social Acceptability   98
    Language, Education and Frames of "Legitimacy"   102
    Conclusion   105

4. **The Significance of Place in Ethnolinguistic Vitality: Spatial Variations Across the Kaike-Speaking Diaspora of Nepal**   109
Maya Daurio

    Kaike Speakers   110
    Language and Identity   115
    Intergenerational Transmission   126
    Conclusion   130

5. **Speaking Chone, Speaking 'Shallow': Dual Linguistic Hegemonies in China's Tibetan Frontier**   137
Bendi Tso and Mark Turin

    The Shape of Linguistic Hegemony: Coercion and Consent   138
    Situating Chone County in Time and Place   140
    Research Methods and Subject Position   144
    Coercion as an Aspect of Linguistic Hegemony   145
    The Role of Consent in Shaping Linguistic Hegemony   154
    Conclusion   159

6. **Concluding Thoughts on Language Shift and Linguistic Diversity in the Himalaya: The Case of Nepal**   163
Mark Turin

List of Tables and Figures   177
Index   179

Contributors

Bendi Tso completed a Master of Arts in Anthropology at the Chinese University of Hong Kong in 2016. She is currently a Ph.D. Candidate in Anthropology at the University of British Columbia. Her research interests lie in linguistic nationalism, linguistic identities, and language ideologies. Her current research explores how the ideology of 'authentic Tibetanness' — the idea that speaking Tibetan is taken as a claim to be an authentic Tibetan person — has been played out among Chone Tibetans in Kanlho Tibetan Autonomous Prefecture by the Chinese state and by Tibetan ethno-nationalists. Her research also examines the ways in which Chone Tibetans engage, mediate, resist, and reject such ideology based on their own linguistic realities and experiences, in history and at present.

Maya Daurio earned a Master of Science in Geography from the University of Montana, where her research focused on language maintenance and social-ecological resilience within an endangered language community in Nepal. She has worked for over eight years in Geographic Information Systems (GIS) and is interested in anthropological, ecological, and humanitarian applications of GIS. Concurrent research interests include language endangerment and maintenance, traditional ecological knowledge, social-ecological resilience, indigeneity, and mountain geographies. Maya will be pursuing a doctorate in Anthropology at the University of British Columbia.

Uma Pradhan is Leverhulme Early Career Research Fellow at Oxford School for Global and Area Studies, University of Oxford. Prior to this, Uma was a Postdoctoral Research Fellow at the Department of

Education Anthropology, Aarhus University, Copenhagen. Uma's research focuses on power-laden dimensions of education and examines the interconnection between state, society, and schooling. Uma holds a DPhil in International Development from the University of Oxford, where she studied the cultural politics of minority language use in schools. She received the Dor Bahadur Bista Prize 2015 and Nations and Nationalism Prize 2018 for articles based on this research. Before joining academia, Uma worked in the development sector for several years.

Gerald Roche is a Senior Research Fellow in the Department of Politics, Media, and Philosophy at La Trobe University, and has previously held positions at the University of Melbourne, Uppsala University, and Qinghai Normal University. His research focuses on the politics of language endangerment and revitalization, particularly within Tibet and the Himalayas. Recent edited publications include the *Routledge Handbook of Language Revitalization* (with Leanne Hinton and Leena Huss) and two open access publications: *Indigenous Efflorescence: Beyond Revitalization in Sapmi and Ainu Mosir* (with Hiroshi Maruyama and Isa Virdi-Kroik), and *Long Narrative Songs from the Mongghul of Northeast Tibet: Texts in Mongghul, Chinese, and English* (with Limusishiden).

Selma K. Sonntag is Professor Emerita of Politics at Humboldt State University in California and Affiliate Professor of Political Science at the University of Colorado, Boulder. Her research area is the politics of language, primarily in South Asia, but also in the United States, Europe and South Africa. Her numerous publications on language politics in South Asia have appeared in *Language Policy, The Journal of Commonwealth and Comparative Politics*, and *Nationalism and Ethnic Politics*, among other journals, as well as in over a dozen edited volumes. Her books include *The Local Politics of Global English: Case Studies in Linguistic Globalization* (2003) and *State Traditions and Language Regimes* (2015). Dr. Sonntag was a Research Fellow at the Jawaharlal Nehru Institute for Advanced Studies in New Delhi in spring 2012 and the recipient of two Fulbright research awards. She recently completed her tenure as chair of the Research Committee on the Politics of Language of the International Political Science Association.

Hiroyuki Suzuki holds a D.Litt. in linguistics from Kyoto University (2007) and is currently a post-doctoral researcher at the Department of

Culture Studies and Oriental Languages, University of Oslo, Norway, and a visiting scholar at the National Museum of Ethnology, Osaka, Japan. His principal research interests are descriptive linguistics, geolinguistics, dialectology, and sociolinguistics of languages in the Tibetosphere. He has published various works on preliminary descriptions of individual Tibetic languages, grammar sketches, geolinguistic analysis, and narrative analysis with interlinear glossing. He is an author of two books: *Dongfang Zangqu Zhuyuyan Yanjiu* (2015) and *100 Linguistic Maps of the Swadesh Word List of Tibetic Languages From Yunnan* (2018).

Tunzhi (Sonam Lhundrop) is a Ph.D. student in linguistics at La Trobe University, Australia. He is writing a descriptive grammar of the rTa'u language, a rGyalrongic language spoken in western Sichuan Province, China. He is a native of the rTa'u community and for the last decade he has been engaged in language and cultural documentation projects.

Mark Turin is an anthropologist, linguist and occasional radio presenter. An Associate Professor of Anthropology at the University of British Columbia, Mark has held research and teaching appointments at Yale, Cambridge, Cornell and Leipzig universities. He directs the World Oral Literature Project, an urgent global initiative to document and make accessible endangered oral literatures before they disappear without record, and the Digital Himalaya Project, which he co-founded in 2000 as a platform to make multimedia resources from the Himalayan region widely available online. Mark has worked in the Himalayan region (Nepal, northern India and Bhutan) since 1992 and is the author or co-author of four books, numerous articles, the editor of nine volumes, and edits a series on oral literature.

Preface

Sameness and difference.

Language is what makes us human, yet languages are also what differentiate us.

The linguistic condition of our species is perhaps no better illustrated than in the Himalaya. As depicted in Edward Lear's timeless painting of Kanchenjunga that graces the cover of this volume, the snow-capped mountains seem like formidable barriers and the foothills an impenetrable jungle to human — and hence language — contact. Yet the mountain range that forms the Himalayan chain is majestic, the foothills and valleys lush, and the high-altitude plateaus expansive — a seeming invitation to human interaction and linguistic exchange. While the geographical determination of linguistic commonality and difference is acute in the Himalayan region, most of the barriers and overtures to language contact are political, particularly with the advent of colonialism, modernity and globalization.

This original and timely collection brings together case studies from salient areas of the Himalayan region — Tibet (China), Assam (India) and Nepal — focused on the politics of language contact. Promoting a historically grounded and theoretically informed perspective, *The Politics of Language Contact in the Himalaya* offers nuanced insights into language and its relation to power in this geopolitically complex region. As editors, we are confident that it will be essential reading for researchers in the fields of language policy and planning, applied linguistics, and language and literary education. The detailed introduction and concluding commentary make the collection accessible to all social scientists concerned with questions of language, and we anticipate that the book as a whole will be of interest to scholars in anthropology, sociolinguistics, political science and Asian studies.

The Politics of Language Contact in the Himalaya is, in many ways, the realization of a decades-long scholarly exchange between us, the editors, about our mutual research interests and experiences in the Himalaya, an exchange made all the more stimulating because of our different disciplinary backgrounds (political science and linguistic anthropology). The 5th Himalayan Studies Conference in Boulder, Colorado in September 2017, provided the ideal scholarly forum at which to launch this new phase of our collaboration: we convened a double-panel session of early-career and established scholars to explore language and politics in the Himalaya. The lively discussion among panel participants and conference attendees was critical to enriching the five new research contributions which comprise this volume. Without the efforts of the Conference Organizing Committee, the Association for Nepal and Himalayan Studies which organizes the regular Himalayan Studies Conferences, and the local conference sponsor, the Center for Asian Studies at the University of Colorado, Boulder, this collection would not be as timely or rich as it is.

We are grateful to a number of people and organizations who helped to bring this book into being. First of all, our thanks to the editorial team and staff at Open Book Publishers, for their professionalism and enduring commitment to reshaping the present and the future of academic publishing. In addition, we have benefitted a great deal from the assistance of Vicki Sear and Erin Guntly, both graduate students at the University of British Columbia, whose careful attention to detail has strengthened the editorial process. We are particularly indebted to Meredith Reba at the Yale School of Forestry and Environmental Studies who designed the map showing the locations of the speech communities covered in this collection.

We would also like to thank the anonymous reviewers who generously gave of their time and insights to strengthen this collection through their constructive feedback. Thanks as well to all of the contributors who submitted their work to this collection: we have enjoyed working with each of you and have learned more about the linguistic richness and diversity of the Himalayan region as a result.

Both of us are fortunate to be part of university communities with fast-growing initiatives that focus on the Himalayan region — the

Tibet Himalaya Initiative at the University of Colorado, Boulder, and the Himalaya Program at the University of British Columbia. We have benefitted enormously from the scholarly networks of faculty, staff, students and community partners that these two initiatives have catalyzed and are grateful to the efforts of our colleagues for nurturing such programs. Finally, our thanks go to you — the reader — for picking up this volume in paper or digital format, and for engaging with the ideas that it contains.

Selma K. Sonntag and Mark Turin
July 2019

Introduction: Language Politics and Language Contact

Selma K. Sonntag

Language politics has always been inherently interdisciplinary, as highlighted by the range of disciplines contributing to and represented in the field — and linguistics and political science are not always the primary ones. The scope of the field is further enlarged by the two different ways that the phrase 'language politics' can be parsed: the *language of politics* versus the *politics of language*. The *language of politics* traces its contemporary roots to George Orwell's celebrated and still relevant novel, *1984*. The study of the manipulation of politics and political attitudes through language, i.e., through choice of words, labels and metaphors as well as grammatical and syntactical structures (e.g., passive versus active voice), gained momentum beginning in the 1980s — appropriate timing given its Orwellian roots — when the linguist George Lakoff promoted the notion of 'framing.' How political issues are 'framed' often determines the parameters of political debate in the public sphere. Dalits throughout South Asia, including the Himalaya, raised their voice in the public sphere by rejecting Mahatma Gandhi's paternalistic framing of them as *Harijan* and the more pejorative label of 'Untouchables' in favor of the agonistic term, 'oppressed' (*dalit*). The framing of local activity against big commercial logging in the Garhwal Himalaya in the 1970s as an environmental movement — the *Chipko andolan* — spread the now renowned 'tree-hugging' trope far beyond the western mountains of the Himalaya (Rangan 2000; DeLoach, Bruner and Gossett 2002). In effect, Lakoff ignited the study of the language of politics in a number of disciplines, including enthusiasm for Critical Discourse Analysis (CDA) in linguistics. Political science was a laggard in embracing the linguistic turn, despite political communication having a long pedigree in the discipline dating back to Harold Laswell, most famous for defining politics as 'who gets what, when and how' in the 1930s.

Political science has also lagged behind other disciplines in the study of the *politics of language*, a field which has come to be populated primarily by applied linguists and sociolinguists under the rubric of Language Policy and Planning (LPP). Thomas Ricento's (2016) four-volume anthology of LPP, published in the series *Critical Concepts in Linguistics*, attests to the growing prominence of the field. The origins of LPP can be traced back to the post-World-War-II decolonization period with the emergence of newly independent, dubbed 'developing', countries. The seminal LPP volume *Language Problems of Developing Nations*, edited by Joshua Fishman, Charles Ferguson and Jyotirindra Das Gupta, appeared in 1968. The choice of language(s) to use in education and administration, among other sectors, in these new nations was typically perceived as a problem needing to be solved by rational planning using 'technical tools for choosing among several alternatives' (Rubin and Jernudd 1971: xiv). Linguists were enlisted for corpus development; they were often joined by other social scientists for the more politically fraught status development in the language planning process. The few political scientists who ventured into the field (see Sonntag 1996 for a list) tended to recommend monolingual language policies or a dual language policy which retained the former colonial language along with a dominant 'native' language. These language policy recommendations were for the most part informed by modernization theory, the mantra of which was that modern nations functioned more efficiently and engendered national loyalty when they adopted policies that promoted societal and individual monolingualism.

The growing critique of modernization theory in the 1970s affected the LPP field, with critical sociolinguistics taking the lead over the more traditional disciplines (Ricento 2000). Critical sociolinguists undertook and published in-depth, nuanced case studies of the politics surrounding language policy choices (see, e.g., Phillipson, Skutnabb-Kangas and

Africa 1986; Tollefson 1986). Many of these were descriptive rather than theoretically-driven, for there was no common theoretical approach in the LPP field to replace modernization theory, despite some dabbling in post-structuralism (Clayton 1999). Recently, the study of the politics of language has been invigorated by political theory, in particular by normative theorists who focus on multiculturalism. In 2003, in the *Annual Review of Applied Linguistics*, Will Kymlicka and Alan Patten announced that 'political theorists in the last few years have started to take an interest in issues of language policy' (Kymlicka and Patten 2003a: 3). That same year, they published an edited volume, *Language Rights and Political Theory* (2003b), launching a prominent intervention into the LPP field by a subfield of political science that heretofore had been absent. Political scientists other than normative theorists have also recently been developing theoretical frameworks for analyzing language politics (see, e.g., Sonntag and Cardinal 2015) that resonate with efforts by LPP scholars (see, e.g., Tollefson 1991).

The present volume reflects and contributes to this burgeoning, interdisciplinary discussion of both theoretical approaches and nuanced case studies in the study of language politics. While the contributors come from an array of traditional disciplines — linguistics, political science, anthropology, geography — all work, and some were trained, in disciplinary interstices. Most are emerging scholars, embarking on research careers that will continue to bridge disciplines. The book is also grounded in the multidisciplinary nature of area studies, focusing on the Himalaya, a transborder region offering a rich bounty of case studies. The contributors all presented, or had planned to present, papers at the 5th Himalayan Studies Conference in Boulder, Colorado, 1–4 September 2017. In their Himalayan case studies, the locations of which are depicted on the map in Figure 0.1, the contributors focus on the second parsing of language politics, the *politics of language*, but they also draw upon the language of politics, or more precisely how language politics is framed by different agents.

A distinctive feature of this book is that all of the contributions address the politics of language *contact*. This welcome feature brings to the scholarly discussion on language politics a more nuanced understanding of language(s) and their relation to power than is often found in traditional social science analyses. For example, in recent

Fig. 0.1 Map of the Himalaya region: areas discussed in this volume highlighted in blue. Created by Meredith Reba, CC BY.

econometric analyses of the politics of language, political scientists and economists (e.g., Ginsburg and Weber 2011; Laitin and Ramachandran 2016) have latched onto 'language distance,' originally proposed by the linguist Joseph Greenberg (1956), as an independent variable with little understanding of the concept's limitations in multilingual environments. In contrast, the focus on language contact in this volume allows for the rich, contextual analyses that area studies afford. In the context of South Asia, the concept of language contact is attuned to Murray Emeneau's (1956) ground-breaking article on India as a linguistic area, published in the same issue of the journal, *Language*, as Greenberg's language-distance article. The insights that interdisciplinary, area-studies scholars can bring to the study of the language politics are significant, as this volume clearly demonstrates.

In the formulation adopted in this book, language contact is a historical constant. However, the multilingualism that language contact generates — whether individual or societal multilingualism — is always contingent (see also Heugh and Stroud 2018). This contingency is primarily dependent on the power dynamics among those in contact. Hence the notion of language contact neither compels a rigid categorization of languages as objects, as they are treated in many social science analyses of language politics (e.g., Liu 2015), nor does it dissolve the category of language as is common among postmodernist renditions (e.g., Makoni and Pennycook 2005; Wee 2011). The first contribution to this volume, 'Language Contact and the Politics of Recognition Amongst Tibetans in China: The rTa'u-Speaking "Horpa" of Khams' by Tunzhi (Sonam Lhundrop), Hiroyuki Suzuki and Gerald Roche, begins by developing the notion of language contact along two dimensions: a horizontal dimension (associated more with linguistics) and a vertical dimension (which brings into focus power dynamics). The authors argue that both dimensions in concert make up the politics of language contact. They then proceed to demonstrate how a rigid categorization of the rTa'u language spoken in the eastern stretches of Tibet can impede a politics of recognition as expatiated by political theorists who expound on multiculturalism. They also warn against the postmodern inclination of dismissing rTa'u as a language, concluding that this would equally impede the politics of recognition for its speakers. According to their analysis, recognition entails not only the politics of language but the language of politics, that is, how rTa'u is labeled in public and academic discourse.

While the authors of this first contribution draw on political theory in their case study of the politics of language contact in the Himalaya, I take a historical-institutionalist approach developed in comparative politics in my chapter, the second in this collection, entitled 'What Happened to the Ahom Language? Language Politics in Assam.' In this contribution I analyze the language shift from a Tai-Kadai language to Indo-Aryan Assamese in the precolonial Ahom kingdom in Northeastern India. While the power dynamics of language shift, a well-established concept in the LPP field (see, e.g., Fishman 1964), usually entails speakers of a subordinate language abandoning their language for the dominant language (see the other chapters in this volume), in the Ahom case those in power abandoned their language in preference of another language in the kingdom's multilingual environment. I employ the concepts of state tradition and language regime to analyze how and why, in the Ahom kingdom, language shift defied the expected trajectory of power dynamics, in which those in power impose their language on their subordinates. Like the first chapter in this book, my contribution problematizes a rigid, genealogical classification of languages. By analyzing the politics of language contact in a historical context, I also expose the implicit assumptions about power and language that tend to adhere to studies of language politics bound to the nation-state model. Throughout the collection, the contributors' focus on the constant of language contact confirms the contingency of the nation-state's monolingual model. This shifts our understanding of the politics of language away from positing monolingualism as the norm, toward multilingualism as both the individual and societal default — what Kathleen Heugh and Christopher Stroud (2018: 1) call a 'southern lens […] for understanding multilingualism.'

In the book's third chapter, entitled 'Transforming Language to Script: Constructing Linguistic Authority through Language Contact in Schools in Nepal,' Uma Pradhan examines the power dynamics — which she conceptualizes as 'linguistic authority' drawing on Pierre Bourdieu's theoretical framework — of language contact in education in contemporary Nepal. Nepal's new policy of MultiLingual Education (MLE) is generating new sites and types of language contact, as Pradhan outlines in her description of the adoption of multilingual textbooks in a school in the southern Tarai region. In the following chapter, entitled

'The Significance of Place in Ethnolinguistic Vitality: Spatial Variations Across the Kaike-Speaking Diaspora of Nepal,' Maya Daurio discusses another prominent feature of the politics of language contact in Nepal: mobility and internal migration. Daurio's case study focuses on the rural-urban dynamics of Kaike speakers in and from the Dolpa region in western Nepal. In addition to a spatial dynamic, Daurio employs a temporal one, showing how the politics of language contact has changed for Kaike speakers over the decades since Jim Fisher's (1986) original anthropological work in the same area.

In their contribution, 'Speaking Chone, Speaking "Shallow": Dual Linguistic Hegemonies in China's Tibetan Frontier,' Bendi Tso and Mark Turin use prolonged language contact between Chone Tibetan and other Tibetan languages, as well as Chinese, as a backdrop to introduce other key concepts in the politics of language. They problematize the concept of 'linguistic hegemony' to demonstrate that the usual binary of dominant versus subordinate/minority language common in research on language politics and particularly in the Language Policy and Planning (LPP) field (see, e.g., Wright 2004) is more complicated in the context of language contact. They develop the notion of 'dual hegemonies' to capture the complex hierarchy of languages in the border region where Tibet interfaces with non-Tibetan populations, particularly with Han Chinese. The language hierarchies they expose are hegemonic in that they are established through coercion and consent — through language policies and ideologies. Their focus on language policy as well as language ideology provides for a more robust analysis than Critical Discourse Analysis (CDA) studies (see Blommaert and Bulcaen 2000) which tend to be limited to ideological representations in documents and other public discourse. Conceiving of language policy as the institutionalization, and not only the representation, of language ideology (Sonntag and Cardinal 2015: 8) enables the authors to analyze the role of language practices stemming from language policies, such as adult literacy programs, in the hegemonic establishment of language hierarchy. The authors of the first chapter of this volume make a similar point about language hierarchies: relying only on a critical analysis of their ideological construction often misses how speakers of the subordinate language(s) consent to and actively seek recognition rather than reject hegemony. These two contributions — the first and the last of the book, and both on the politics of language contact in Tibet — suggest that the counter-hegemonic agency that critical sociolinguists (e.g., Canagarajah 1999; Pennycook 1995) tend to impute to non-dominant language speakers can be quite ephemeral.

The endurance of established language hierarchies is a theme addressed throughout the volume. Uma Pradhan's analysis in her chapter suggests that an upheaval or reversal of the historically prevailing language hierarchy in Nepal is unlikely, despite the opening — what I would call a 'critical juncture' — provided by Nepal's new MLE policy. Only when established language hierarchies are disrupted because of a significant change in the power dynamics — which, according to Uma Pradhan and others (e.g., Turin 2006), hasn't yet happened in Nepal, notwithstanding its new political regime — is it likely that a new language hierarchy will emerge. In the case study that I present of the Ahom kingdom's shift from a Tai-Kadai language to Indo-Aryan Assamese, the critical juncture marked the expansion of the ranks of the elite hierarchy to include Assamese speakers, causing Assamese to be valued over the Ahom language. Focusing on the local level in her case study in a relatively isolated rural area in Nepal, Maya Daurio demonstrates that power dynamics can change and evolve to alter a local language hierarchy. Uma Pradhan's analysis also indicates that there is space at the local level for negotiating linguistic authority, albeit within the context of the prevailing linguistic hierarchy implicit in Nepal's national framework for education.

While the focus of Maya Daurio's study is the linguistic vitality of Kaike — much improved in recent decades from what Jim Fisher (1986) worried was a dying language — all of the contributions in this book at least touch upon the theme of language vitality and language loss. Perhaps the most dramatic case of language loss among those covered in this volume is that of the Ahom language in upper Assam, providing a fitting title for my case study: 'What Happened to the Ahom Language?' Unlike the other cases of language loss discussed in this book, Ahom was not a subordinate or bottom-of-the-hierarchy language. I explain the loss in terms of, in effect, the erosion of state traditions that had fostered a non-territorially-demarcated multilingual environment with a very high degree of language contact. Incorporation in territorially-defined modern 'nation-states' with their 'monoglot nationalism' — as

Tunzhi (Sonam Lhundrop), Hiroyuki Suzuki and Gerald Roche put it in their contribution to this collection — has been the bane of linguistic diversity. This is amply demonstrated by the two contributions on Tibet in this volume which highlight the impending language loss of rTa'u and Chone Tibetan. As the authors of the first chapter note, Tibet is 'typically viewed as linguistically homogeneous,' leading to a somewhat simplistic view of language politics in Tibet as that of a Tibetan language endangered by Chinese linguistic hegemony. Such a narrow reading belittles, albeit most likely unintentionally, a serious concern over the loss of internal Tibetan linguistic diversity.

In Nepal, where the nation-state was 'imagined' fairly early (in the eighteenth century), language loss — although not language contact — was somewhat impeded by the relative lack of infrastructure in a predominantly rural environment, at least until the era of *bikas* (modernity/development), which started in the 1950s. More recently, fitting Nepal's linguistic diversity into discrete, identifiable 'languages' that can be preserved and even revitalized has been a formidable undertaking in the Nepalese nation-state's transition from a monolingual to at least a nominally multilingual language regime (see Sonntag 1995). The hope is that this new regime will stem language loss, but as Uma Pradhan points out, in Nepal's new MLE, identifying the languages to be saved involves 'transform[ing] language to script,' as the title of her contribution to this book indicates. In the context of Nepali linguistic hegemony, she demonstrates that this transformation results in a heavy dose of Nepali inserted into the local Tharu language to make the newly written Tharu in the textbooks *rāmro* (good). According to Pradhan, what connotes 'good' language in this case is the visual impact of language contact between dominant (e.g., Nepali) and subordinate (e.g., Tharu) written languages.

The complex relation between the spoken and written forms of language contact is an important element in language politics, as is well demonstrated in this volume. One aspect of the relationship on which several contributions expound is linguistic purity. Tunzhi (Sonam Lhundrop), Hiroyuki Suzuki and Gerald Roche observe that written Tibetan serves as the benchmark of purity and authenticity for Tibetans, hence the source of loanwords in the hierarchically subordinate rTa'u language whose speakers seek recognition as Tibetan. But such borrowing also marks the rTa'u as not an authentic Tibetan language, further impeding its speakers' claims to be Tibetan. In their chapter, Bendi Tso and Mark Turin explain that Chone Tibetan speakers attribute what they perceive as their language's 'shallowness' to the high number of Chinese loan words. In contrast, Amdo Tibetan, standardized in written form by the Chinese government for use in schools and administration, is perceived to be more authentically Tibetan. Both of the chapters on the politics of language contact in Tibet in this book demonstrate how linguistic purity reinforces and reflects linguistic hierarchy. Uma Pradhan's research suggests that incorporating loan words from the dominant language can help elevate the status of the subordinate language. In this case, Nepali loan words help 'sanitize' Tharu.

The power of the written standard language over spoken language is a common theme in this book, as the above examples suggest. As Uma Pradhan observes in her chapter, '"Writing" [...] became a way to prevent a language from being labelled as a dialect of another language.' In my contribution, I note that an important aspect of the critical juncture marking the shift from Tai-Kadai Ahom to Indo-Aryan Assamese was when court chronicles started to be written in Assamese by new entrants into the ruling hierarchy who were literate in Assamese. Yet the relationship between written and spoken language(s) is often muddled or overlooked by scholars of language politics. Political scientists tend to conflate the written and spoken language (e.g., Laitin and Ramachandran 2016) and LPP scholars tend to wall off their discipline from literary studies where written language is the focus. The chapters in this volume help overcome these deficits in the study of language politics by, as Pradhan puts it, 'drawing attention to the often-overlooked dynamics of written language contact' and contributing to a further broadening of the field of language politics through a more interdisciplinary lens.

This book also addresses the relationship between language and ethnicity, a topic which tends to be overdetermined in scholarship on language politics (May 2008: 8). The contributions demonstrate that this relationship, like the multilingualism generated by language contact, is temporally and spatially contingent. Maya Daurio's chapter illustrates the spatial contingency of ethnolinguistic identity: diasporic Kaike speakers tend to identify their language as a marker of their ethnicity more so than those who remain in the Tichurong Valley in Dolpa. Furthermore, both diasporic and valley-dwelling Kaike speakers identify Kaike as their language and not their ethnicity. Instead they identify ethnically as Tarali — which Daurio points out can also cover non-Kaike-speaking Tichurong residents. Identification with their larger ethnic group, the Magars of Nepal, is even less common, particularly for Tichurong residents. When Kaike speakers do identify as Magar, it is primarily for instrumental reasons. The temporal contingency of the relation between language and ethnic identity is highlighted in the first two chapters of the volume. Tunzhi (Sonam Lhundrop), Hiroyuki Suzuki and Gerald Roche analyze the exonyms used for rTa'u speakers which historically identify them as non-Tibetan. Yet rTa'u speakers self-identify as Tibetans. This self-identification, argue the authors, should be recognized and respected, no matter that rTa'u can be linguistically classified as a non-Tibetan language. As Mark Turin (2018: 265) has contended, 'There is no reason that communities should be expected to define or categorize themselves based upon externally imposed linguistic criteria that have a lot to say about grammar but nothing to say about belonging.' In my chapter, I argue that the Ahom were not an ethnic group, and linguistic identity was not a meaningful identifier of belonging in precolonial Assam, despite the intensity of ethnolinguistic identity in Assam today. The 'essentializing link between language and identity,' as Tunzhi (Sonam Lhundrop), Hiroyuki Suzuki and Gerald Roche put it in their contribution, is a colonial and modern nation-state construct. Most states engaged in nation-building have attempted to link national identity to a single language, resulting in language policies that promoted monolingualism. This clearly was the case in Nepal, as Uma Pradhan demonstrates in her contribution. Only recently has the Nepali state entertained demands for mother-tongue education, legalizing multilingual education practices of the type that Pradhan details in her chapter. Her analysis indicates that the process of transforming the mother tongue of Tharus into a Tharu language to be used in schools belies a simple equation between language and ethnicity.

The scholarly enterprise of mapping ethnicities onto languages or languages onto ethnicities is not the straightforward, objective activity that is often assumed in studies of ethnolinguistic politics, particularly those that negatively correlate ethnolinguistic diversity within a nation with poor national economic performance (e.g., Easterly and Levine 1997; Liu 2015). Situating their case study in a key transborder region, Bendi Tso and Mark Turin demonstrate the limitations of confining analyses of the relationship between language and ethnicity to the national context. According to their research, Chone Tibetans tend to evaluate their language in terms of both the Tibetan ethnolinguistic context and the Chinese national context. Both contexts devalue Chone Tibetan, a politics of language that can best be understood by focusing on language contact, as exemplified throughout this volume. This lack of isomorphism between language and ethnicity — so apparent in the Himalaya — should be the starting point, the basic assumption, of scholarly analyses of language politics. As Mark Turin (2018: 264) argues, scholarly 'thinking that fuses ethnicity together with language' is not only sloppy but potentially 'dangerous' to adducing the politics of language by neglecting the role of language contact in group identity (see also Wee 2018). Recent work on language politics elsewhere (see, e.g., Albaugh and de Luna 2018 on Africa) similarly challenges the assumption of the universality of a one-to-one correspondence between language and ethnicity — an assumption that emanates from the historical experience of the West/North. In this regard, this volume, based in interdisciplinary area studies, makes an important contribution to the study of language politics beyond the Himalaya. To quote Turin (2018: 263) again, 'the collapsing of ethnicity and language into one category [is] a "political act".'

The themes of language contact, language and ethnicity, written and spoken forms of language, purity and authenticity, linguistic hegemony and hierarchy, and language vitality and language loss that are addressed in the contributions to this book in the context of Himalayan area studies are crucial to advancing our understanding of language politics. The interdisciplinary nature of the volume is a vital ingredient to this advancement, in both the Himalaya and beyond.

References

Albaugh, Ericka A. and de Luna, Kathryn M. 2018. 'Toward an Interdisciplinary Perspective on Language Movement and Change,' in *Tracing Language Movement in Africa*, ed. by Ericka A. Albaugh and Kathryn M. de Luna (New York: Oxford University Press), pp. 1–25.

Blommaert, Jan and Bulcaen, Chris. 2000. 'Critical Discourse Analysis,' *Annual Review of Anthropology* 29 (October): 447–66.

Canagarajah, A. Suresh. 1999. *Resisting Linguistic Imperialism in English Teaching* (Oxford: Oxford University Press).

Clayton, Thomas. 1999. 'Decentering Language in World-System Inquiry,' *Language Problems & Language Planning* 23 (2): 133–56.

DeLoach, Mark, Michael S. Bruner and John S. Gossett. 2002. 'An Analysis of the 'Tree-Hugger' Label,' in *Enviropop: Studies in Environmental Rhetoric and Popular Culture*, ed. by Mark Meister and Phyllis M. Japp (Westport: Praeger), pp. 95–110.

Easterly, William and Levine, Ross. 1997. 'Africa's Growth Tragedy: Policies and Ethnic Divisions,' *Quarterly Journal of Economics* 112: 1203–50.

Emeneau, Murray. 1956. 'India as a Linguistic Area,' *Language* 32: 3–16.

Fisher, James F. 1986. *Trans-Himalayan Traders*. Berkeley and Los Angeles: University of California Press.

Fishman, Joshua A., Charles A. Ferguson, and Jyotirindra Das Gupta (eds.). 1968. *Language Problems of Developing Nations* (New York: John Wiley & Sons).

Fishman, Joshua A. 1964. 'Language Maintenance and Language Shift as a Field of Inquiry,' *Linguistics* 2 (9): 32–70.

Ginsburgh, Victor and Weber, Shlomo. 2011. *How Many Languages Do We Need? The Economics of Linguistic Diversity* (Princeton: Princeton University Press).

Greenburg, Joseph. 1956. 'The Measurement of Linguistic Diversity,' *Language* 32: 109–15.

Heugh, Kathleen and Stroud, Christopher. 2018. 'Diversities, Affinities and Diasporas: A Southern Lens and Methodology for Understanding Multilingualisms,' *Current Issues in Language Planning*, https://doi.org/10.1080/14664208.2018.1507543

Kymlicka, Will and Patten, Alan. 2003a. 'Language Rights and Political Theory,' *Annual Review of Applied Linguistics* 23: 3–21.

Kymlicka, Will and Patten, Alan. 2003b. *Language Rights and Political Theory* (Oxford: Oxford University Press).

Laitin, David D. and Ramachandran, Rajesh. 2016. 'Language Policy and Human Development,' *American Political Science Review* 110 (3) (August): 457–80.

Liu, Amy H. 2015. *Standardizing Diversity: The Political Economy of Language Regimes* (Philadelphia: University of Pennsylvania Press).

Makoni, Sinfree and Pennycook, Alastair. 2005. 'Disinventing and (Re) Constituting Languages,' *Critical Inquiry in Language Studies* 2 (3): 137–56.

May, Stephen. 2008. *Language and Minority Rights: Ethnicity, Nationalism and the Politics of Language* (New York and London: Routledge (Taylor & Francis Group)).

Pennycook, Alastair. 1995. 'English in the World/the World in English,' in *Power and Inequality in Language Education*, ed. by James W. Tollefson (Cambridge: Cambridge University Press), pp. 34–72.

Phillipson, Robert, Tove Skutnabb-Kangas and Hugh Africa. 1986. 'Namibian Educational Language Planning: English for Liberation or Neo-colonialism?', in *Language and Education in Multilingual Settings*, ed. by Bernard Spolsky (Clevedon: Multilingual Matters), pp. 77–95.

Rangan, Haripriya. 2000. *Of Myths and Movements: Rewriting Chipko Into Himalayan History* (London: Verso).

Ricento, Thomas. 2000. 'Historical and Theoretical Perspectives in Language Policy and Planning,' *Journal of Sociolinguistics* 4 (2): 196–213.

Ricento, Thomas (ed.). 2016. *Language Policy and Planning* (Critical Concepts in Linguistics series), Vols. I–IV (London and New York: Routledge (Taylor & Francis Group)).

Rubin, Joan and Jernudd, Björn H. 1971. 'Introduction: Language Planning as an Element in Modernization,' in *Can Language Be Planned? Sociolinguistic Theory and Practice for Developing Nations*, ed. by Joan Rubin and Björn H. Jernudd (Honolulu: The University Press of Hawai'i), pp. xiii–xxiv.

Sonntag, Selma K. and Cardinal, Linda. 2015. 'Introduction: State Traditions and Language Regimes: Conceptualizing Language Policy Choices,' in *State Traditions and Linguistic Regimes*, ed. by Linda Cardinal and Selma K. Sonntag (Montreal: McGill-Queens University Press, 2015), pp. 3–26.

Sonntag, Selma K. 1996. 'Political Science and Contact Linguistics,' in *Contact Linguistics: An International Handbook of Contemporary Research*, ed. by Hans Goebl, Peter H. Nelde, Zdeněk Stary and Wolfgang Wölck (Berlin: Walter de Gruyter), pp. 75–81.

Sonntag, Selma K. 1995. 'Ethnolinguistic Identity and Language Policy in Nepal,' *Nationalism and Ethnic Politics* 1 (4) (Winter): 116–28.

Tollefson, James W. 1986. 'Language Policy and the Radical Left in the Philippines: The New People's Army and it Antecedents', *Language Problems and Language Planning* 10: 177–89.

Tollefson, J. W. 1991. *Planning Language, Planning Inequality: Language Policy in the Community* (New York: Longman).

Turin, Mark. 2018. 'Situating Language, Recognizing Multilingualism: Linguistic Identities and Mother Tongue Attachment in Northeast India and the Region,' in *Geographies of Difference: Explorations in Northeast Indian Studies*, ed. by Mélani Vandenhelsten, Meenaxi Barkataki-Ruscheweyh and Bengt G. Karlsson (London and New York: Routledge (Taylor & Francis Group)), pp. 253–71.

Turin, Mark. 2006. 'Minority Language Policies and Politics in Nepal,' in *Lesser Known Languages in Nepal: Status and Policies, Case Studies and Applications of Information Technology*, ed. by Anju Saxena and Lars Borin (Berlin and New York: Mouton de Gruyter), pp. 161–74.

Wee, Lionel. 2011. *Language without Rights* (Oxford: Oxford University Press).

Wright, Sue. 2004. *Language Policy and Language Planning: From Nationalism to Globalization* (New York: Palgrave Macmillan).

1. Language Contact and the Politics of Recognition amongst Tibetans in the People's Republic of China
The rTa'u-Speaking 'Horpa' of Khams

Tunzhi (Sonam Lhundrop), Hiroyuki Suzuki, and Gerald Roche

Vertical and Horizontal Politics of Language Contact in Tibet

Language contact has both horizontal and vertical dimensions. The horizontal dimension refers to the exchange of linguistic features that takes place during language contact. This includes the flows of lexicon, phonemes, syntactic structures, and so on, that occur via practices of borrowing, code-switching, and the intergenerational transmission of languages acquired in adulthood. Over time, such horizontal exchanges lead to linguistic convergence, the emergence of creoles and pidgins, and the formation of language areas. The vertical dimension of language contact, meanwhile, refers to the ordering of populations into hierarchies according to their language practices, through various processes of domination and subordination (Grillo 1989). Whilst the horizontal dimension of language contact is primarily associated with convergence, the vertical dimension is associated with linguistic differentiation (Gal 2016) and language shift — the replacement of one language by another (Pauwels 2016).

Both horizontal and vertical dimensions of language contact influence one another, and both are inherently political. Regarding the horizontal dimension, we often see, for example, the existence of purist ideologies (Thomas 1991) underlying resistance to loanwords in accordance with the position of language varieties and their speakers in a vertical hierarchy; purism typically targets terms from threatening dominant languages, but is indifferent to borrowing from subordinate languages. The features that are exchanged in horizontal contact are also coded as indexing various types of vertically arranged categories of languages (beautiful/ugly, expressive/restrictive, etc.) and people (good/bad, superior/inferior, competent/incompetent, etc.) (Alim, Rickford, and Ball 2016; Piller 2016). The various interactions between the vertical and horizontal dimensions of language contact produce the multitude of language ecologies present today — the rich diversity of how multiple language forms are differentiated and organized in social and physical space (Haugen 2001).

In this chapter we focus on the vertical dimension of the politics of language contact, with a discussion of 'recognition' as a key process through which vertical sorting takes place in language contact situations. From within the vast literature on the politics of recognition, we focus on key sources in order to introduce how this concept can be used to think about the vertical dimension of language contact. Cillian McBride (2013) distinguishes two subtly distinct varieties of 'recognition', which we will gloss as 'individual recognition', and 'collective recognition' — we focus on the latter. Both concepts draw on Hegel's foundational work on the intersubjective nature of identity (Cudd 2006) — the way that individual and collective identities are formed through relationships with others, rather than arising from the inherent qualities of the individual or collective self. In this view, recognition by others is a key component of the development of self-identity. For theorists of collective recognition such as Charles Taylor and Nancy Fraser, the recognition of a person's belonging to a larger group is foundational to healthy identity formation. Injustice arises when such identities are denied (non-recognition) or are denied equal respect to mainstream identities (mis-recognition). Both non- and mis-recognition lead to various harms, including social exclusion, economic marginalization, interpersonal discrimination against members of non- and mis-recognized groups, and a distorted sense of self and self-worth. We argue that in the context of language contact and the creation of language hierarchies, language shift can also be viewed as a harm resulting from mis-recognition.

We examine recognition and the formation of language hierarchies in the Tibetan context. Although typically viewed as linguistically homogenous, with diversity existing only between dialects of a single Tibetan language, Tibet is actually home to significant linguistic diversity (Roche 2014, 2017). The region's language ecology is now dominated by the national language of the People's Republic of China (PRC), Putonghua, whilst an imagined, standard Tibetan language, represented by the written language, acts as a regionally dominant, but nationally minoritized, language. Meanwhile, this standard Tibetan language is positioned in a vertical hierarchy above the region's spoken Tibetic varieties (Tournadre 2014) and its minority (i.e., non-Tibetic) languages (Roche and Suzuki 2018). An important factor conditioning the prestige and vitality of these minority languages is their lack of official recognition by the Chinese state, which renders them invisible to formal language policy and planning initiatives (Roche and Yudru Tsomu 2018). However, in this article we do not discuss state policies and practices, but instead draw attention to another way in which Tibet's minority languages are subordinated in a language hierarchy — their mis-recognition by the 'mainstream' Tibetan population.

We examine the mis-recognition of Tibet's minority languages through an exploration of the case of the rTa'u language. rTa'u is spoken by approximately 45,000 people in western Sichuan Province, primarily in dKar mdzes (Ganzi) Tibetan Autonomous Prefecture. All its speakers are classified as Tibetans within the state's ethnic classification system, and also consider themselves as such. rTa'u has a long history of contact with Tibetan, as evidenced by the numerous Tibetan loanwords it contains (Wang 1970–71). However, this contact has intensified in the past three decades in the context of rapid, state-led development and increasing human mobility. A recent investigation into the vitality of rTa'u found it to be 'clearly endangered' (Tunzhi 2017), with widespread language shift towards Tibetan underway. rTa'u is widely known in the linguistic literature as Horpa, and Tunzhi (2017) has argued that the use of this exonym by linguists potentially contributes to rTa'u speakers' negative attitudes towards their language and thus also contributes to undermining the language's vitality. In this chapter, we extend this argument in two parts. First, we examine how debates about the origin of rTa'u speakers and the 'notorious ambivalence' (Wang 1970–71) of the term Hor both contribute to mis-recognition, insofar as they bring into question the rTa'u speaker's deeply-felt Tibetan identity. Secondly, we look at how this mis-recognition articulates with the broader position of rTa'u speakers in the context of contemporary debates and social movements amongst Tibetans in the PRC. We argue that this mis-recognition in two social domains — the academic and the everyday — contributes to the overall subordination of the rTa'u language within the Tibetan hierarchy of languages, which in turn is driving language shift.

In the conclusion, we examine the implications of these arguments for understanding language contact in Tibet and the Himalaya more broadly, addressing our conclusions to both analytical and normative concerns. Analytically, we argue that the concept of recognition, despite having been critiqued by both anthropologists and linguists, is nonetheless useful in understanding the politics of language contact. Secondly, our normative conclusions examine how a more nuanced consideration of the dynamics of recognition can be used to formulate ameliorative projects that could help foster linguistic diversity in the region, and reverse the widespread language shift currently underway throughout Tibet and the Himalaya; we contrast this perspective with current local approaches to language politics in Tibet, which are, as we show below, based in essentializing and purist discourses that are likely to be contributing to, rather than resisting, language loss.

The rTa'u-speaking 'Horpa': Ambiguous Origins and Shifting Polysemy

A great deal of scholarly attention in the PRC has been focused on placing rTa'u speakers within the broader Tibetan community. Within these debates, the fact that rTa'u speakers are Tibetans, but speak a non-Tibetan language, is viewed as a 'problem' that requires solving, often through historical investigations seeking a single baptismal origin for

1. Language Contact in Tibet

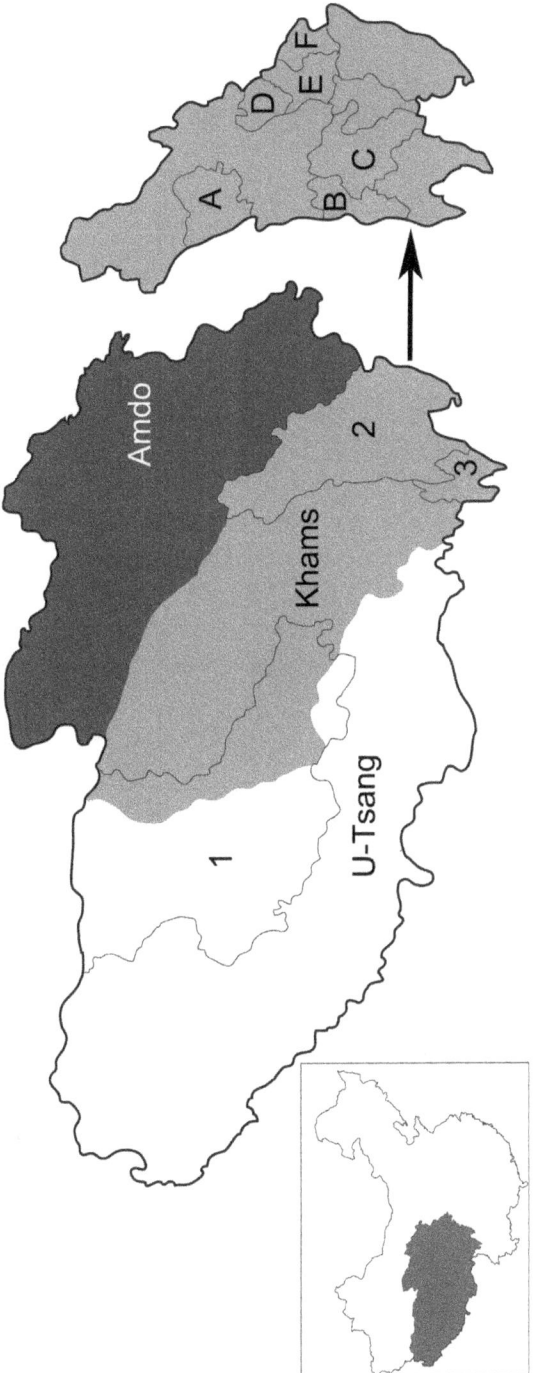

Fig. 1.1. Map of Tibet with cultural regions and prefectures. Created by the authors, CC BY.

This map shows major locations mentioned in this chapter. The inset (left) shows the location of the Tibetan Plateau within the People's Republic of China. The central map shows the Tibetan Plateau divided into three main cultural regions (Amdo, Khams, and U-Tsang), and also shows prefectures mentioned herein: 1) Nag chu; 2) dKar mdzes, and; 3) bDe chen. At right, dKar mdzes Prefecture is shown, with counties mentioned in the text: A) sDe dge; B) 'Ba' thang; C) Li thang; D) Brag 'go; E) rTa'u, and; F) Rong brag.

the population, which would supposedly resolve the issue of their contemporary identity. This search for a single origin is complicated by the polysemy of the term Hor that is applied to rTa'u speakers in literary Tibetan, and which is also used in Chinese and English texts to refer to their language. We argue that the search for origins, and the polysemy of Hor, are part of a broad regime of mis-recognition that does not take into account rTa'u speakers' professed identity as unproblematically Tibetan, despite their linguistic distinctiveness. Following, we briefly examine the main competing theories of the origins of the Horpa people before discussing the polysemy of the term Hor.

Numerous scholars trace the origin of rTa'u speakers to the Mongols, typically Eastern or Khalkha Mongols (Zeng 2006; Ren 1981; Gele 1988; Ganzi Xianzhi 1999; Daofu Xianzhi 1997). The Mongol invasion of what is now dKar mdzes Tibetan Autonomous Prefecture is an unequivocal historical fact. Proponents of the theory that rTa'u-speakers originate with Mongols trace the term Horpa directly to the legacy of having been invaded, and then ruled over, by Mongols, known as Hor, from the Yuan Dynasty (1271–1368) to the early Qing Dynasty (1644–1912) (Tunzhi 2017). Although no linguist today considers rTa'u to be a Mongolic language, there has nonetheless been speculation that rTa'u is related to Mongolian, such as in Zeng (2007: 186):

> We departed from Dajianlu (Kangding), setting out to explore the Hor region. As we passed through Songlinkou, we discovered that the Horpa people are different from Khams-Tibetans. Our interpreter, who was from Kangding told us [...] that the language spoken by Horpa people is a mixture of Mongolian and Tibetan called Dijiaohua, which is incomprehensible to neighboring Tibetans.

Zeng (2007) further cites reference to local toponyms in identifying Mongolian influence.[1]

A second theory that seeks to explain rTa'u origins is what we call the nativist theory. This theory has received little attention — only a few scholars from dKar mdzes Prefecture have written on the topic, though it is widely discussed in local intellectual circles. A key proponent of

---

1   For instance, the township located about ten kilometers east of Luhuo County town called Srib mo (Simu) is said to be a Mongolian term, as is the village name Shwa ba thang (Xialatuo), which is said to mean 'Yellow Plain'.

this view is Ran (2004), who, in addition to his published work, has also given several oral presentations on the theory, and has written a number of unpublished manuscripts on the topic. The nativist theory argues that place names in the Tibetan-speaking area to the west of the rTa'u-speaking region provide good evidence that the rTa'u language predates the arrival of the Tibetan language. Ran (2004: 27) provides a list of mountain and place names which he argues are rTa'u in origin, e.g., that use the prefix /zæ/, meaning mountain in rTa'u, but having no meaning in Tibetan. This is significant given that rTa'u language is today no longer spoken in this area. Ran (2004: 26–37) thus argues that rTa'u speakers or the rTa'u language are native to the area,[2] and prominent local Tibetan scholar Thubtan Phuntshog (Thub bstan Phun tshogs, p.c.) concurs with Ran's argument.

Although situating rTa'u speakers as indigenous might be viewed as an attempt to raise their status within local language hierarchies, like the theory of Mongol origins, it still constitutes a form of mis-recognition in treating Tibet's minority language speakers as a problem that needs to be solved — an aberrance from an assumed mainstream population — and in not taking seriously speakers' professed identities. Such debates about the origin of rTa'u speakers can be understood in the broader situation of the numerous ways in which the term Hor is used in Tibetan contexts. An exploration of how the meaning of this term has changed over time, and shifts according to context, will show that the mis-recognition found in the search for Horpa origins is also perpetuated by the use of this polysemous label.

The word Hor appears in both written and spoken varieties of Tibetan. For instance, Powers and Templeman (2012: 299) define Horpa as: 'a term used by Tibetans to refer to Uyghurs, and sometimes to Mongols. It generally refers to Turkic or Mongolian people living near Tibetan populations in northern Tibet and modern Qinghai.' Edgar (1932: 71) states in a description regarding the people called Hor in the dKar mdzes area that, 'the "Yugurs" and the "Hor" are the same people.' In the following discussion of the term Hor, we first examine and compare definitions in several modern Tibetan dictionaries, and then, with reference to Moriyasu (1977), explore the shifting meaning

---

2   Ran (2004: 26–37) dates the antiquity of this settlement to approximately the fifth and sixth centuries AD.

of Hor over time. Finally, we survey the different meanings of Hor in a variety of local contexts throughout the eastern Tibetosphere.

Amongst modern Tibetan dictionaries, Jäschke (1881: 598) defines Hor according to two historical periods: formerly, it designated a Mongol, whilst at the time of writing it referred to Tibetans living near Lake Nam (gNam mtsho) in Central Tibet, or to Turkic peoples in Western Tibet. Les Missionnaires Catholiques du Thibet (1899: 1066) first defines Hor as a term for both regions and people, namely, in the western Tibetan area it refers to Turkestani people, whereas in central Tibet it denotes various pastoral tribes in the North Plains (Byang thang) region. Additionally, Hor is also claimed to designate Le thang [sic],[3] 'Ba' thang, and sDe dge, as well as a large region referred to as the Hor zar Khag lnga [sic][4] or Hor po Khag lnga [sic].[5] Das (1902: 1329, 1330) defines Hor as 'a Tatar', and Hor pa as 'a Dzungarian; also a Tibetan from the northern provinces, a herdsman of North Tibet.' Zhang (1985: 3071–72), meanwhile, defines Hor as describing various ethnic groups in different periods, i.e., Yugur (Uyghur) before the Yuan; Mongol in the Yuan; 'A zha and Tuyuhun in the Yuan-Ming transition; and at present, pastoralists in the Byang thang, and members of the Tu nationality (*minzu*) of Qinghai. Zhang also provides two additional meanings: *a po hor*, for pastoralists living in northern Tibet, and people of the Khams Tre Hor region, although the Chinese description in the dictionary is 'Mongolians living in five regions: Daofu, Luhuo, Zhuwo, Ganzi, and Donggu'.[6] Goldstein (2001: 1175) provides two meanings: firstly, referring to either Mongolia or Mongols or, secondly, to the pastoralists living in Northern Tibet.

We see both variation and overlap in these definitions. Whereas Goldstein (2001: 1175) does not distinguish Mongols and pastoralists in Northern Tibet, Jäschke (1881: 598) clearly mentions the temporal distinction between these two; however, as a modern synchronic description, Hor in the sense of Mongol also appears in compounds

---

3   Li thang in Literary Tibetan. However, local Tibetans in Li thang consider the toponym as Le thang which has the same sense as Li thang 'grassland as a bronze mirror'. The local pronunciation follows the spelling Le thang, not Li thang.
4   Hor sras khag lnga 'five districts ruled by the Hor prince' in Literary Tibetan.
5   Hor dpon khag lnga 'five Hor chieftain's states' in Literary Tibetan. There are also other Literary forms, such as hor khog khag lnga and hor khag sde lnga.
6   Each of them in Literary Tibetan is rTa'u, Brag 'go, Tre hor, dKar mdzes, and sTong skor. However, the components of 'five regions' are not consistent in literature and narratives.

such as *Hor glu* 'Mongol song', *Hor gos* 'Mongol clothing', and *Hor zla* 'Mongol calender'. Jäschke (1881: 598), Les Missionnaires Catholiques du Thibet (1899: 1066), and Zhang (1985: 3072) point out that the meaning of Hor differs according to region, denoting pastoralists of northern U-Tsang, Turkic people in Western Tibet,[7] and people in five Hor districts in Khams. Therefore, Hor is a polysemic word when viewed synchronically. Finally, as Goldstein (2001: 1175) makes clear, the meaning also varies depending on whether a text is in Classical or Modern Tibetan.

Moriyasu (1977) provides a diachronic perspective on the polysemy of the term Hor through a detailed analysis of the Dunhuang document,[8] *Pelliot Tibétain 1283*,[9] together with other primary sources in Chinese, Old Uyghur, and Literary Tibetan. He argues that Hor originally denoted non-Tibetan groups living on the northern Tibetan plateau, regardless of their specific ethnicity, but excluding the Han of the Tang and Qing Dynasties, and the Uyghur (1977: 43–44). He divides changes in the object denoted by Hor into five periods (see Table 1.1):

Table 1.1. Changes in the meaning of Hor over time.

Era	Meaning of Hor
7th c. to mid 8th c. (until early 9th c.)	ethnic groups in northern Tibet, between Tibet and Tang
late 8th c. to 9th c.	equivalent to Dru gu (Turkic or Uyghur)
13th c. to 15th c.	Mongol
(16th to) 17th c. (until 18th c.)	ethnic groups of Qinghai and Turkic and Mughal people in Western Tibet
19th c. to 20th c.	ethnic groups of Northern Tibet (Byang thang) and Eastern Tibet (sDe dge)

Source: Moriyasu 1977

---

7   Not giving a detailed description on the usage of *hor* in the western Tibetosphere within the article, we note here that in the present Ladakh, Tibetic-speakers employ *hor* to designate Turkic groups, especially Uyghur and Uzbek as well as *hor pa* for these people (Nicolas Tournadre, p.c.).
8   This collection of documents, found in the Mogao caves in contemporary Dunhuang, Gansu Province, in the People's Republic of China, includes some of the earliest known Tibetan texts.
9   The transliteration of this document is available at http://otdo.aa.tufs.ac.jp/archives.cgi?p=Pt_1283.

He concludes by defining Hor as 'ethnic groups except for the Han living on the northern Tibetan plateau, as well as those living in contact with the border of Tibet' (Moriyasu 1977: 45). Moriyasu thus claims that for Tibetans, Hor denotes non-Tibetan ethnic groups on the northern Tibetan plateau, which is why it excludes Han, who are the counterpart to the east of Tibet. Based on this conclusion, we can understand that the polysemy of the word Hor is partially due to an accumulation of various meanings, and the meaning denoted by the word depends on the era and region.

If we turn to contemporary usages of the term, we find significant differences from this historical situation. Moreover, there are differences between Hor as an autonym and an exonym. We will examine how Hor is used in the regions of U-Tsang, Amdo and Khams, following an introduction to Hodgson's (1853) distinction between Hor and Sog.[10] Hodgson (1853: 122–23) describes Hórsók as a compound of two Literary Tibetan words *hor* and *sog*; however, no modern Tibetan dictionary we consulted includes this compound (Jäschke 1881; Les Missionnaires Catholiques du Thibet 1899; Zhang ed. 1985; Goldstein 2001). Oidtmann (2014) also discusses Hor Sog as a copular expression appearing in the title of a text[11] by Welmang Pandita Konchok Gyaltsen,[12] and analyses Hor Sog as 'Hor and Sog', referring to the Yuan and then later Mongol khanates, especially that of Gushri Khan (2014: 306). Both Ahmad (1970: 110) and Tucci (1999: 256n128) make a similar distinction between Hor and Sog as representing distinct Mongol populations.

In the context of the U-Tsang, Hor primarily denotes Tibetan people living in the Nag chu region, and is used as both an exonym and autonym; people in Nag chu call themselves Hor pa, whilst outsiders call them *a pho hor*,[13] an appellation that typically carries a derogatory connotation. Nag chu Tibetans nonetheless express strong attachment

---

10   In the earlier period, *sog* denoted countries and states to the west of Tibet, mainly the present Iran as *sog po stag gzi*, and at present Turkey, *sog po du ru ka*: (Zhang ed. 1985: 2961).
11   *rGya bod hor sog gyi lo rgyus nyung brjod pa byis pa 'jug pa'i 'bab stegs*.
12   dBal mang paN Di ta dKon mchog rGyal mtshan (1764–1863). Although Oidtmann (2014) transcribes the first name as Belmang, we provide the local pronunciation — Welmang.
13   Zhang (1985: 3072, 3121) provides a spelling *a po hor*, which might follow the pronunciation of Central Tibet.

to their identity as Hor, and in particular to their place within the thirty-nine Hor tribes, Hor tsho So dgu (Karmay 2005; Shi and lHa mo thar 2012). Linguistically, the Nag chu Hor language is considered a member of the Khams pastoralists' dialect group by previous works such as Qu (1996) and sKal bzang 'Gyur med and sKal bzang dByangs can (2002), and as a member of the southeastern section together with many Khams Tibetan subgroups (Tournadre 2014).[14]

In Amdo, the northeastern part of the Tibetosphere, Roche (2011) mentions that Turkic-, Sinitic-, and Mongolic-speaking peoples of Amdo are often construed as and referred to as Hor, and he documents how Tibetans in Xing'er Township (Minhe County) refer to local Mangghuer people as Hor. Nowadays, many Amdo Tibetan speakers primarily understand Hor as a term designating the people of Tu nationality (*hor rigs*). However, in referring to the Tu as Hor, the term Hor pa is not used in Amdo.

In Khams, especially within the present dKar mdzes Prefecture of Sichuan Province, we find Hor as an appellation of ethnic groups as well as toponyms. According to Moriyasu (1977), Tibetans in Central Tibet began, in the nineteenth century, to use Hor to refer to inhabitants of the 'five Hor regions': rTa'u, Brag 'go, Tre hor, dKar mdzes, and sTong skor in today's dKar mdzes (cf. Zhang 1985: 3071); inhabitants of this region are referred to as Hor pa, and toponyms containing Hor are widespread. However, it is crucial to note that Hor in this context is an exonym. Although some contemporary Tibetans of the 'five Hor regions' now refer to themselves as Horpa, the term appears to have originated as an exonym approximately 200–300 years ago, in the Yongzheng period of the Qing Dynasty, i.e., the early eighteenth century (Li 2015: 120–21).

The extent of the Hor khog Khag lnga is limited to the northern part of the contemporary dKar mdzes Prefecture, from dKar mdzes County in the north to rTa'u County in the south. However, we can find toponyms containing Hor even in southern Khams, up to the present gTor ma rong valley in bDe chen Prefecture, where we find a hamlet called Hor gzung,[15] which locals interpret to mean 'the place grasped

---

14 This group was previously named Kham-Hor in Tournadre (2005).
15 Huorong. Here and following, the Chinese pinyin for Tibetan place names are provide in the footnotes.

(controlled) by Hor'. Tibetans living in this hamlet consider Hor to mean 'Mongol', referring to Mongols who came to the area during the Yuan Dynasty. Li thang and Nyag chu kha counties also have several toponyms such as Hor lung (township),[16] Hor chu (river),[17] and Hor rnying a.k.a. Hor ra rnying ba (township).[18] Locals also interpret these names to be connected to Mongols of the Yuan Dynasty.

Throughout Khams, the term Hor (for Mongols) is typically conflated with Sog. In interviews with local Tibetans residing in or near hamlets containing Hor, the term Sog was consistently used to refer to Mongols, not Hor. No one was able to explicitly distinguish Hor from Sog. Some outsiders suggest that Hor in Li thang and Nyag chu kha can be interpreted as Hor in Hor khog Khag lnga; however, except for the mention of Les Missionnaires Catholiques du Thibet (1899: 1066) that Hor also designates Le thang [sic], 'Ba' thang, and sDe dge, nowhere else is it recorded that Li thang and Nyag chu kha were part of Hor khog Khag lnga. Furthermore, we can note that in some toponyms in dKar mdzes Prefecture, Sog often refers to 'Mongol', even in relation to the Yuan Dynasty, such as Sog pho (township) of Rong mi Brag 'go (a.k.a. Rong brag) County. Local Tibetans trace their origins to Mongol soldiers who did not complete the journey to Yunnan. Contemporary residents are Khams Tibetan speakers, and are generally unfamiliar with the term Hor. Lastly, we refer to Giraudeau and Goré's (1956) French-Tibetan dictionary, which primarily reflects spoken varieties from the southern Khams area. They give a single Tibetan word for 'Mongolian': *sog po*, followed by an example *Sog po gong ma*, denoting 'Mongolian or Manchurian emperor' (1956: 185). This means that they understand *Sog po* both as Mongolian and Manchurian in the historical context, whereas it only means Mongolian in the contemporary context. This view, except for the sense of Manchurian, is widely shared by Tibetans in southern Khams today. The word Hor as a designation of Mongol does not appear in this dictionary.

To summarize, then, local Tibetans in Khams often understand both Hor and Sog to mean Mongol, but use Sog for Mongols in the modern age, and Hor in a historical context related to the Yuan Dynasty. As

---

16   Honglong.
17   Huoqu.
18   Heni or Heranniba.

Moriyasu (1977) points out, Mongolians in the Yuan Dynasty were called Hor by Tibetans; however, Tibetans in the contemporary era hardly recognize the historical difference between the two lexemes, and thus understand them as synonyms.

Taken together, the debates around the origins of rTa'u speakers, and the polysemy of the term Hor suggest the same thing — that rTa'u speakers are somehow less than Tibetan; that their identity is a problem that needs to be solved, since they are distinct from a perceived Tibetan norm. Both the search for origins and the exonym Hor suggest that somewhere there is an unproblematic, standard Tibetan to whom rTa'u speakers are being compared. The polysemy of the term Hor is particularly telling in this regard, since the only point at which all possible meanings of the term converge is around the concept of a 'non-Tibetan' inhabitant of Tibet. Meanwhile, the debates around the origin of rTa'u speakers enact mis-recognition in a more subtle way, in that, even when finding rTa'u speakers to be indigenous, they serve the 'metacultural' function (Urban 2001) of validating a link between historical origins and contemporary identity, and thus overriding the views and beliefs of contemporary rTa'u speakers, whilst also perpetuating the status of rTa'u speakers as a problematic population that necessitates special explanation for their distinctiveness. These academic infatuations with the supposedly problematic nature of rTa'u speakers and the Hor stand in stark contrast to rTa'u speakers' self-perception as unproblematically Tibetan, despite their linguistic distinctiveness. Even though most rTa'u speakers are unaware of these debates — only two college graduate interviewees out of a total of thirty had even heard the term Hor[19] — we nonetheless argue that these debates are significant in that they form part of a larger regime of mis-recognition when viewed in the broader context of contemporary discussions around Tibetan identity and language in the PRC.

---

19 The following section is based on two periods of fieldwork, in 2014 and 2017. Data were collected mainly through qualitative, semi-structured interviews, with a sample of twenty in the former and ten in the latter, by way of cluster sampling.

rTa'u-speakers and Contemporary Tibetan Language Politics

Within contemporary discussion around language and identity amongst Tibetans, minority languages such as rTa'u are faced with a pervasive climate of mis-recognition. This primarily manifests as the assertion of monoglot nationalism (Dorian 1998; Heinrich 2012), a standard language ideology (Lippi-Green 1997) that portrays all Tibetans as speaking a single language. This singularity is often explained in terms of common origins and descent, with all the languages of Tibet typically viewed as rooted in the written form. In this view, non-standard languages are thought to be corrupted, degraded forms of the written language, as expressed in the following quote from the Tibetan historian Tsepon WD Shakabpa (2009: 13).

> The spoken and written forms of Tibetan are closely related, although there are modest corruptions in the spoken form in widespread areas: Lhodruk, Sikkim, Ladakh, Monpa, Sherpa, Tamang, and so forth [...] although there is one original language for the three provinces of Tibet, regional accents have evolved. Because of these corruptions, if one does not listen carefully, it is difficult to understand.

Such a view portrays rTa'u and other minority languages of Tibet as corrupted forms of written Tibetan, thus placing them beneath the written language in a prestige hierarchy organized around the principle of purity. This view of non-standard languages as degraded forms of the written language can be gleaned from Teichman's (1922: 65, emphasis added) description of rTa'u, which most likely reproduces the views of local interlocutors: 'The language spoken at Dawu (perhaps akin to that used in the Gyarong States further east) is a *very corrupt* form of Tibetan, if indeed it is a Tibetan dialect at all.'[20] Similarly, Rockhill's (2004 [1891]: 263) description of rTa'u language as 'a wonderful mixture of Tibetan and Chinese' is most likely derived from his local informants, and represents the Tibetan standard language ideology that diversion from an ancestral language comes about via 'corruption' from other languages.

---

20 Teichman then goes on to discuss the 'curious racial mixture' of local Tibetans, suggesting that he viewed linguistic and biological types as related.

When not tied to the written language by a process of temporal degradation, minority languages such as rTa'u may be connected to written Tibetan by an imagined process of fossilization; divergence as stasis rather than change. A number of online commentaries[21] have attempted to establish some sort of relationship between Old Tibetan and contemporary rTa'u, in support of the theory that rTa'u is a 'living fossil' of Old Tibetan. One online article[22] by a rTa'u-speaker suggests that rTa'u speakers are the descendants of soldiers sent by Tibetan kings to safeguard the eastern entrance to the Tibetan plateau. According to the author, this explains the supposed character traits of contemporary rTa'u speakers: negotiation skills and a tendency to fight. The author even suggests that the language itself was developed as a secret code for spying purposes. This article, from a native perspective, if nothing else, emphasizes the desire of rTa'u people to be identified as Tibetans.

Alongside such attempts to identify rTa'u with Old Tibetan, local discourses also draw attention to the language's radical difference from spoken Tibetan. When referring to the language, non-rTa'u speakers typically refer to it not as Horpa (as in Literary Tibetan) or rTa'u (as speakers refer to it), but as *logs skad* — a widespread Tibetan term used to refer to non-standard languages in the eastern Tibetosphere. This term has been defined as referring to a 'kind of speech not understood by others in a certain region, line of work, etc.'[23] And although this definition appears merely descriptive and non-pejorative, rTa'u speakers consider *logs skad* to have definite negative connotations; it is not a term they themselves use.[24] Another term applied by other Tibetans to the rTa'u language, but not used by rTa'u speakers themselves, is *'dre skad*, which literally means 'ghost speech/language.'[25] As with *logs skad*, this term carries negative

---

21 A speech on Mdo Kham rTa'u area by 'gyaur Med Tshering, 26 April 2014: http://ti.zangdiyg.com/Article/detail/id/2620.html; a brief talk on Mdo Kham rTa'u language by Orgyan rDorje, 12 March 2015: http://www.tibetcm.com/contemporary/critical/2015-03-12/7472.html
22 A short take on the relationship between rTa'u language and written Tibetan by rTa'u rGyal Mtshan, 25 June 2016: http://www.gltadra.com/kb/ndbw.asp?id=1321&Zhg=001&NdRak_ID=ZamqowLc#ndbwNdCam
23 The Tibetan & Himalayan Library, Tibetan text archive, English definition of *logs skad*, http://dictionary.thlib.org/internal_definitions/public_term/123461
24 Suzuki and Sonam Wangmo (2016) discuss the term *logs skad*.
25 In addition to 'ghost', other suggested translations for *'dre* include 'demon', 'imp', 'goblin', and 'devil', all strongly suggestive of the term's negative connotations (see

connotations. Furthermore, these derogatory terms for the rTa'u language are generally associated with broadly negative stereotypes regarding its speakers: that rTa'u speakers are shrewd business people (and are therefore by implication greedy and dishonest), have a tendency to fight, and have no appreciation for (mainstream) Tibetan culture.

These portrayals of Tibetan as a prestige ur-language, and rTa'u as either a degraded or fossilized (but always radically different) derivative, take on heightened significance in the contemporary context of widespread social mobilization in defense of the Tibetan language. Although the vitality of Tibetan is certainly greater in comparison to the region's minority languages, concern for, and mobilization in defense of, the Tibetan language has intensified in the twenty-first century (Robin 2014; Roche 2017). Such concerns have emerged, in particular, in responses to changes in schooling, which have increasingly seen the promotion of what is called the 'type two educational model,'[26] which has basically instituted Chinese-medium education and relegated Tibetan to a subject, rather than a medium of education (Henry 2016). In response to this, and other pressures on the Tibetan language, two major programs have emerged as part of a broader language movement: one promoting the use of 'pure father-tongue', (*pha skad gtsang ma*) and the other advocating grassroots literacy.

The 'pure father-tongue' movement is a form of 'verbal hygiene' (Cameron 1996) aimed primarily at avoiding loanwords in spoken and written Tibetan, and promoting Tibetan neologisms (Thurston 2015, 2018). The underlying logic of the movement is that the Tibetan language is threatened by an increasing number of loanwords from Chinese, particularly as the language expands into new domains. Rather than a discrete, organized social movement with a clear organizational structure and program of activities, the pure-father-tongue movement is a diffuse, decentralized, grassroots movement (Roche and Lugyal Bum 2018). It is promoted through social media and in essays, poems, memes, and songs, as well as by word of mouth. The following examination of pure-father-tongue discourses is suggestive of the ways in which they

---

http://dictionary.thlib.org/internal_definitions/public_term/11031). Interestingly, Thurston (2018: 205) provides another possible interpretation for '*dre skad* as 'blended language'; the word '*dre* is also a verb stem denoting 'mix, blend.'

26 For further discussion of this system, see Chapter 5 of this volume, by Bendi Tso and Mark Turin.

constitute a form of mis-recognition for speakers of rTa'u and other minority languages, in positing an essentializing link between language and identity that elides the existence of Tibetan minority languages and speakers.

One can easily find many poems dedicated to the pure father-tongue, as in the following sample by Tibetan poet Pedma Trashi (Pad ma bkra shis).[27] In this poem, the Tibetan language is considered a cornerstone of Tibetan identity, along with other important elements such as being compassionate and abstaining from alcohol. Such poems are recited at school ceremonies and other social events. A common theme in all such poetry is that language is the keeper of culture, and that without culture one group of people is no different from any other, and therefore the key to maintaining Tibetan identity is the maintenance of a pure father-tongue.[28]

ཨོཾ། ཁ་བ་ཅན།
ཨོཾ། བྱམས་སེམས་ཅན་གྱི་མི་རིགས་ཡིན།
ཨོཾ། ཆང་དང་ཨ་རག་ཁྱེད་ཀྱིས་བཅུང་བ་མིན།
གཞིས་རྒྱུད་བལ་ལས་འཇམ་བའི་བུ་མོ་དང་།
ལ་རྒྱ་སྟེ་པོར་བཀུར་བའི་ཕོ་གཏོང་ཚོ་ཨོཾ།
བོད་ཆས་གཙང་མ་གྱོན་དང་ཕ་བཟང་བུ།
བོད་སྐད་གཙང་མ་ཤོད་དང་རིགས་བཟང་རྒྱུད།

Oh, people of the Snowland
Oh, people of compassion
Oh, you forbid alcohol
Women's personality is softer than wool
Men honor dignity the highest of all. Oh!
Wear authentic Tibetan clothes, good sons and daughters,
Speak pure Tibetan language, people of good lineage.[29]

---

27 See the poem online here, http://www.inalco.fr/sites/default/files/asset/document/jpo_chants_pema_tashi_final_final_0.pdf
28 Here and elsewhere, the Tibetan texts have been transcribed faithfully according to the original, even when they include 'errors'.
29 Translation by Sonam Lhundrop.

The most popular way that such ideas reach the general population is undoubtedly through song. Many songs in recent years have highlighted the importance of speaking pure Tibetan.[30] In 2015, a song titled 'Father-tongue (*Pha skad*)' was the main theme at the New Year Gala of Khampa TV, which featured the young Tibetan singer Gergyal Pedma (*dGe rgyal Pad+ma*) singing the following lyrics:[31]

ལོ་རྒྱུས་ཀྱི་གཡས་སྦུབ་ནས་ཤུད་པའི།
སྙན་འཇེབས་ཀྱི་རོལ་དབྱངས་དྭངས་མ།
ཡབ་མེས་ཀྱི་བྱངས་ཁྲག་གིས་བསྐྲུན་པའི།
ཉམས་མེད་ཀྱི་རྟོགས་བརྗོད་རིང་མོ།
ཕ་སྐད། དེད་ཅོང་གི་ཕ་སྐད།
སྦྱང་དཀར་རྩམ་པ་ལས་ཞིམ་བའི་ཕ་སྐད།
ཕ་སྐད། ཕ་སྐད། དེད་ཅོང་གི་ཕ་སྐད།

Nourished in the wealth of history,
The melodious sound,
Created by the unvanishing spirits of ancestors,
Embodiment of the long-lasting tales of our ancestors,
Father-tongue — our father-tongue,
Sweeter than sweet *tsampa*,
Father-tongue, father-tongue — our father-tongue.[32]

Another clear example of such promotion is the song 'Manifestation of the Father-tongue (*Pha skad kyi Rang mdangs*)' by the well-known singer Shertan (*Sher bstan*):[33]

---

30 In addition to the two songs described below, another extremely popular song on this theme is Three Lamas are Seated Up There (sTod gan na bla ma rnam gsum bzhugs) by Rigdzin Drolma (Rig 'dzin sgrol ma), which can be accessed at: https://www.youtube.com/watch?v=wDQdwn3fCOw
31 You can view Gergyal Pedma performing the song here: https://www.youtube.com/watch?v=pmz_ojUfYzs
32 Translation by Sonam Lhundrop.
33 See the song performed here: https://www.youtube.com/watch?v=PFD4M5ffZHI

ང་འི་བསིལ་ལྡན་གངས་རིའི་ཞིང་ཁམས་ལ།
དགུང་ནི་ཉི་ཟླ་སྐར་གསུང་ལམ་མེ་ལམ།
ནང་སྨྱུང་ཆར་ཆེལ་མ་ཤིག་སི་ཤིག
ང་བོད་པའི་རྟེན་འབྲེལ་རང་འགྲུབ་རེད།

In my heavenly land of snow
High above shine the sun, moon and stars
Within, blessings rain down —
The fortunate blessings of the Tibetan people

གནས་གཙིག་ལག་ཁང་བཟང་པོ་བྱང་ན།
ཆོས་མདོ་སྔགས་བཀའ་བསྟན་རི་རབ་བརྩིགས།
ནང་རིག་གནས་ཆེ་ཆུང་རྒྱ་མཚོ་འཁྱིལ།
ང་བོད་པའི་རྟེན་འབྲེལ་རང་འགྲུབ་རེད།

In the palace of monastic universities
Great teachings pile up like a great mountain
Within, a great ocean of wisdom swirls —
The fortunate blessings of the Tibetan people

བློན་སྟན་མི་ཨ་ནུའི་སྐུ་དྲིན་ལ།
བོད་དབུས་ཡིག་གསལ་བྱེད་གསེར་འོད་འཕྲོ།
ནང་ཤེས་རིག་སྟོང་གི་མེ་ཏོག་འཛུམ།
ང་བོད་པའི་རྟེན་འབྲེལ་རང་འགྲུབ་རེད།

To the benevolence of the great minister Thunmi
The Tibetan letters shine with glory
Within, the flowers of great civilization blossom —
The fortunate blessings of the Tibetan people

ངའི་ཕ་སྐད་རིན་ཆེན་གསེར་དག་རེད།
ངའི་མ་ཡིག་དྭངས་གཙང་འོ་མ་རེད།
ནང་མཐུན་སྦྱེལ་དར་དཀར་རིན་མོ་རེད།
ང་བོད་པའི་རྟེན་འབྲེལ་རང་འགྱུར་རེད།

My father-tongue is as pure as gold
My writing system is as pure as fresh milk
Within us, unity is pure as a white silk strip —
The fortunate blessings of the Tibetan people

སྐད་གཙང་མ་བོད་པའི་ཕ་ནོར་རེད།
དབྱངས་ཨ་ཡིག་བོད་པའི་རྒྱན་ཆ་རེད།
ནང་ཆ་ལུགས་བོད་པའི་རང་གཞིས་རེད།
བོད་མི་ནན་གནམ་གི་སྲུང་རྒྱ་ཚོ།

Pure language is Tibetans' treasure
The letters of the alphabet are Tibetans' adornments
Within, the cultural manifestation reflects who we are —
Do not lose that which the sky has protected[34]

Some have even seen it as a marketing strategy to include such songs in albums so that they reach even larger audiences. In the music industry, a new term has been invented in light of this, *phake chedruk* (*pha skad ched bsgrigs*) 'pure-father-tongue album', meaning that such albums include only Tibetan language songs.

Although informal groups sometimes form to encourage people to speak 'pure' Tibetan, it is more often promoted by individuals, particularly those with some level of formal education. One impact of the movement has been to establish a value hierarchy that promotes 'pure' language as both prestigious and morally valuable, and hence a source of pride, and denigrates 'mixed' language as non-prestigious, immoral, and shameful. This is significant for minority languages such

---

34 Translation by Sonam Lhundrop.

as rTa'u in that, as we have seen above, they are typically viewed as mixed languages. Television has been a popular medium for propagating such purist language ideologies: an example will suffice to demonstrate. In one well-known clip, a pastoralist goes to a city to purchase goods for the upcoming Tibetan New Year. He enters a shop and starts speaking a 'mixed' language, assuming that the shopkeeper must be Han Chinese. To his surprise, the shopkeeper is a Tibetan. Nonetheless, instead of speaking Tibetan to the shopkeeper he continues in 'mixed' language, now thinking to impress her and show his superiority. To his disappointment and embarrassment, the shopkeeper reprimands him and lectures him on the importance of speaking 'pure' language (Thurston 2015 discusses the role of comedy in propagating language ideologies in the Tibetan context).

In addition to this focus on verbal hygiene, the contemporary Tibetan language movement has also focused on adult literacy. People from different backgrounds, such as college students, monks, and business people, have been organizing village-level programs to teach written Tibetan to illiterate pastoralists and farmers. These programs have also appeared in the rTa'u area amongst rTa'u speakers, including in Tunzhi's village. His mother is sixty-five years old at the time of writing, and has never been to school, but has participated in a village-level illiteracy eradication program since 2014 (each household is expected by the monastery to send at least one member to attend these classes). She is now able to read several common Buddhist scriptures and chant them while following a recording on audiocassette. Cases such as hers are now common in the rTa'u area. And although we acknowledge that such programs are very much welcomed by local communities, we argue that they contribute to the mis-recognition of rTa'u speakers insofar as they reaffirm the essentializing, monoglot link between language and identity, whilst also undermining the perceived value of the spoken language and precluding efforts to develop a writing system for it.

Also known as the 'eradicating illiteracy' (*yig rmongs sel*) program, the adult literacy program aims to teach adults basic Tibetan literacy so that they can independently read Buddhist scriptures. Each monastery oversees a specific district, and conducts such programs in communities within its district. Often the monastery develops the textbooks. Classes are continued until participants are able to recite a designated scripture.

No comprehension lessons are offered; the pedagogical content simply includes how to pronounce the letters, how to combine them into syllables, and some provide chances to practice reciting simple texts. A typical program lasts about 15–20 days and is carried out annually prior to the New Year, a time when all residents are back in the community from their seasonal work at construction sites far away. In the case of the first author's community, the local monastery sends a head teacher who teaches the advanced classes, while local college students who are back in the community during the winter holiday teach the beginners. Students are divided into different classes based on their reading proficiency. During class, students repeat letters and portions of text after the teacher. There are simple tests at the end of each program, in which students recite a given text. However, there are reports and pictures on the social media platform, WeChat, of other communities with more advanced and long-term classes, and videos circulated on WeChat show adults memorizing long Buddhist texts and demonstrating their mastery of the content through debate. In many cases, college students and local monks collaborate on such programs.

Pressure to learn written Tibetan and to speak Tibetan in a manner that conforms to the written standard is increased by the language's association with Tibetan Buddhism and religious figures. Many rTa'u speakers describe feeling anxious when *lamas* are present, especially when they are invited to perform rituals in family homes, because such figures sometimes scold locals who speak Tibetan with an accent, or even simply for speaking rTa'u in their presence. For rTa'u-speakers, their identity and sense of belonging to a community are strongly linked with their religious affiliation, and therefore such pressures from religious figures, combined with Buddhist institutional support for purism and literacy, are felt as a heavy burden. For many rTa'u speakers, such pressures are viewed as a choice between their language, on the one hand, and their religion and identity on the other.

In this context, literacy in Tibetan becomes a nexus for maintaining ethnic boundaries through purist practices, promoting alternative visions of modern Tibetan identity through literacy, and accessing the sacred. It is perhaps not surprising, then, that when asked if there is any value in maintaining the rTa'u language, most interviewees directly compare its value with the maintenance and development of the Tibetan language. They claim that maintaining rTa'u is valuable only insofar as it contributes to the maintenance of the Tibetan language. Otherwise, the maintenance of the language for its own sake is seen as meaningless. One particular interviewee, the head of a school for orphans in the rTa'u area (and therefore the bearer of significant responsibility for the transmission of the language) stated that one language is enough for Tibet, and all effort should be directed towards the development and promotion of a single Tibetan language, even at the expense of the rTa'u language. This is demonstrative of the hegemonic position of monoglot language ideologies in relation to contemporary visions of Tibetanness.

This unwillingness to maintain rTa'u manifests in resistance to efforts to develop the language, for instance, by creating a writing system for it. This contributes to a vicious cycle where the language is seen as useless and therefore not worth maintaining, but cannot be made useful without such initiatives. This can be seen particularly in the educational context. Although most rTa'u speakers are unwilling to develop a writing system for their language, the lack of a writing system can be seen as one of the factors that deprives rTa'u of social and cultural prestige, and places pressure on speakers to abandon their language for Tibetan. Children are encouraged to speak Tibetan at school (even when the majority of students are rTa'u speakers), and only use rTa'u at home.

However, even this last bastion of the language is now under pressure, as it is commonly thought that speaking rTa'u hinders one's capacity to learn Tibetan well, as rTa'u is seen as a corrupting influence on pure Tibetan. However, the challenges faced by rTa'u speakers in learning Tibetan can more accurately be explained by the failure of the educational system to account for the fact that they are learning a second language, not 'their own' first language. Nonetheless, prevailing views amongst rTa'u speakers blame the children themselves for being poor students, and also blame the rTa'u language for 'corrupting' the Tibetan language. Such views have convinced rTa'u-speaking parents that speaking Tibetan at home with their children is in their best interests.

One interviewee in particular shared a story that reflects the motives that lead rTa'u speakers to experience persistent linguistic anxieties in relation to their spoken Tibetan. She is from a community where all households but hers speak rTa'u, so she has become fluent in both her home language, pastoralist Tibetan (*'brog skad*), and rTa'u since an early age. However, she said that since she moved to the city of Chengdu a few years ago due to health issues, 'Other Tibetans say I speak Tibetan with an accent… this made me very embarrassed.' For the vast majority of rTa'u speakers, such moments of mis-recognition based on their accent are incidents of great embarrassment and shame; rather than being recognized and esteemed as multilingual Tibetans, rTa'u speakers are thus mis-recognized as aberrant, and disesteemed.

Conclusion

Above, we have discussed how mis-recognition of rTa'u speakers functions in two distinct arenas: the academic and the quotidian. Within the academic field, knowledge production focuses on attempting to clarify the origins of the 'Horpa.' The 'notorious ambivalence' (Wang 1970–71) of this term, both diachronically and synchronically, suggests that its only stable function has been to imbue various populations with contrastive alterity, as Others to the Tibetan Self. Meanwhile, the everyday lived reality of rTa'u speakers is increasingly characterized by mis-recognition within the context of an essentializing language movement that seeks to tie Tibetan identity to a single, 'pure' language. In both cases, rTa'u speakers are denied recognition by significant social others — Tibetan academics, clergy, and laymen. The claims of rTa'u speakers to be Tibetan whilst speaking a non-Tibetan language are at best problematized, and at worst outright rejected, resulting in various harms for rTa'u speakers, including linguistic anxiety and insecurity, ultimately leading to language endangerment and shift.

We believe that the preceding discussion demonstrates the analytical value of applying the concept of recognition to examinations of how hierarchies emerge in language contact situations. However, we acknowledge that not everyone shares our enthusiasm for the analytical usefulness of the concept. Scholars such as Coulthard (2008, 2014), Povinelli (2002), and Vincent (2017), for example, have argued that although a focus on recognition helps reveal the existence of diffuse and often concealed symbolic value hierarchies, it nonetheless leaves power hierarchies in place. These authors claim that since recognition is usually *given* by dominant groups to the subordinated, it continues the disempowerment of minoritized groups and thus both perpetuates and conceals existing power structures, rather than eradicating them. Simpson (2014) has offered the concept of *refusal* as an alternative to the asymmetrical and disempowering notion of recognition; to refuse is to reject the power structures inherent in recognition, and to assert Indigenous identities and practices on the basis of continuing sovereignty, rather than intersubjective processes that entangle the Indigenous subject with practices of settler dominance. In reply to such criticisms, we note that these analyses were all developed in Western, settler-colonial, liberal-democratic, multicultural societies, where those offering recognition (and perpetuating mis-recognition) are viewed by subaltern populations as dominating, oppressive Others. In the present case, however, we have been examining a situation in which a linguistic minority is facing mis-recognition from a dominant, mainstream group with which it identifies, and which *it does not wish to refuse*. As such, appropriate recognition is likely to be deemed by them not only apt, but, given the important role that religion plays in setting the boundaries of the desired collective belonging, also morally good. This therefore opens up the possibility that structures of recognition and mis-recognition, whilst always implying power asymmetries, do not necessarily imply oppression.

A second line of argument that should be considered here relates specifically to recognition and languages. Although typically not discussed explicitly in terms of recognition, or with reference to authors such as Taylor and Fraser, there has been ongoing debate amongst linguists for at least the past twenty-five years regarding the value of 'differentiating' languages as bounded, stable 'objects.' We regard this conversation to be, in important ways, about recognition, and not only the differentiation of linguistic types and the creation and reinforcement of symbolic hierarchies. Criticism of the politics of recognition as it relates to language include: that such practices can impose inappropriate, etic standards for what constitutes a language (Mülhäusler 2006); that it may lead to the commodification of and competition between languages (Dobrin, Austin, and Nathan 2007); and that it often reproduces standard language ideologies and essentialist theories of language and identity that underlie much language endangerment (Heller and Duchêne 2007). Such views are also bolstered by broader poststructuralist critiques that view language as a fundamentally dynamic, fluid, fuzzy set of resources

(Makoni and Pennycook 2005), rather than as a preexisting structure to which individuals belong; in this view, the assertion of stable identity categories, rather than their organization into hierarchies, is the source of injustice. In response to these criticisms, we note that the existence of distinct linguistic types is not in question in the context we are examining; rTa'u speakers recognize the distinctiveness of their language from that of mainstream Tibetans, who, in turn, recognize the distinctiveness of rTa'u. To refute these salient local categories would thus be to engage in both 'epistemic violence' (the rejection of the subaltern subject's capacity to know, see Spivak 2010), as well as 'ontological violence' (violence against the conceptual order and lifeworld constructed by subaltern subjects). In contexts where discrete, bounded languages are already part of local views, we therefore see discussions of recognition as analytically appropriate.

Beyond the analytical value of engagement with the concept of recognition in understanding the construction of language hierarchies, and in nuancing our understanding of recognition in different contexts, we also argue that the concept has a normative role to play in efforts to support individual languages and maintain linguistic diversity. We argue that greater recognition for the rTa'u language by the mainstream Tibetan community would help in its maintenance, and we therefore make the following recommendations. Firstly, academics in the PRC and elsewhere who speculate about the identity of rTa'u speakers should take seriously the expressed opinions of rTa'u speakers. Secondly, given that the polysemy of the term *Hor* reduces its discursive role to something like 'un-Tibetan', scholars would be well advised to avoid this term. Thirdly, proponents of adult literacy and the 'pure-father-tongue' movements could give greater recognition and esteem to minority languages such as rTa'u in relation to the 'standard' Tibetan that they promote. Finally, the Tibetan community at large, including local religious figures, could contribute to this increased recognition for the language by avoiding negative terms such as *logs skad* and *'dre skad*, and by valorizing, rather than dis-esteeming, minority languages such as rTa'u; and by tolerating 'accents' in people who speak Tibetan as a second language, and even esteeming such individuals for their multilingual repertoires, rather than viewing such capacities as barriers to Tibetanness. These changes would go a long way to improving an ideological environment which is, to say the least, currently unsupportive of the maintenance of the rTa'u language.

Finally, it is worth noting that many of Tibet's minority languages, all of which are endangered to some degree, are in a similar predicament to rTa'u, facing a double bind between maintaining a language but having their Tibetanness questioned, or abandoning their language in order to claim a Tibetan identity. State structures that deny recognition to Tibet's minority languages are unlikely to change, and thus the exclusion of these languages from major social institutions is likely to persist. Any attempts to reverse language shift in those domains is therefore unlikely to succeed. However, it is possible that a change in attitudes towards these languages by other Tibetans, and greater recognition of their social and cultural value, would help support these languages into the future, and thus help reverse the broader decline in linguistic diversity currently apparent in Tibet and the Himalaya.

References

Ahmad, Zahiruddhin. 1970. *Sino-Tibetan Relations in the Seventeenth Century*, Serie Orientale Roma XL (Roma: Istituto Italiano per il Medio ed Estremo Oriente).

Alim, H. Samy, Rickford, John, and Ball, Arnetha. 2016. *Raciolinguistics*: *How Language Shapes our Ideas About Race* (Oxford: Oxford University Press), https://doi.org/10.1093/acprof:oso/9780190625696.001.0001

Calvet, Louis-Jean, trans. by Andrew Brown. 2006. *Toward an Ecology of World Languages* (Cambridge: Polity).

Cameron, Deborah. 1996. *Verbal Hygiene* (London: Routledge).

Coulthard, Glen. 2008. 'Beyond Recognition: Indigenous Self-Determination as Prefigurative Practice', in *Lighting the Eighth Fire*: *The Liberation, Resurgence, and Protection of Indigenous Nations*, ed. by Leanne Simpson (Winnipeg: Arbeiter Ring Publishing), pp. 187–204.

Coulthard, Glen. 2014. *Red Skins, White Masks*: *Rejecting the Colonial Politics of Recognition* (Minneapolis: University of Minnesota Press).

Cudd, Ann. 2006. *Analyzing Oppression* (Oxford: Oxford University Press).

Daofu xianzhi 道孚县志 [*Daofu County Annals*]. 1997 (Sichuan Renmin Chubanshe 四川人民出版社 [Sichuan People's Press]).

Das, Sarat Chandra. 1902. *A Tibetan-English Dictionary with Sanskrit Synonyms* (Calcutta: Bengal Secretariat Book Depot).

Dobrin, Lise, Austin, Peter K., and Nathan, David. 2007. 'Dying to Be Counted: The Commodification of Endangered Languages in Documentary Linguistics', in *Proceedings of the Conference on Language Documentation and Linguistic Theory* (London: School of Oriental and African Studies, University of London), https://www.dnathan.com/eprints/dnathan_etal_2007_commodification.pdf

Dorian, Nancy. 1998. 'Western Language Ideologies and Small Language Prospects', in *Endangered Languages: Language Loss and Community Response*, ed. by Lenore Grenoble and Lindsay Whaley (Cambridge: Cambridge University Press), pp. 3–12, https://doi.org/10.1017/CBO9781139166959.002

Edgar, J. H. 1932. 'The Horpa of the Upper Nya or Yalung', *Journal of the West China Border Research Society* 5: 69–72.

Fraser, Nancy. 2000. 'Rethinking Recognition', *New Left Review* 3: 107.

Fraser, Nancy. 2003. 'Social Justice in the Age of Identity Politics: Redistribution, Recognition, and Participation', in *Redistribution or Recognition?: A Political-Philosophical Exchange*, ed. by Nancy Fraser and Axel Honneth (London: Verso), pp. 7–109.

Gal, Susan. 2016. 'Sociolinguistic Differentiation', in *Sociolinguistics: Theoretical Debates*, ed. by Nikolas Coupland (Cambridge: Cambridge University Press), pp. 113–38. https://doi.org/10.1017/CBO9781107449787.006

Ganzi xianzhi 甘孜县志 [*Ganzi County Annals*]. 1999. (Chengdu: Sichuan Kexuejishu Chubanshe 四川科学技术出版社 [Sichuan Science and Technology Press]).

Gele 格勒. 1988. *Lun Zangzu wenhua de qiyuan, xingcheng yu zhoubian minzu de guanxi* 论藏族文化的起源、形成与周边民族的关系 [*On the Origin of Tibetan Culture and Its Relationship with the Neighboring Ethnic Groups*] (Guangzhou: Zhongshan Daxue Chubanshe 中山大学出版社 [Zhongshan University Press]).

Giraudeau, Pierre-Philippe and Goré, Françis Louis Noël. 1956. *Dictionnaire français-tibétain (Tibet oriental)* (Paris: Adrien-Maisonneuve).

Grillo, Ralph. 1989. *Dominant Languages: Language and Hierarchy in Britain and France* (Cambridge: Cambridge University Press).

Haugen, Einar. 2001. 'The Ecology of Language', in *The Ecolinguistics Reader: Language, Ecology, and Environment*, ed. by Alwin Fill and Peter Mühlhäusler (London: Continuum), pp. 57–66.

Heinrich, Patrick. 2012. *The Making of Monolingual Japan: Language Ideology and Japanese Modernity* (Toronto: Multilingual Matters).

Hodgson, Brian. 1853. 'Sifan and Hórsók Vocabularies', *Journal of the Asiatic Society of Bengal* 22: 121–51.

Honneth, Axel. 1995. *The Struggle for Recognition* (Cambridge: Polity).

Jäschke, Heinrich August. 1881. *A Tibetan-English Dictionary*: *With Special Reference to the Prevailing Dialects* (London: Kegan Paul).

Karmay, Samten G. 2005. 'The Thirty-nine Tribes of Hor: A Historical Perspective', in *The Arrow and the Spindle*: *Studies in History, Myths, Rituals, and Beliefs in Tibet*, Vol. 2 (Kathmandu: Mandala Book Point), pp. 181–204.

Les Missionnaires Catholiques du Thibet. 1899. *Dictionnaire thibétain-latin-français* (Hong Kong: Imprimerie de la Société des Missions Étrangères).

Li, Shaoming 李绍明. 1980. 'Tangdai Xishan zhu qiang koolüe 唐代西山诸羌考略 [Research on various Qiang groups in West Mountains during Tang Dynasty]', *Sichuan Daxue Xuebao* 四川大学学报 [Sichuan University Journal] 1: 83–95.

Li, Zhiying 李志英. 2015. 'Kangqu "Baili tusi" kao 康区"白利土司"考 [On "Beri chieftain" in Khams]', *Zangxue Xuekan* 藏学学刊 13: 107–22.

Lippi-Green, Rosina. 1997. *English with an Accent*: *Language, Ideology, and Discrimination in the United States* (London: Routledge).

Makoni, Sinfree and Pennycook, Alistair. 2005. 'Disinventing and (Re) Constituting Languages', *Critical Inquiry in Language Studies*: *An International Journal* 2 (3): 123–57. https://doi.org/10.1207/s15427595cils0203_1

McBride, Cillian. 2013. *Recognition* (Cambridge: Polity).

Moriyasu, Takao. 1977. 'Tibet-go siryoo tyuu ni arawareru hoppoo minzoku — DRU-GU to HOR — [A propos des tribus de l'Asie Centrale qui se trouvent dans les sources tibétaines: DRU-GU et HOR]', *Journal of Asian and African Studies* 14: 1–48.

Mühlhäusler, Peter. 2006. 'Naming Languages, Drawing Language Boundaries, and Maintaining Languages, with Special Reference to the Linguistic Situation in Papua New Guinea', in *Language Diversity in the Pacific*: *Endangerment and Survival*, ed. by Dennis Cunningham, D. E. Ingram and Kenneth Sumbuk (Clevedon: Multilingual Matters), pp. 24–39, https://doi.org/10.21832/9781853598685-006

de Nebesky-Wojkowitze, René. 1956. *Oracles and Demons of Tibet*: *The Cult and Iconography of the Tibetan Protective Deities* ('s-Gravenhage: Mouton).

Oidtmann, Max Gordon. 2014. *Between Patron and Priest*: *Amdo Tibet Under Qing Rule, 1792–1911* (PhD Dissertation, Harvard University), http://nrs.harvard.edu/urn-3:HUL.InstRepos:11745702

Pauwels, Anne. 2016. *Language Maintenance and Shift* (Cambridge: Cambridge University Press).

Piller, Ingrid. 2016. *Linguistic Diversity and Social Justice*: *An Introduction to Applied Sociolinguistics* (Oxford: Oxford University Press).

Povinelli, Elisabeth. 2002. *The Cunning of Recognition*: *Indigenous Alterities and the Making of Australian Multiculturalism* (Durham, NC: Duke University Press).

Powers, John and Templeman, David. 2012. *Historical Dictionary of Tibet* (Lanham: The Scarecrow Press).

Qu, Aitang. 1996. *Zangzu de yuyan he wenzi* 藏族的语言和文字 [*Language and Script of Tibetan*] (Beijing: Zhongguo Zangxue Chubanshe 中国藏学出版社 [China Tibetology Press]).

Ran, Changsheng 冉长生. 2004. *Xianshui hepan - Huoer zhi mi* 鲜水河畔-霍尔之谜 [*Riversides of Xianshui - The Mystery of Horpa*] (Chengdu: Bashu Shushe 巴蜀书社 [Bashu Press]).

Ren, Naiqiang 任乃强. 1981. *Qiangzu yuanliu tansuo* 羌族源流探索 [*Exploration of the Origin and Development of Qiang People*] (Chongqing: Chongqing Chubanshe 重庆出版社 [Chongqing Press]).

Robin, Françoise. 2014. 'Streets, Slogans and Screens: New Paradigms for the Defense of the Tibetan Language', in *On the Fringes of the Harmonious Society: Tibetans and Uyghurs in Socialist China*, ed. by Trine Brox and Ildikó Bellér-Hann (Copenhagen: NIAS Press), pp. 209–34.

Roche, Gerald. 2011. *Nadun: Ritual and the Dynamics of Diversity in Northwest China's Hehuang Region* (PhD dissertation, Griffith University).

Roche, Gerald. 2014. 'The Vitality of Tibet's Minority Languages in the Twenty-first Century: Preliminary Remarks', *Multiethnica* 35: 24–30.

Roche, Gerald. 2017. 'The Transformation of Tibet's Language Ecology in the Twenty-first Century', *The International Journal of the Sociology of Language* 245: 1–35, https://doi.org/10.1515/ijsl-2017-0001

Roche, Gerald, and Suzuki, Hiroyuki. 2018. 'Tibet's Minority Languages: Diversity and Endangerment', *Modern Asian Studies* 52.4: 1227–1278, https://doi.org/10.1017/S0026749X1600072X

Roche, Gerald, and Lugyal Bum. 2018 'Language Revitalization of Tibetan', in *The Routledge Handbook of Language Revitalization*, ed. by Leanne Hinton, Leena Huss, and Gerald Roche (London: Routledge), pp. 417–26. https://doi.org/10.4324/9781315561271

Roche, Gerald, and Yudru Tsomu. 2018. 'Tibet's Invisible Languages and China's Language Endangerment Crisis: Lessons from the Gochang Language of Western Sichuan', *China Quarterly* 233: 186–210. https://doi.org/10.1017/S0305741018000012

Rockhill, William Woodville. 2004 [1891]. *The Land of the Lamas: Notes of a Journey Through China, Mongolia and Tibet* (Delhi: Sri Satguru Publications).

Shi, Shuo 石硕, and lHa mo thar 拉毛太. 2016. 'Tantao Zangwen wenxian zhong "hor" (huoer) de gainian ji fanwei 探讨藏文文献中"ཧོར"(霍尔)"的概念及范围 [Exploring the notion and range of Hor in Tibetan documents]', *Qinghai Minzu Yanjiu* 青海民族研究 [*Qinghai Minzu Research*] 2: 149–54.

Simpson, Audra. 2014. *Mohawk Interruptus: Political Life Across the Borders of Settler States* (Durham, NC: Duke University Press).

sKal-bzang 'Gyur-med 格桑居冕 and sKal-bzang dByangs-can 格桑央京. 2002. *Zangyu fangyan gailun* 藏语方言概论 [*An Introduction to Tibetan Dialects*] (Beijing: Minzu Chubanshe 民族出版社 [Minzu Press]).

Spivak, Gayatri. 2010. 'Can the Subaltern Speak?', in *Can the Subaltern Speak? Reflections on an Idea*, ed. by Rosalind Morris (New York: Columbia University Press), pp. 21–80.

Suzuki, Hiroyuki and Sonam Wangmo. 2016. 'Lhagang Choyu: A First Look at its Sociolinguistic Status', *Studies in Asian Geolinguistics* 2: 60–69.

Taylor, Charles. 1994. 'The Politics of Recognition', in *Multiculturalism: Examining the Politics of Recognition*, ed. by Amy Gutman (Princeton, NJ: Princeton University Press), pp. 25–74.

Teichman, Eric. 1922. *Travels of a Consular Official in Eastern Tibet: Together with a History of the Relationship between China, Tibet, and India* (Cambridge: Cambridge University Press).

Thomas, George. 1991. *Linguistic Purism* (New York: Longman).

Thurston, Timothy. 2015. *Laughter on the Grassland: A Diachronic Study of Amdo Tibetan Comedy and the Public Intellectual in Western China* (PhD dissertation, Ohio State University).

Thurston, Timothy. 2018. 'The Purist Campaign as Metadiscursive Regime in China's Tibet', *Inner Asia* 20: 199–218, https://doi.org/10.1163/22105018-12340107

Tournadre, Nicolas. 2005. 'L'aire linguistique tibétaine et ses divers dialectes', *Lalies* 25: 7–56.

Tournadre, Nicolas. 2014. 'The Tibetic Languages and their Classification', in *Trans-Himalayan Linguistics: Historical and descriptive linguistics of the Himalayan area*, ed. by Thomas Owen-Smith and Nathan W. Hill (Berlin: Walter de Gruyter), pp. 105–29, https://doi.org/10.1515/9783110310832.105

Tsepon Wangchuk Deden Shakabpa. 2009. *One Hundred Thousand Moons: An Advanced Political History of Tibet* (Leiden: Brill), https://doi.org/10.1163/ej.9789004177321.1-1260

Tucci, Giuseppe. 1999 [1949]. *Tibetan Painted Scrolls*. 2 vols., 2nd ed. (Bangkok: SDI Publications).

Tunzhi (Sonam Lhundrop). 2017. 'Language Vitality and Glottonyms in the Ethnic Corridor: The rTa'u Language', *International Journal of the Sociology of Language* 245: 147–68, https://doi.org/10.1515/ijsl-2017-0006

Urban, Greg. 2001. *Metaculture: How Culture Moves Through the World* (Minneapolis: University of Minnesota Press).

Vincent, Eve. 2017. *'Against Native Title': Conflict and Creativity in Outback Australia* (Canberra: IATSIS Press).

Wang, Stephen S. 1970–71. 'Consonant Clusters of Tibetan Loanwords in Stau', *Monumenta Serica* 29: 631–58, https://doi.org/10.1080/02549948.1970.11745006

Zeng, Xianjiang 曾现将. 2006. 'Kangbei Huoer ren de laiyuan ji lishi yanbian lice 康北霍尔人的来源及历史演变蠡测 [The origin of Hor people in Northern Kham and their historical development]', *Minzu Yanjiu* 民族研究 [Nationality Research] 5: 79–84.

Zeng, Xianjiang 曾现将. 2007. *Hu xi minzu yu Zangyi Zoulang - yi Mengguzu wei zhongxin de lishixue kaocha* 胡系民族与藏彝走廊-以蒙古族为中心的历史学考察 [The Hu-related Ethnic Groups and the Tibetan-Yi Corridor: A Historical Investigation Based on Mongolian] (Chengdu: Sichuan Renmin Chubanshe 四川人民出版社 [Sichuan People's Press]).

2. What Happened to the Ahom Language?
The Politics of Language Contact in Assam

Selma K. Sonntag

The modern nation-state, emanating from post-Westphalia Europe, is frequently characterized by linguistic homogeneity, if not always empirically then at least ideologically. A common language is ideologized as the glue of the nation, the emotional tie needed to foment a sense of national identity rising above parochial proclivities. Furthermore, the modern state has an interest in impelling linguistic homogeneity: 'linguistic rationalization' (Laitin 1988) allegedly promotes administrative and economic efficiency and, some argue (e.g., Patten 2001), democratic participation. Even multilingual states, such as India, engage in these processes: in the Indian federal system, states, including Assam, are the site of linguistic rationalization (Laitin 1989) and cultivation of the affective ties that fuel linguistic nationalism (Mitchell 2009; Sonntag 2014).

The association of a common language with the nation-state, both as a marker of identity and a vehicle of communication, has been avowed by such acclaimed scholars as Benedict Anderson (1991), Ernst Gellner (1983) and Eric Hobsbawm (1990). They attribute the association to print capitalism, industrialization, and nationalism, respectively. These attributions impart a sense of inevitability to linguistic homogenization in the modern nation-state, as if linguistic homogenization is the only outcome of modernization and nation-building. They also shift focus away from the state as the purposeful perpetrator of linguistic rationalization to forces beyond the state's control. But we know that, despite state attempts at linguistic rationalization, most modern states are not monolingual and that, despite Anderson's claim that historically as well as currently 'the bulk of mankind is monoglot' (1991: 38), a majority of the global population remain polyglots (Meyerhoff and Stanford 2015: 3). Moreover, despite its Herderian origins, the modern nation-state fixes its territorial boundaries, which do not always correspond to more fluid linguistic boundaries. Thongchai Winichakul (1996: 67) has chastised Anderson, Gellner and Hobsbawm and their followers for failing to 'pa[y] attention to the most obvious constitutive element of a nation-state, namely its territory, as if it were merely a non-effective container of [...] essential elements [of the nation].' Refocusing on the agency of the state, i.e., 'bringing the state back in' (Evans et al. 1985) to our analyses of language politics, exposes the historical and geographical contingency of the Western European nation-state model of linguistic homogeneity and debunks its accompanying ideology of linguistic nationalism.

A historical-institutionalist approach to the study of language politics, as developed by Sonntag and Cardinal (2015), lends itself to analyzing language politics in a variety of geographically and temporally dispersed and diverse states, rather than being limited to the modern nation-state. Central to our theoretical framework are the analytical concepts of state tradition and language regime. We posit that state traditions inform language regimes. State traditions are representational sedimentations of how a state governs. They are reflected in historical patterns of institutionalized practices of governance. For example, federalism represents a state tradition of territorial governance that informs the language regime in India, Canada and the erstwhile Soviet Union. In the United States, liberalism, rather than federalism, has been the dominant tradition informing language policy choices (Sonntag 2019). Language policies compatible with state traditions are institutionalized, comprising a language regime. Language regimes are, then, the institutionalized practices of language governance. Because state traditions inform these institutionalized practices, a language regime has a representational or ideological component as well. As such, language regimes tend to be hegemonic and therefore relatively stable. Although specific language policies within the regime may be tinkered with around the edges, the range of policy options is circumscribed by state tradition. In the terminology of historical institutionalism, language policies are said to be path dependent. Only at critical junctures is a wider range of policy choices considered. Critical junctures can, but do not always, disrupt state traditions, leading to new policy regimes. More often, state traditions endure even though the policy path may shift.

Using this historical institutionalist framework of state traditions and language regimes, my chapter is a case study of Assamese language politics. I cover three different polities or states — the Ahom kingdom, British India, and independent India — and their associated language regimes, all located in the same complex linguistic environment marked by language contact and diversity. My primary focus, however, will be on the Ahom kingdom. As a precolonial state in the Himalayan border region between what we categorize today as South Asia and Southeast Asia, the Ahom kingdom's state traditions, and by extension its language regime, were decidedly different from either the colonial state or independent India. What makes the study of the Ahom kingdom intriguing is that, at the height of its power during the seventeenth century, prior to British colonization, the Ahom kingdom shifted from using the Tai-Kadai Ahom language to using the Indo-Aryan Assamese language, suggesting a rupture in the language regime. This shift appears to have been subsequently reified under the colonial language regime, setting the stage for postcolonial linguistic nationalism in Assam. Hence the framing of this chapter's theme as 'What happened to the Ahom language?'

I will proceed on the assumption that the Ahom kingdom was similar to other 'mandala states'[1] in Southeast Asia. The key traditions of the mandala states that I discuss below are their non-territoriality and elite hierarchy. I then sketch out a probable linguistic environment of the Ahom kingdom, speculating on its language regime given its mandala-state traditions. I attempt to identify the critical juncture at which the language shift from Tai Ahom to Assamese occurred. I argue that this

---

1   The metaphor of the mandala invokes a cosmic universe depicted as a circle radiating outward, the center of which is the most spiritually enlightened or, in the case of states, the most politically powerful.

critical juncture indexed a change in the language regime informed by incipient changes in the Ahom kingdom's traditions of non-territoriality and elite hierarchy. I will then discuss how this shift was consolidated under the colonial state and its attendant linguistic ideology. Finally, I will address language politics in post-independence Assam, starting with nationalist representations of the Ahom kingdom and its language regime. My research is based on secondary sources, most of them historiographical and using scant or sketchy records, hence my use above of less-than-analytical terms, such as 'assumption', 'sketch', 'attempt' and 'speculate'.

The Mandala State

Given the dominance of the Western nation-state model, scholars have grappled with identifying and defining 'Asian forms of the nation' (Tønnesson and Antlöv 1996). Historians of Southeast Asia have reached a consensus to some extent on the precolonial state, after sifting through the historiography of the region:

> historians have found the state-as-mandala productive in their thinking for two reasons. First, it is an 'indigenous' model and therefore 'protects' early Southeast Asia from Eurocentric concepts. Actually, of course, it is not indigenous; it is Indic. Second, it is a cultural concept, and its very resistance to pat definition as a model of state formation gives it interpretative power (Reynolds 1995: 427).

James Scott (2009) defines the classical mandala or *padi* state in opposition to Zomia, the anarchic, swidden-agricultural swathe of highlands across Southeast Asia and Northeast India. Largely missing from his analysis is the flip-side of his dichotomy between the mandala state and Zomia: the mandala state in interaction with a transregional Sanskrit cosmopolis, to use Sheldon Pollock's (1998a) terms. Both Scott's and Pollock's analyses are useful in reconstructing the dynamics of the politics of language contact in Assam.

One of the most significant characteristics of the mandala state is its non-territoriality. In mandala states, '[t]he political sphere could be mapped only by power relationships, not by territorial integrity' (Thongchai 1994: 79). Yet scholars of language politics (e.g., Laponce 1987) often identify territoriality as essential to the vitality of a language. Pollock labels the transition from Sanskrit's transregional cosmopolitanism to vernacularization as 'literary territorialization' (Pollock, 1998b: 49), when 'new notions of geocultural frameworks [were developed] for [...] literary narrative representations [...] in which [...] texts would circulate' (Pollock 1998a: 28). The lack of territoriality as a political concept in the mandala states — what we can call a state tradition of non-territoriality — suggests a different type of language politics and language regime from that of the modern nation-state.

Instead of sovereignty being defined territorially in precolonial Southeast Asia, power radiated out of the center, hence the mandala trope. Shifting and overlapping alliances, and multiple, shared sovereignty were the norms (Thongchai 1994: chap. 4). There were no fixed territorial boundaries where one mandala state started and another stopped. And they differed in the range or scope of their mandala. The 'unit of political order' (Scott 2009: 430) that indexed the state tradition of non-territoriality was *muang*, a Tai/Thai term that Thongchai Winichakul (1994: 81) glosses as 'governed area' and Charles Keyes (2003: 184) translates as 'principality'. A *muang* could be within the mandala of one or more powerful states, often called *muang* themselves (Keyes 2003: 179), and could have subordinate *muang* within its mandala orbit. A *muang* could shift territorially from, for example, one side of the Mekong River to the other but remain the same *muang* (Miles 2014: chap. 6). *Muang* could divide and separate, and, less frequently, coalesce and combine. Moreover, 'a subject of a local authority could be at the same time a subject of another authority' (Thongchai 1994: 73). At least in northern Thailand, spoken languages were referred to as *Kammüang*, or language of the *muang* (Keyes 2003: 184). Because of the shifting nature of *muang* and their populations, people also 'shift[ed] their language practices' (Scott 2009: 39). Languages were no more delineated or objectified than territory was. Language contact, diversity and multilingualism were constants. As Oliver Wolters (1999: 159), the historian usually credited for the mandala trope, puts it: 'There are probably few more influential cultural features in earlier Southeast Asia than multilingualism.'

At the center of the mandala states was the king or deva-raj. Kings were considered to be reincarnated divinities legitimizing their centrality and rule in what Victor Lieberman (2011) refers to as river-valley civilizations. The 'Indianization' of Southeast Asian kingdoms

(Coedès 1967) provided legitimation of hierarchical rule centered around the king. As Coedès (1967: 15–16) defines it:

> Indianization must be understood essentially as the expansion of an organized culture that was founded upon the Indian conception of royalty, was characterized by Hinduist or Buddhist cults, the mythology of the *Purāṇas*, and the observance of the *Dharmaśāstras*, and expressed itself in the Sanskrit language. It is for this reason that we sometimes speak of 'Sanskritization' instead of 'Indianization'.

Sanskritization in this context refers to the adoption of Sanskrit as the aesthetic, political-cultural, and literary language of the court and the legitimation this provided, and not necessarily to emulation by those lower in the sociopolitical hierarchy, as the term implies today throughout South Asia. Sanskrit was never used as an 'everyday medium of communication [...] [n]or even functioned as a chancery language for bureaucratic or administrative purposes' in the mandala states (Pollock 1998a: 12). However, its use introduced writing to the mandala states; literacy, or in Pollock's terms 'literariness', provided the trappings of hierarchical rule. According to Pollock (1998a), inscriptions from this period would usually begin with accolades to the king in Sanskrit, then revert to details in the local language(s), written in Sanskritic script. Sanskrit functioned as the expressive, aesthetic language, whereas local languages were for enumerative, constative uses (Pollack 1998a: 12). We can identify Sanskritization or Indianization as the source of the mandala-state tradition of socio-political hierarchy. Along with the state tradition of non-territoriality, it informed a cosmopolitan Sanskritic language regime. With the 'spread of political Sanskrit', Southeast Asia became part of what Pollock (1998a: 12) refers to as the 'Sanskrit cosmopolis'.

This Sanskrit cosmopolis was ecumenical according to Pollock (1998a, 1998b) — religion per se was not the driver of the spread of Sanskrit; instead Pollock attributes its spread to the aesthetic, universalistic traits of Sanskrit's hyperglossia and accompanying cultural-political practices. And yet it seems that this hyperglossia began to break down with the spread of Theravada Buddhism from Sri Lanka and its attendant Sanskritized Pali liturgy in the early centuries of the second millennium CE. Nevertheless, consistent with Pollock's analysis, Steven Collins (2003) suggests that the adoption of Pali Buddhism in mandala states was not necessarily or primarily for religious purposes.

According to Collins (2003: 681), Pali Buddhism 'began to be imported by kings as part of their state-building enterprises [...] [Its] ideology operated among the elite, primarily as an element in a nexus of power, as local power-holders were organized by a king into a *maṇḍala*.' Pali or Theravada Buddhism '[i]n its sociopolitical aspect [...] had to do with naturalizing inequality in social hierarchies' (Collins 2003: 681), i.e., it was instrumental in reinforcing the hierarchical state tradition at a time when mandala kingdoms, particularly newer ones in Siam and Burma, were coming into their own.

It also appears that the importation of Pali Buddhism and its liturgy spurred the development of local writing systems, albeit derived from Pali's Sanskritic script (Collins 2003: 683). Hence, with the adoption of Buddhism by the Siamese king in the thirteenth century, royal inscriptions began to appear in what was to become the Thai script (Keyes 2003: 183; Collins 2003: 684). The Burmese script dates about a century earlier, while other orthographic systems in what is now Burma, such as Mon and Arakanese scripts, appeared even earlier, predating Pali Buddhism to some extent (Collins 2003: 683–84). The change in the literary language regime of the Siamese and Burmese mandala states corresponds to Pollock's vernacularization, that is, a shift from Sanskrit being the ascetic language of royal accolades and poetry to vernaculars playing this role. The language regimes of the mandala states became more parochial and local — in effect, remaining multilingual and multiscriptal but without the Sanskrit hyperglossia.

Although the development of local scripts appears to signal a language regime change, there was not necessarily a corresponding political change: mandala states tended to endure up until colonial conquest. In particular, state traditions endured. As suggested above, the state tradition of hierarchy was actually reinforced by the introduction of Pali Buddhism. Thongchai Winichakul (1994) argues that what I am calling the mandala-state tradition of non-territoriality was not disrupted in Siam until colonial powers began to vie for power in Southeast Asia, at which time the Siamese kingdom managed to escape colonization by quickly adopting the technology of mapping and territorial-administrative control. Yet Pollock's vernacularization rests on an assumption of new 'geocultural frameworks' enabling 'literary territorialization' (Pollock 1998b: 49). So what were the new geocultural conceptions that marked the change in language regime? Culturally, Theravada Buddhism percolated down the social hierarchy (Collins 2003; Keyes 2003), which hadn't happened with the Brahmanical Hinduism of the Sanskrit cosmopolis (Coedès 1967: 369). Geographically, the spread of Tai peoples south and west from Yunnan had reinforced the *muang* concept as the primary 'unit of political order' (Scott 2009: 430). These cultural and geographical shifts framed the 'turn [...] to the use of local languages for literary expression in preference to the translocal language[s]' of Sanskrit and Pali (Pollock 1998a: 6). The 'local' was not defined territorially but rather according to its place in the mandala of state power. The shift to the vernacular was a conscious choice, according to Pollock (1998a: 7) — it was a policy option that had opened up at a critical juncture.

The state traditions of hierarchy and non-territorialization endured at this juncture, during the shift in the literary language regime from Sanskrit hyperglossia to vernacularization. Nevertheless, the new regime enabled 'literary territorialization' (Pollock 1998b: 49) which was not equivalent to political territorialization but undoubtedly impacted, and gradually transformed, political-cultural concepts of space. Institutionally, this transformation took the form of 'a more uniform and efficient tax regime and administration, and [...] kingdomwide economic integration and militarization' (Scott 2009: 253) in the increasingly centralized mandala states on the eve of colonialism. In turn, '[t]he process of valley homogenization' along the Chao Phraya, Salween and Irrawaddy 'was much advanced by increasing state centralization between 1600 and 1840', with 'the valley states [...] busy fabricating more uniform Burmese, Siamese [...] and Shan' (Scott 2009: 253, referencing Lieberman). Zomia remained outside of the mandala states' hierarchy in Scott's rendition, not least because of the mandala states' lack of territorial sovereignty and integrity.

However, the mandala states were dependent on Zomia for their agricultural and military manpower needs, which they would obtain by periodically raiding Zomia, often for slaves (Scott 2009; Wolters 1999: 164). The mandala states also battled each other, albeit for control of manpower rather than territory (Wolters 1999: 164). Given the lack of fixity of the states and their subjects (including slaves), there was a great deal of fluidity in identity. Although we need not accept Scott's emphasis on Zomians-versus-the-state as the most relevant distinction, there is a general consensus that neither language nor ethnicity were salient identity markers in the mandala state. As Scott (2009: 253) puts it, '[a] certain plasticity of identity was built into precolonial power relations.' While the elite literary component of the language regimes of mandala states was initially characterized by Sanskrit hyperglossia, followed by literary vernacularization, the 'constant movement back and forth between the valleys and the hills' (Scott 2009: 27) meant that quotidian language practices were undoubtedly multilingual and involved constant language contact, often between unrelated languages. Despite valley homogenization — particularly in terms of governmentality — on the eve of colonialism, most scholars concur that it is indeed difficult to say that there was any concept of ethnolinguistic identity, as we now conceive of it, in the mandala state (Scott 2009: 253).[2]

The Ahom Kingdom

Hence the difficulty of identifying the Ahom. Yasmin Saikia (2004: 252) insists that the Ahom are not an ethnic group, despite an ethnolinguistic dimension to their current-day efforts at mobilization. More probably, they initially were identifiable as warriors migrating with a Tai king from the east, and constituted the military-bureaucratic class once the Ahom kingdom was established in the upper Brahmaputra Valley in the thirteenth century (Saikia 2004: chap. 3). This 'class' of 'nobles' (Saikia 2004: 20, 126, 252) shared power with the king, or *swargadeo*, as 'Ahoms' (Guha 1983: 19–20). According to Saikia (2004: 133), these initial Ahoms, i.e., the royalty and the warrior-administrators, were all men and 'espoused local women'. Amalendu Guha (1983: 39), who more easily uses Ahom as an identitarian category, claims that the initial Ahoms separated from a *mung* or *muang* in upper Burma. Guha (1983: 12, 32) glosses *mung* as 'political society'; accordingly 'the Ahom polity started as a loose confederacy of several mungs around a dominant one of the Tai model.'

---

2   Sudipta Kaviraj (2010: 141–43) argues that likewise in Bengal prior to colonialism, there was 'no linguistic identity'. He points to the 'fuzziness' of space and time in pre-colonial India, distinct from the enumeration and mapping of the colonial world.

It appears, then, that the establishment of the Ahom kingdom in the early thirteenth century was based on mandala-state traditions. The *muang* geocultural framework and a sociopolitical hierarchy with a noble class were its foundation. Moreover, it was founded in a complex, multilingual environment, which was neither 'politically void' (Guha 1983: 12) nor literately void (Gohain 1999: 101), at the critical juncture when mandala states were vernacularizing. As I argue below, this put the Ahom language regime on a different policy path, setting the stage for the replacement of the Tai-Kadai Ahom language with Indo-Aryan Assamese at another critical juncture: when the kingdom's traditions of non-territoriality and elite hierarchy were changing, although not completely disrupted. I will first reconstruct the Ahom language regime by elucidating how the Ahom kingdom's mandala-state traditions informed it, then analyze its shift to Assamese.

Like other mandala states, the Ahom kingdom was not dependent on territorial control, but rather control of manpower for wet-rice-agricultural as well as military purposes (Guha 1983: 34; Saikia 2004: 128–29). Accordingly, there was no land tax imposed in the kingdom, only a labor, and at times military, service requirement (Bhattacharya 2005: 21; see also Gurung 2018: 199, n14; Parwez 2018: 133). Indeed, the institutionalization of manpower in 'the Ahom peasant-militia' system of corvée labor was deemed 'the most important component of the Ahom political system' by Edward Gait, a colonial authority on the Ahom (quoted in Saikia 2008: 154). The nobility was responsible for acquiring the manpower, usually by absorbing and/or enslaving the diverse population, often through military ventures. These populations could be Zomians: Guha's (1983) account has been characterized by Nayanjot Lahiri (1984: 60) as 'the absorption of stateless shifting cultivators into [the *padi* Ahom] polity' (see also Saikia 2004: 155). Manpower could also be secured from other *muang* — usually militarily although without necessarily absorbing the *muang* themselves, as was typical of mandala states. Some of the earliest secured, if not absorbed, were the Tibeto-Burman-speaking Barahis and Morans (Guha 1983: 15; Saikia 2004: 2), whose women the initial Ahom espoused (Saikia 2004: 32). The acquired manpower was organized at its base into *paik*, which consisted of three to four individual laborers (or militiamen) who then shared rotation in labor units known as *khel* (Saikia 2004: 126–27; Guha 1983:

8–9; Terweil 1983: 58). *Khel* were further aggregated into *faid* or 'service groups' (Saikia 2004: 126). Neither *khel* nor *faid* had any territorial base. Nor did they necessarily contain *paik* from the same locale or speaking the same language: 'To inhibit khel solidarity, paiks were constantly moved from place to place and between khels' (Saikia 2004: 127). This system undoubtedly both reflected and reinforced an extremely diverse multilingual environment.

Khel were under the control of the Ahom nobility. The structure of the nobility was hierarchical, with the rungs expanding and growing more numerous over time. At the apex initially were two great *gohain* (Terweil 1983: 21), followed by lesser *gohain* in the hierarchical ranking. The *gohain* 'control of the labor force [...] made these nobles very powerful, often more powerful than the [royal] princes' (Saikia 2004: 126). Their relation with the Ahom royalty cohered to mandala-state traditions: according to Barend Terweil (1983: 54), *gohain* is the Assamese term for Ahom nobility; in Ahom Tai, the titles of these high-ranking *gohain* contained the word *mung*, the Ahom cognate of the Thai *muang* — reflecting the Tai model of political society as a loose confederation, as identified by Guha (1983) quoted above. Also quite powerful, and more numerous, were the *phukan* and *barua*, nobles who were responsible for large *khel* which served in both wet-rice agriculture production and military ventures (Saikia 2004: 126; Guha 1983: 8). Lower ranks, such as the *saikia*, also constituted the Ahom, or nobility class. Beyond the initial warrior migrants, the Ahom were drawn from earlier populations and autochthonous groups, and possibly from earlier as well as more recent Tai migrations from upper Burma (Guha 1983; Gohain 1999: 102; Saikia 2004: 27). Saikia (2004: 286) cites a source claiming that the third great *gohain*, created in the late fifteenth century, was initially filled by a Naga (see also Baruah 1999: 32). In Scott's (2009) terminology, Nagas would be considered Zomians; that they could be enlisted as both *paik* and the highest-ranking Ahom demonstrates the political-cultural, and by extension linguistic, fluidity of the Ahom kingdom.

Just as fluid was the literary environment of the Ahom kingdom. The Ahom mandala state most probably was part of, or at least influenced by, the Sanskrit cosmopolis (see Saikia 2004: 118). At a minimum, the kingdom was sandwiched by it — between Southeast Asia and ancient Kamarupa in the lower Brahmaputra Valley, where the spoken and written linguistic heritage was Indo-Aryan (Saikia 2008: 160–64), dating from the fifth century onward (Gohain 1999: 101). According to Guha (1983: 12), the 'political heritage of ancient Kamarupa had not left upper Assam totally untouched.' Other lower Brahmaputra kingdoms, such as the Kachari, Koch and Jaintia, had developed writing systems as well (Saikia 2004: 123). Pollock dates Assamese vernacularization from the mid-fourteenth century when the Ramayana was first composed in Assamese 'at the request of the Barāhi king'. Although the Barahi king to whom Pollock attributes vernacular Assamese patronage appeared to be further down the valley than the Tibeto-Burman-speaking Barahi with whom the Ahom initially interacted (see above), Pollock's dating suggests that not long after their arrival in upper Assam from Southeast Asia, the Ahom came into contact with vernacularizing trends originating in the South Asian, as opposed to the Southeast Asian, Sanskrit cosmopolis.[3]

It appears that the Ahom brought a writing system with them in the early thirteenth century, possibly pre-dating the emergence of the Thai script in Siam, but post-dating vernacularization in the mandala states in Burma. B. K. Gohain (1999: 101), referencing scholars such as Terweil, claims that the script of the Ahom kingdom was 'specific only to Ahom' and that it was 'derived from old Mon as it was written in the first centuries of the second millennium A.D.' — the Mon kingdom being one of the first vernacularizing mandala states among the Southeast Asian mandala states, as noted above.[4] Other scholars, such as Guha (1983),

---

3   In a personal conversation (29 October 2018, Dibrughar University, Assam) I had with Jahnabi Gogoi Nath, a historian of the Ahom kingdom (see, e.g., Gogoi Nath 2002), she expressed doubt whether the king whom Pollock references was Barahi. Given my argument that ethnonyms had little or no identitarian significance, or that kingdoms were not territorially defined and marked by a specific language before vernacularization, whether the royal patron of the first Assamese Ramayana was Barahi or not is less significant than that he was Hindu and probably a Tibeto-Burman speaker.

4   This assessment that the Ahom script was similar to the Mon script was also expressed by Girin Phukon, Director of the Institute of Tai Studies and Research in Moranhat, Assam during my visit there on 30 October 2018. However, in an article in the Institute's journal, Phukon (2018: 212) speculates that the Ahom 'acquired the script from the Pyu in Upper Burma'. Phukon's assessments are not necessarily inconsistent, given that the Pyu (Tibeto-Burman speakers) could have themselves adopted the script in which Mon, an Austro-Asiatic language, was written. But they do indicate the high degree of both written and spoken language contact that was prevalent throughout the region historically.

refer to the Ahom writing system as 'Tai script'. Ahom literariness took shape in the *buranji*, which were primarily court chronicles celebrating and delineating the genealogy and exploits of the kingdom's rulers. The *buranji* were under the keep of the *deodhai*, or priests, of the Ahom kingdom. But there is little, if any, historical evidence that the *deodhai* were Buddhists (or Hindus). The critical juncture in literary vernacularization marked by the introduction of Pali Buddhism in other mandala states, as discussed above, was apparently absent in the Ahom case. Or at least the religious component was absent, but perhaps not the literary marker: Gait, the British colonial 'expert' on the Ahom kingdom, claimed that the Ahom language was 'written in a character derived from Pali' (quoted in Saikia 2004: 285). If indeed the Ahom script was based on the Mon script, which, as discussed above, pre-dated full-scale adoption of Pali Buddhism, then this dates the establishment of the Ahom kingdom on the cusp of literary vernacularization in Southeast Asia spurred on by Pali Buddhism.

At least initially, then, the written language regime of the Ahom kingdom was neither the cosmopolitan Sanskrit language regime nor a fully vernacularized one in terms of literary territorialization, but rather a very fluid, multiscriptal language regime. While Sarharuddin Ahmed (2008: 22) claims that '[t]he inscriptions of the Mediaeval Assam (Āhom period) are written partly in Sanskrit and partly in local Tai language',[5] indicative of the language regime of the Sanskrit cosmopolis, the Ahom *buranji*, which are more literary and included origin myths as well as royal chronologies and military exploits, 'were never written in Sanskrit but rather in Assamese, and occasionally in a Tai language that is sometimes referred to as Ahom' (Saikia 2004: 123). The Ahom language regime was also likely characterized by fluid multilingualism. With literacy limited to the very few, primarily the priestly and royal/nobility classes in mandala states, 'there was no pressure to impose linguistic uniformity on the peoples' of these 'premodern' mandala polities (Keyes 2003: 186). We can assume that the spoken means of communication in the Ahom kingdom comprised a variety of languages, including pidgins (Baruah 1999: 31). As Terweil (1983: 44) has put it, '[t]he Ahom developed sophisticated communication systems and organizational hierarchies [...] Generally they succeeded in keeping a tight hold over a

---

5 Ahmed (2008), unfortunately, does not specify to which inscriptions he is referring.

large populace of great diversity.' Linguistic contact between Tai-Kadai, Indo-Aryan, Tibeto-Burman and Austro-Asiatic 'language families' must have been constant in speech interactions among and between the different 'classes' and *muang* in the Ahom kingdom. The language regime of the Ahom kingdom, at least up until the seventeenth century, is therefore probably best characterized as institutionalized multilingual and multiscript/multiliterate contact.

In the early sixteenth century, the sphere of the Ahom mandala state began expanding through military ventures to include the older Chutia kingdom to the northeast. The recently Hinduized Chutia, who may have been either Tibeto-Burman or Tai-Kadai speakers or both, had supposedly developed 'a Tai script' (Saikia 2004: 6) — another example of the very complex environment of language contact throughout upper Assam. Guha (1983: 27) emphasizes the resulting influence of Hinduism on the Ahom kingdom from not only the Chutia but also from further Ahom expansion westward: 'By 1539, the Ahom territory became at least twice as big as what it was in size around 1407. More important, its Assamese-speaking Hindu subjects were now more numerous than the Ahoms themselves.' Soon thereafter, in 1562, according to Guha (1983), the Koch invaded from the west, having already absorbed Assamese-speaking Hindu Kamarupa, only to have the Ahom reverse their fortunes by the mid-seventeenth century. Also by the mid-seventeenth century, the Ahom had finally managed to stave off repeated Mughal military incursions. Hence, '[a]t its peak in the seventeenth century the Ahom kingdom stretched from Sadiya [the earlier Chutia capital] in the east to Guwahati in the west' (Saikia 2004: 8). As Jahnabi Gogoi Nath (2002: 30) phrases it, the 'small [Ahom] state formed in the extreme south-east corner of the Brahmaputra valley in the early part of the 13th century became the single largest state of Assam covering almost the entire region of the valley by the last part of the 17th century.'

Evidence of territory becoming a political category in the wake of successful Ahom military expansion can be gleaned by comparing the Ahom kingdom's early 1500s census with census categories of the mid-seventeenth century. The early sixteenth century census focused on manpower, i.e., counting the adult male population, with no territorial component, according to Guha (1983: 34). In comparison, the mid-seventeenth-century census was much more complex, although still oriented toward addressing manpower needs. Its purpose was 'to facilitate the swargadeo's [king's] mission to become the most powerful king of the region' by expanding and rationalizing the administrative nobility's functions through new regulations on land division for wet-rice agriculture (Saikia 2004: 127–28). Guha (1983: 34, 32) also notes that there was a 'total absence of any land survey and measurement in the Ahom Kingdom until the end of the 16th century' and that 'land surveyors' (as well as scribes) were brought into the kingdom from the Mughal empire in the early seventeenth century. By 1681, the Ahom had 'started [a] countrywide detailed land survey' (Parwez 2018: 133).

The mid-seventeenth century can be taken as the critical juncture for the Ahom kingdom, with its military victories, particularly over the Mughals, and its ensuing expansion up and down the Brahmaputra Valley disrupting the mandala-state tradition of non-territoriality. It was also a period of substantial political and economic reform (Guha 1983). Terweil (1983: 43–44) claims that with the defeat of the Mughals, 'a new, invigorated Ahom rule was established, ready to try new methods of administration.' A significant example of these new administrative methods was the adoption of the Mughal system of territorial-administrative control — the *pargana* system of collecting land revenue — at least in the newly acquired Ahom territories in lower Assam (Goswami 1986: 16–18; Parwez 2018: 132; Gogoi Nath 2002: 46–47). Not only did new administrative policy options and pathways open up at this critical juncture, the language regime also shifted. Terweil (1983: 44) continues: 'From this time onward the Ahom were firmly set on the path towards full assimilation of Assamese Hindu culture, and the Ahom tongue became obsolete. Assamese script took over from the old Ahom characters.'

Guha (1983) also dates the culmination of the switch from the Tai Ahom language to Assamese to the mid-seventeenth century. As Guha (1983: 10) puts it: 'the literate Ahoms retained the Tai language and script well until the end of the 17th century [...] In this century, this [Tai Ahom] language first co-existed with and then was progressively replaced by Assamese at and outside the [Ahom] court.' Saikia (2004: 120) points to the seventeenth century as well, when 'several Brahmin families were invited to take high positions in the swargadeo's [Ahom king's] administration', testifying to what Guha (1983: 25–30) claims as nearly a century of increasing Brahmanical influence. The literary impact of this evolving state tradition of expanding the ranks of the Ahom nobility can be ascertained from Saikia's (2004: 121) assertion that '[a] close reading of the [Ahom kingdom's] chronicles to evaluate their prose style, orthography and language, narrative structure, and stories indicates that buranji writing developed and took off in the late seventeenth century' — and that these *buranji* were written in Assamese (Saikia 2004: 123).

It was not only through the expansion of the elite that Assamese was replacing the Ahom language. Neo-Vaishnavism with its bhakti and anti-Brahmanical practices was spreading rapidly eastward, up the valley, bringing with it poetry and prose in Assamese to both the literate and illiterate (Guha 1983: 30–31, 44). Although Pollock (1998a: 29) argues that bhakti was not a primary 'dynamic in the history of South Asian vernacularization', its spread corresponds to what appears to be political and cultural changes in the Ahom kingdom, and to parallel the role of Pali Buddhism in the vernacularization of Southeast Asian mandala states. The Ahom kingdom had converted to Hinduism by the mid-seventeenth century, but it wasn't until the late seventeenth century that neo-Vaishnavism received official Ahom royal patronage (Guha 1983: 30–32). This patronage — presumably, in linguistic terms, of 'vernacularizing' Assamese — may have been more significant than neo-Vaishnavism itself (Pollock 1998a: 31).[6]

Equally important as linguistic patronage was the political-economic patronage given to the neo-Vaishnavites. The Ahom kings gave land grants to the neo-Vaishnavite leaders, which dramatically increased from the mid-seventeenth century (Gogoi Nath 2002: 38) — mostly on the huge riverine island of Majuli in the Brahmaputra. These land grants were not subject to the new land taxation system that the Ahom state had adopted from the Mughals. Along with these land grants, *paik* were allocated to the neo-Vaishnavite *satra* (monastaries) (Gurung 2018: 101). The *satra* may have also provided a 'zone of refuge', in Scott's (2009: 22–26) sense of the term, for the *paik*: according to Tejimala Gurung (2018: 113) a 'large number of *paiks* […] escape[d] from periodic paik duty and

---

6   For comparison's sake, according to Carmen Brandt (2015), in the early eighteenth century, the Meitei king converted to Vaishnavism and, legend has it, destroyed the Meitei (Tibeto-Burman) script in the process of switching to a Devanagari-based script.

settle[d] down at *satra* lands.' Another option to those seeking to escape *paik* service was also emerging: 'in the Ahom territories the relatively affluent *paiks* wanted, frequently, to commute their service obligation into cash or kind payments' (Parwez 2018: 133). By the early eighteenth century, 'commutation of paik services for money was encouraged by the Ahom state which needed money for payment of wages to the soldiers' of the increasingly mercenary Ahom army (Gurung 2018: 124, n77). Edward Gait (2015: 184, n1) cites figures for the number dead in a battle in which the Ahom defeated the Jaintia kingdom at the beginning of the eighteenth century: of the 2336 men lost on the Ahom side, approximately 60% were from lower Assam, and hence presumably Assamese speakers, compared to only 40% from upper Assam. Although Gait does not provide information on this, we can speculate that the foot-soldiers from upper Assam were more likely *paik* rendering military service than those from lower Assam, where territorial-administrative control through land taxation had been adopted.

In the end, the Ahom kingdom was brought down by what Guha (1983: 38) calls 'peasant revolts under a [neo-Vaishnavism] religious garb', which 'became endemic' after 1770 (see also Purkayastha 2008: 193). The revolts were at least partly in response to '[t]he Ahom state [...] increasing the duration of service a *paik* had to render' to offset the reduction of manpower resources that had resulted from the increasing demand for commutation of *paik* services (Gurung 2018: 101). Also, the 'grant of large numbers of *paiks* [in the mid-eighteenth century to religious institutions such as *satras*] ultimately drained the state treasury in the form of loss of man-power-revenue' (Gogoi Nath 2002: 40). This was a period of dramatic riverine changes as well (Cederlöf 2014: 23), undoubtedly contributing to the revolts and the kingdom's manpower crisis. The implication in analyses of the decline of the Ahom kingdom is that, while a more territorial notion of political control was emerging, control over manpower remained a significant resource for exercising political authority. The Burmese invaded the weakened Ahom kingdom in the early nineteenth century, after the British attempted to help the Ahom king to get the rebellions under control (Cederlöf 2014: 4). In the subsequent Anglo-Burmese war of 1825, the British took control of the Ahom kingdom, first establishing indirect rule, then direct rule in 1838 (Saikia 2004: 97, 101).

Assuming that the above narrative is more or less accurate, what kind of conclusions can we draw? Using the framework of state traditions and language regimes introduced above, we can postulate that the Ahom kingdom's mandala-state traditions most likely informed a heavily multilingual and multiscriptal language regime. The critical juncture, crowning language regime change, appears to have been when the Ahom kingdom reached its height in the mid-seventeenth century, after nearly a century of expansion that increasingly took on a territorial dimension and accelerated a 'liberal policy of offering respectable official positions to new entrants' (Purkayastha 2008: 180). These newest entrants were in effect 'a new social class related to state power' (Purkayastha 2008: 180). They legitimized their new status by having their own *buranji* written in Assamese (Purkayastha 2008: 180; Saikia 2004: 121, 140). This Assamese *buranji* writing had an expanded 'circle of authors and readers', given the increased extent of the Ahom kingdom (Purkayastha 2008: 180). Adding in the increasing political and linguistic influence of neo-Vaishnavism, it seems, then, at the height of state power, the language of literature, and probably spoken language as well, shifted. The new language regime was informed by state traditions that were morphing into more of a territorial notion of the kingdom and a flatter hierarchy through expansion of the elite. Although these emerging state traditions seem closer to those of the modern state, the language regime they informed remained different. Despite the shift to Assamese, the path dependency of multilingualism through language contact most likely remained.[7]

The Colonial State

By all accounts, the Ahom kingdom's shift from a Tai-Kadai language to Indo-Aryan Assamese predates colonialism. While new 'geocultural' concepts may well have underlain the 'literary territorialization' of Assamese (Pollack 1998b: 49), and the Ahom kingdom's mandala-state tradition of non-territoriality appeared to be changing, the political concepts of fixed borders and territorial sovereignty were a colonial

---

7   The linguistic effects of language contact is apparent today, according to Chelliah and Lester (2016: 305): 'Assamese developed a classifier system unusual to Indo-Aryan on the basis of contact with Tai-Ahom.'

introduction. 'Valley homogenization', including some degree of linguistic homogenization, probably also preceded colonial conquest (Scott 2009: 253). However, the linguistic ideology of a 'language' being a discrete, identifiable object 'belonging' to a particular people in a fixed territory was a colonial imposition. There was a fundamental congruence between 'colonial geography' (Baruah 1999: chap. 2) and the colonial language regime. Colonial geography spawned a 'new property regime' informed by the 'Orientalist view that [...] emphasized the discreteness of each village' (Baruah 1999: 48), just as the colonial language regime was based on the 'dogma that those who speak a particular language form a unique, definable unit and that this unit had a particular culture and a particular history' (Scott 2009: 239, quoting Leach 1954: 48). British colonial rule 'provide[d] a radically new representation of the relation of the speaker to his speech (one language, one name, one identity)' (Montaut 2005: 81). Under colonial rule, the recognition and status of Assamese as the language of the erstwhile Ahom kingdom was consolidated, and extended to the colonial political-geographical construct of Assam and ethnolinguistic construct of the Assamese people.

Integral to this consolidation and extension was the colonial patronage of written texts (Mitchell 2009). Colonial patronage differed from the previous royal patronage of what Pollock (1998a) would call aesthetic texts, such as poetry or royal accolades. Because the new colonial rulers assumed that texts were examples of spoken language (Errington 2008: 58), they patronized the production of grammars and dictionaries of Indian vernaculars, often undertaken by missionaries, spurring standardization. Saikia (2004: 6) notes that 'the written language of Assamese was [...] standardized' by the American Baptist Mission printing a translation of the bible in 1835, 'merg[ing] into one' the various scripts used at the time. Written standardization of Assamese in effect reduced, if not eliminated, the multiscriptal characteristic of the previous Ahom language regime. It also undoubtedly accelerated homogenization of spoken Assamese, a process that began, according to Guha (1983: 44), with the 'neo-Vaishnavite missionaries'. Standardization reflected and reinforced the colonial linguistic ideology that ascribes a discrete, identifiable language as the marker of a discrete, identifiable people or ethnicity. It is the key component of linguistic rationalization (Laitin 1988). The colonial state's language regime was founded on the enumeration and delineation, and then standardization, of indigenous languages.

Philology furnished the 'scientific' vindication of the colonial linguistic ideology (Errington 2008: chap. 4). Through the comparison of the 'languages' in written texts, relations — both spatial and temporal — between languages could be established, according to the philological approach. Since languages mapped onto ethnicities/peoples in the colonial language regime, philology provided the groundwork for establishing historical relations between peoples and ethnicities (including races). Those relations were perceived to be hierarchical. Although philologically Sanskrit was related to Greek, Latin and Persian, as Sir William Jones 'discovered', and had spawned 'daughter' or descendent languages such as Assamese (albeit several nodes down the language family tree), the spatial and temporal distance between Sanskrit and its European sisters indicated to colonialists that Sanskrit and by extension India had fallen into decay (Errington 2008: 56 ff). It was a relatively short step from Jones' 'discovery' in 1786 to Macaulay's declaration in 1835 that 'a single shelf of a good European library was worth the whole native literature of India'. Although the Orientalists, such as Jones, and the Anglicists, such as Macaulay, disagreed over language policy choices for Britain's colonial possession (Sonntag 2011), the colonial state's hierarchical and racist tradition reinforced by colonial linguistic ideology informed the language regime of the colonial state.

The 'history' of the Tai Ahom language and the Ahom kingdom's shift to Assamese challenged some of the tenets of colonial linguistic ideology. The language shift seemed to indicate that the Ahom 'conquerors' did not impose their language on their subjects. This did not quite fit with the biologically-based racist ideology of the inherent superiority of conquerors over the conquered that informed colonial language regimes (Errington 2008: 65, 87). As mentioned above, one of the earliest and best known colonial officials to study Assam, and hence the Ahom kingdom, was Edward Gait in the late nineteenth century. According to Arupjyoti Saikia (2008: 152),

> Gait proclaimed that philology could not be a 'real test of race' [...] [because of] numerous examples where one language had supplanted another, or where conquerors adopted the language of the vanquished.

Here he provided the example of the Ahom, who abandoned their 'tribal dialect' in favor of Assamese.

Gait's 'texts' for his history of Assam were primarily *buranji* which, as noted above, were written mainly in Assamese. *Buranji* were somewhat unusual in that, unlike vernacular texts in many other parts of India, they could be 'read' not only philologically but also as historical texts according to the colonial regime of history (Chatterjee 2008: 14). These local circumstances of Gait's inquiry may have led him to discount philology as providing the 'scientific' evidence of racial inferiority in the case of the Ahom and, by extension, the Assamese. But for Gait, Assamese was undoubtedly a more developed language, with its Sanskrit derivation, than the 'tribal dialect' of the Ahom. Hence linguistic superiority — a strong ideological tenet of the colonial language regime — was nevertheless reinforced in the Assamese case albeit not linked to race. The colonial language regime rendered the Ahom language as 'dead' (Saikia 2004: 80), fitting in with philology's biological metaphors (Errington 2008). The demoting of the Ahom language vis-à-vis Assamese in the colonial regime facilitated the demotion of Ahoms and, by extension, the Assamese as a race in the colonial mentality, despite Gait's reservations.

Further reinforcement of the colonial mapping of racial and ethnic hierarchy was accomplished through a new colonial territorial-administrative 'hard boundary' between hill peoples and supposedly more 'advanced' valley peoples (Baruah 1999: 29; Saikia 2004: 57–58). This new colonial territorial regime disrupted the constant exchange between river valley *padi* states and Zomia that had been a defining feature of mandala kingdoms, including the Ahom kingdom (Scott 2009). This disruption facilitated the dismantling of precolonial economic relations and the introduction of a tea plantation economy. For example, slave-hunting was prohibited by the British in the 1830s, for the alleged protection of hill tribes/Zomians, and then slavery itself was abolished in 1860 (Guha 1977: 3, 10). According to Guha (1977: 10–11), '[t]he abolition of slavery almost crippled the old Ahom aristocracy.' The British took over the sale of opium, which had become an important product for trade and consumption during the decline of the Ahom kingdom. Poppy cultivation was banned at the behest of tea plantation owners in order to coerce the Assamese peasantry into laboring on the plantations (Guha 1977: 6, 9–10, 19). A new land tenure system favored the tea plantations and agriculturally marginalized the peasantry (Baruah 2005: chap. 4). The tea plantations and the colonial administration in Assam tended to employ Bengalis, rather than Assamese, in managerial positions (Saikia 2004: 102). In this new colonial hierarchy, the Ahom, now defined as Assamese — and concomitantly the Assamese language — were ranked below the Bengalis and the Bengali language (although above the tribals in the highlands, i.e., Scott's Zomia). The colonial language regime, informed by Western European state traditions, set the stage for the demotic politics of the modern state, which in Assam have taken the form of intense linguistic nationalism.

The Modern State

Language politics have featured prominently in independent India. A significant component of India's postcolonial language regime has been linguistic federalism, institutionalized by the 1956 States Reorganization Act: major Indian languages, including Assamese, form the basis of most states in India's federal union. The vitality of India's major regional languages seems assured with this linguistic territorialization, while minority languages within the linguistic states remain for the most part unprotected. Linguistic rationalization, i.e., the institutionalized linguistic homogenization of the nation-state model, happens within India's linguistic states (Laitin 1989) — in effect, '[l]inguistic federalism has shifted the politicization of language downward, to the state level' (Sonntag 2014: 96). Major Indian languages are also enhanced through another component of the language regime: the Eighth Schedule of the Indian constitution confers the status of national language on an original fourteen languages (including Assamese), now twenty-two (Sarangi 2015). These two components of modern India's language regime provide it with the 'pan-Indian cultural grammar of the nation-province', to use Baruah's (1999: 113) terminology. Language politics play out primarily in the linguistic nation-provinces or states within India. Linguistic nationalism is the ideological fuel for language politics within the Indian states; multiple 'subnationalisms' (Baruah's terminology again) make up India writ large. Hence, despite state-level linguistic rationalization and nationalism, India can be described as having a multilingual, and multiscriptal, language regime.

The intensity of language politics in various states of India since independence has been attributed to colonialism: '[l]inguistic consciousness [...] seemed to have stemmed from the classificatory passion of the colonial agenda [...] providing the grounds for a distinctive language consciousness later on to develop into language claims and conflicts' (Montaut 2005: 87–88). The raising of a distinctive language consciousness in Assam began soon after the British annexed Assam in 1826. The British had made Bengali the official language in 1837 as they were transitioning to direct rule. According to Uddipan Dutta (2016: 68), '[w]hile this was an administrative decision, it created a situation where Assamese was regarded as a dialect of Bengali.'[8] The colonialists also ruled, or administered, Assam from Bengal, not constituting it as a separate colonial province until 1874 (Baruah 1999: 24), a year after they partially restored Assamese for official use (Saikia 2004: 60; Guha 1977: 22). This colonial rendering of Assam as a territorial and linguistic appendage of Bengal sparked Assamese intellectuals, many of them residing in Calcutta and familiar with the Bengal renaissance, to 'make the case that they [the Assamese] were a distinct people with a distinct language and culture' (Baruah 1999: 71). Their case against the British colonial language policy in Assam was paradoxically based on the colonial — and modern — linguistic ideology of discrete peoples having their own discrete language, and their demands therefore resonated with the language regime (Sonntag and Cardinal 2015: 8). It was consequently unsurprising when they allied with missionaries complicit with the colonial regime who promoted the Assamese language as the distinctive feature of Assam, for the purpose of disseminating Christian scriptures to the local population in their own language (Baruah 1999: 71; Saikia 2004: 60). Ironically, the tea industrialists helped cultivate Assam's territorial distinctiveness from

---

8   The view that Assamese is a dialect of Bengali still finds expression in such prominent places as the Oxford Dictionary. The 2010 edition's definition of Assamese as '[t]he Indic language which is the official language of Assam, related to Bengali and spoken by around 23 million people, roughly half in Assam and half in Bangladesh' recently generated an online petition pointing out both its linguistic and territorial errors (https://www.change.org/p/oxford-university-press-wrong-definition-of-assamese-in-oxford-dictionary-of-english?recruiter=38274722&utm_source=share_petition&utm_medium=facebook&utm_campaign=fb_send_dialog&utm_term=autopublish). My thanks go to Mark Turin for informing me about this petition.

Bengal, given the increasing brand recognition of Assamese tea (Baruah 1999: 27). With the association between the Assamese language and the regional territory solidifying, '[l]anguage politics became the channel for new demands' for the Assamese (Saikia 2004: 60).

By the early twentieth century, Assamese intellectuals were wedding their anti-colonialist discourse to the nationalist cause. While some nationalists identified ancient Kamarupa in the lower Brahmaputra Valley as the source of pride in Assamese, others, such as the Assamese historian Surya Kumar Bhuyan, attempted to bond the (Indo-Aryan) Assamese with the (Tai-Kadai) Ahom kingdom in order to authenticate a distinctive ethnolinguistic consciousness, especially distinct from Bengali (Saikia 2008: 161; Purkayastha 2008: 196). The singularity of Assamese consciousness was crucial: 'Bhuyan's portrayal of a generic Assamese society evolving within the Ahom state trie[d] to assure homogeneity by playing down the legacy of a composite culture' (Purkayastha 2008: 194). Bhuyan 'argu[ed] for a language-based nationalism for Assam', with language being 'identified as a central feature defining Assamese culture', for which he 'used the *buranji* texts as a powerful weapon [...] to assert an Assamese linguistic identity' (Purkayastha 2008: 196). Furthermore, Bhuyan made the vital territorial linkage: 'The name (Asam = Ahom) was a symbol of the territorial identity of modern Assam' for him (Purkayastha 2008: 195).

The language-territory-people association, reified under the colonial regime, now resonated in the struggle for independence and beyond. Bhuyan had made the territorial linkage, but in Assam linguistic homogenization remained precarious despite Bhuyan's and others' attempts. Sylhet, which had been considered 'as part of the mostly Bengali-speaking Surma Valley as opposed to the mostly Assamese-speaking Brahmaputra Valley' by colonial authorities was hived off from Assam at Partition, when its population voted by referendum to join (East) Pakistan rather than remain in India (Baruah 1999: 101). However, Cachar, also in the Surma Valley, remained part of Assam. Nagaland was formed in 1963 in a rather unsuccessful attempt to contain an insurgency. Further reorganization of Assam, which had linguistic implications, was postponed until the early 1970s, when Meghalaya, Mizoram and what became Arunachal Pradesh were detached. Even then, linguistic homogenization within Assam remained incomplete: according to the 1991 census, only about 58% of the population claimed

Assamese as their first language (Baruah 1999: 19). By the 2011 census, that figure had dropped to 48% ('Assamese Language Under Threat' 2018). The Assam state government's inability to carry out linguistic rationalization has been at the base of much of the conflict, often violent, in recent decades.

Assam's claims to legitimately constitute a linguistic state in modern India's language regime has been further compromised by the emergence of a Tai-Ahom identity movement in recent decades. As Saikia (2004: 11) puts it, 'the assertion of Ahoms as separate from the Assamese is a problematic sign of the internal breakdown of the composite Assamese identity.' Some self-identifying Ahoms are attempting language revitalization of Tai-Ahom, claiming Thai spoken in Thailand is a related language and seeking assistance from Thai scholars (Saikia 2004: 185–87, 216–21). In this regard, they are downplaying language contact and the multilingualism it has entailed in Assam in their reconstruction of Ahom historical experience, opting for a philological basis to their new, distinct linguistic identity in Assam. The movement also identifies a territorial component to Tai-Ahom identity: the upper Brahmaputra Valley (Saikia 2004: 232). Interestingly, however, one of the main organizations of the movement, the *Ban Ok Publik Muang Tai* (translated as the *Tai-Ahom Sahitya Sabha* in Assamese or Eastern Tai Literary Society), whose 'main agenda [i]s to produce a memory of the Ahom as an ethnic group' through a reinterpretation of the historical records (Saikia 2004: xv, 180), retains in its name the mandala geocultural concept of *muang*. The likelihood of success of the movement is minimal, especially compared to the better-known Bodo movement in Assam. In 2003, Bodos attained territorial recognition through the establishment of a territorial council under their governance; the Bodo are now demanding a separate state in India's federal union. The Bodo language also received recognition in 2003, through its addition to the Eighth Schedule (Sarangi 2015), even though there are, unsurprisingly, many Bodo languages and many Bodo have assimilated linguistically to Assamese (Baruah 1999: 180–83). In contrast, Tai-Ahom activists' ethnolinguistic demands have not gained the same amount of traction in India's current language regime. As suggested throughout this chapter, this may be because by invoking the Ahom kingdom as the historical basis of their ethnolinguistic identity, the activists are also unintentionally invoking the legacy of a multilingual, multiscriptal language regime informed by mandala-state traditions.

Conclusion

Colonial and postcolonial language regimes are palimpsests, imposed not on blank slates but in complex political and cultural environments marked by historically dynamic language contact. While language contact has been recognized as a prominent and ongoing feature of the linguistic environment in South Asia (Emeneau 1956), and certainly characterized precolonial language regimes, it was not institutionalized in India's colonial or postcolonial language regime. In contrast to these latter language regimes, conceptions of language and language use as language contact, without discrete associations with a particular territory or people, informed the language regime of the precolonial Ahom kingdom.

The Ahom kingdom's shift from the Tai-Kadai Ahom language to the Indo-Aryan Assamese language signaled the vernacularization of the Sanskrit cosmopolis in Assam, at a critical junction when the kingdom's mandala-state traditions were being disrupted. Pollock (1998a: 31–32) references the argument that when the kingdoms in the Sanskrit cosmopolis started being spatially defined, then vernaculars took over from Sanskrit, suggesting a close, if not symbiotic, relationship between territorialization and vernacularization. At the height of the Ahom kingdom, the two processes of vernacularization and territorialization were intertwined. That vernacularization happened in Assamese, rather than in the Ahom language, is at least partially explained by the flattening of the elite hierarchy through an influx of Assamese speakers at the critical juncture.

While the legacy of the Ahom language regime can still be detected in the rich linguistic diversity in Assam today, as well as perceived in India's 'multilingual ethos' (Montaut 2005), language politics in Assam today resonate with the modern nation-state's language regime of linguistic rationalization — albeit modulated by India's linguistic federalism, in that linguistic rationalization is the political agenda of states within the Indian union, rather than the nation-state writ large. In Assam's case, linguistic rationalization grates against its linguistic diversity. That diversity reflects the legacy of Assam's multilingualism emanating from a historical constant of language contact. The historically and theoretically grounded case study of Assam that I have presented above exposes the contingency of contemporary language politics informed by a language regime that is path-dependent on linguistic homogeneity.

References

2018 (5 November). 'Assamese Language Under Threat: AXX', *The Sentinel* (Dibrugarh edition), p. 1, https://www.sentinelassam.com/news/assamese-language-under-threat-axam-xahitya-xabhaaxx/

Ahmed, Sarharuddin. 2008. 'Cultural Ties Between India and Ancient Cambodia', *Bulletin of the Assam State Museum* 18: 19–23.

Anderson, Benedict. 1991. *Imagined Communities* (London: Verso).

Baruah, Sanjib. 2005. *Durable Disorder: Understanding the Politics of Northeast India* (New Delhi: Oxford University Press).

Baruah, Sanjib. 1999. *India Against Itself: Assam and the Politics of Nationality* (Philadelphia: University of Pennsylvania Press).

Bhattacharya, Sudhindra Nath. 2005. 'The North-East Frontier — The Land, the People and their Early History' (excerpt from author's *A History of Mughal North East Frontier Policy* [1929]), in *Discovery of North-East India*, Vol. 1: *North-East India — A Panoramic View*, ed. by S. K. Sharma and Usha Sharma (New Delhi: Mittal Publications), pp. 1–39.

Brandt, Carmen. 2015. 'Writing off Domination: The Revival of the Chakma and Meitei Scripts', presentation in the Script Systems and Identity Formation in South Asia panel at the 44th Annual Conference on South Asia, October, Madison, WI.

Cederlöf, Gunnel. 2014. *Founding an Empire on India's North-Eastern Frontiers 1790–1840: Climate, Commerce, Polity* (New Delhi: Oxford University Press).

Chatterjee, Partha. 2008. 'Introduction: History in the Vernacular', in *History in the Vernacular*, ed. by Raziuddin Aquil and Partha Chatterjee (Ranikhet: Permanent Black), pp. 1–24.

Chelliah, Shobhana and Lester, Nicholas. 2016. 'Contact and Convergence in the Northeast', in *The Languages and Linguistics of South Asia: A Comprehensive Guide*, ed. by Hans Henrich Hock and Elena Bashir (Berlin: Walter de Gruyter), Section 2.5.

Coedès, George. 1967. *The Indianized States of Southeast Asia*, ed. by Walter F. Vella; translated by Susan Brown Cowing (Honolulu: East-West Center Press).

Collins, Steven. 2003. 'What is Literature in Pali?', in *Literary Cultures in History: Reconstructions from South Asia*, ed. by Sheldon Pollock (Berkeley: University of California Press), pp. 649–88.

Dutta, Uddipan. 2016. '*Sarbabhoumo Asom*: Three Public Discourses', in *Unheeded Hinterland: Identity and Sovereignty in Northeast India*, ed. by Dilip Gogoi (New York: Routledge), pp. 49–69.

Emeneau, Murray. 1956. 'India as a Linguistic Area', *Language*, 32: 3–16.

Errington, Joseph. 2008. *Linguistics in a Colonial World: A Story of Language, Meaning, and Power* (Malden, MA: Blackwell Publishing).

Evans, Peter, Dietrich Rueschemeyer and Theda Skocpol (eds.). 1985. *Bringing the State Back in* (Cambridge: Cambridge University Press).

Gait, Edward. 2015. *A History of Assam* (Delhi: Surjeet Publications, 8th Indian Reprint).

Gellner, Ernst. 1983. *Nations and Nationalism* (Ithaca: Cornell University Press).

Gogoi Nath, Jahnabi. 2002. *Agrarian System of Medieval Assam* (New Delhi: Concept Publishing Co.).

Gohain, B. K. 1999. *Origin of the Tai and Chao Lung Hsukapha: A Historical Perspective* (New Delhi: Omsons Publications).

Goswami, Surendra Kumar. 1986. *A History of Revenue Administration in Assam, 1228–1826 A.D.* (Guwahati: Spectrum Publications).

Guha, Amalendu. 1983. 'The Ahom Political System: An Enquiry into the State Formation Process in Medieval Assam: 1228–1714', *CSSSC Occasional Paper* (Calcutta: Centre for Studies in Social Sciences) 64 (October): 5–56 https://opendocs.ids.ac.uk/opendocs/handle/123456789/3259

Gurung, Tejimala. 2018. 'Crisis of Sustenance and Decline of the Ahom State in Eighteenth Century Assam', in *The Falling Polities: Crisis and Decline of States in North-East India in the Eighteenth Century*, ed. by Tejimala Gurung (Guwahati: DVS Publishers), pp. 95–124.

Guha, Amalendu. 1977. *Planter-Raj to Swaraj: Freedom Struggle and Electoral Politics in Assam, 1826–1947* (New Delhi: People's Publishing House).

Hobsbawm, Eric. 1990. *Nations and Nationalism Since 1780* (Cambridge, UK: Cambridge University Press).

Kaviraj, Sudipta. 2010. *The Imaginary Institution of India: Politics and Ideas* (Ranikhet: Permanent Black).

Keyes, Charles F. 2003. 'The Politics of Language in Thailand and Laos', in *Fighting Words: Language Policy and Ethnic Relations in Asia*, ed. by Michael E. Brown and Šumit Ganguly (Cambridge, MA: MIT Press), pp. 177–210.

Laitin, David D. 1988. 'Language Games', *Comparative Politics* 20 (3) (April): 282–302.

Laitin, David D. 1989. 'Language Policy and Political Strategy in India', *Policy Sciences* 22: 415–36.

Lahiri, Nayanjot. 1984. 'The Pre-Ahom Roots of Medieval Assam', *Social Scientist* 12 (6) (June): 60–69.

Laponce, Jean. 1987. *Languages and their Territories* (Toronto: University of Toronto Press).

Leach, Edmund. 1954. *Political Systems of Highland Burma* (Cambridge: Harvard University Press).

Lieberman, Victor. 2011. 'What *Strange Parallels* Sought to Accomplish', *Journal of Asian Studies* 4 (November): 931–38, https://doi.org/10.1017/S0021911811001628

Meyerhoff, Miriam and Stanford, James N. 2015. '"Tings Change, All Tings Change": The Changing Face of Sociolinguistics with a Global Perspective', in *Globalizing Sociolinguistics: Challenging and Expanding Theory*, ed. by Dick Smakman and Patrick Heinrich (London: Routledge), pp. 1–15.

Miles, William F. S. 2014. *Scars of Partition: Postcolonial Legacies in French and British Borderlands* (Lincoln: University of Nebraska Press).

Mitchell, Lisa. 2009. *Language, Emotion, and Politics in South India* (Ranikhet: Permanent Black).

Montaut, Annie. 2005. 'Colonial Language Classification, Post-Colonial Language Movements, and the Grassroot Multilingualism Ethos in India', in *Living Together Separately. Cultural India in History and Politics*, ed. by Mushirul Hasan and Asim Roy (New Delhi: Oxford University Press), pp. 75–106.

Parwaz, M. 2018. 'Crisis in the Ahom State in Eighteenth Century', in *The Falling Polities: Crisis and Decline of States in North-East India in the Eighteenth Century*, ed. by Tejimala Gurung (Guwahati: DVS Publishers), pp. 125–48.

Patten, Alan. 2001. 'Political Theory and Language Policy', *Political Theory* 25 (5) (October): 691–715.

Phukan, Girin. 2018. 'Socio-religious Knowledge Culture of the Ahoms', *Indian Journal of Tai Studies*, 18 (October): 193–225.

Pollock, Sheldon. 1998a. 'The Cosmopolitan Vernacular', *Journal of Asian Studies* 57 (1): 6–37.

Pollock, Sheldon. 1998b. 'India in the Vernacular Millennium: Literary Culture and Polity, 1000–1500', *Daedalus*, 127 (3) (Summer): 41–74.

Purkayastha, Sudeshna. 2008. 'Restructuring the Past in Early-Twentieth-Century Assam: Historiography and Surya Kumar Bhuyan', in *History in the Vernacular*, ed. by Raziuddin Aquil and Partha Chatterjee (Ranikhet: Permanent Black), pp. 172–208.

Reynolds, Craig J. 1995. 'A New Look at Old Southeast Asia', *The Journal of Asian Studies*, 54 (2) (May): 419–46.

Saikia, Arupjyoti. 2008. 'Gait's Way: Writing History in Early-Twentieth-Century Assam', in *History in the Vernacular*, ed. by Raziuddin Aquil and Partha Chatterjee (Ranikhet: Permanent Black), pp. 142–71.

Saikia, Yasmin. 2004. *Fragments of Memories: Struggling to be Tai-Ahom in India*. (Duke University Press).

Sarangi, Asha. 2015. 'India's Language Regime: The Eighth Schedule', in *State Traditions and Language Regimes*, ed. by Linda Cardinal and Selma K. Sonntag (Montreal: McGill-Queen's University Press), pp. 205–18.

Scott, James C. 2009. *The Art of Not Being Governed: An Anarchist History of Upland Southeast Asia* (New Haven, CT: Yale University Press).

Sonntag, Selma K. 2011. 'The Changing Global-Local Linguistic Landscape in India', in *English Language Education in South Asia*, ed. by Lesley Farrell, Udaya N. Singh and Ram A. Giri (New Delhi: Foundations Books), pp. 24–35.

Sonntag, Selma K. 2014. 'Depoliticizing Hindi in India', in *Defining the Indefinable: Delimiting Hindi*, ed. by Agnieszka Kuczkiewicz-Fraś (Frankfurt am Main: Peter Lang), pp. 95–105.

Sonntag, Selma K. 2019. 'The Liberal Tradition in America: A Historical-Institutionalist Approach to U.S. Language Policy', in *Language Politics and Policies: Perspectives from Canada and the United States*, ed. by Thomas K. Ricento (Cambridge: Cambridge University Press), pp. 27–44.

Sonntag, Selma K. and Cardinal, Linda. 2015. 'Introduction: State Traditions and Language Regimes: Conceptualizing Language Policy Choices', in *State Traditions and Language Regimes*, ed. by Linda Cardinal and Selma K. Sonntag (Montreal: McGill-Queen's University Press), pp. 3–26.

Terweil, Barend Jan. 1983. 'Ahom and the Study of Early Tai Society', *Journal of the Siam Society* 81 (2): 42–62.

Thongchai Winichakul. 1994. *Siam Mapped: A History of the Geo-Body of a Nation* (Honolulu: University of Hawai'i Press).

Thongchai Winichakul. 1996. 'Maps and the Formation of the Geo-Body of Siam', in *Asian Forms of the Nation*, ed. by Stein Tønnesson and Hans Antlöv (Richmond, UK: Curzon) pp. 67–92.

Tønnesson, Stein and Antlöv, Hans (eds.). 1996. *Asian Forms of the Nation* (Richmond, UK: Curzon).

Wolters, Oliver W. 1999. *History, Culture, and Region in Southeast Asian Perspective*, rev. ed. (Ithaca: Cornell University Press, in cooperation with the Institute of Southeast Asian Studies, Singapore).

3. Transforming Language to Script
Constructing Linguistic Authority through Language Contact in Schools in Nepal

Uma Pradhan

'Earlier they used to speak *phohor* (unclean) and *je pāyo tyehi* (unsystematic) Tharu. Now they speak *rāmro* (good) Tharu, while also learning Nepali', one of the parents told me as he described his child's progress in Jana Kalyan Higher Secondary School (JKHSS).[1] JKHSS had been implementing a Multi-Lingual Education (MLE) program since 2010, with the financial and technical support of United Mission to Nepal (UMN) and the Government of Nepal. As a part of the MLE program, the school used Dangaura Tharu[2] — the language spoken by ninety per cent of the student population — as the language of instruction for all subjects in Grades I–III. In line with this, JKHSS also developed a set of textbooks using three different languages — Tharu, Awadhi, and Nepali simultaneously. As I inquired further about this, the Vice Principal of the school, who is also the chief editor of textbooks, explained the process of MLE implementation and textbook preparation: 'When we started mother-tongue education in our school, we refined our language

---

1 The school requested the use of their actual name, rather than the pseudonym, so that their efforts in mainstreaming mother-tongue education could be publicly recognized.
2 Tharu language is a contested category. Sonntag (1995: 115) notes that 'Tharus are an ethnic group in search of a language'. Though Tharus have succeeded in coalescing pan-Tharu identity, they do not have a singular linguistic identity. Guneratne (1998) identifies at least nine different Tharu languages spoken across Nepal. The variant spoken at JKHSS, Kapilbastu, is commonly known as Dangaura Tharu.

[*parimarjit garyaū*]; we removed 'bad words',³ systematized it and made it suitable for the textbooks.' (Interview, 3 Jan 2014).

This apparent sanitization of the language is one of the ways in which JKHSS prepared the Tharu language for school education. The practice of removing what are seen to be profanities, jargon, bad grammar and mispronunciations — a process that also aims towards linguistic hygiene — is a result of an urge to improve and clean up language (Cameron 1995). In JKHSS, this process of cleansing the language was animated by three main challenges. First, while the MLE program opened up official space for minority language education in JKHSS, it also put a spotlight on its putative lack of appropriate vocabulary, standardization, and grammar. As in many other mother-tongue education schools, the teachers and the school administration of JKHSS had become acutely aware of an "inadequate" level of literary development in their language, especially when developing new textbooks. Second, the MLE program brought minority languages such as Tharu in close contact with the national education system and the dominant language, Nepali. Third, this language contact created a process of negotiating linguistic authority, albeit within the confines of nationally-mandated guidelines. In order to use Dangaura Tharu for education, the school and textbook writers had to change this primarily oral language into a written language, and prepare it for the purpose of education. This chapter explores the ways in which local languages are being reshaped through the process of transforming a spoken language into a written language, and how this dynamic is revealing the understandings of the nation that are currently being reconfigured through language contact in schools.

Methodologically, this chapter is based on fieldwork conducted between August 2013 and March 2014 in Jana Kalyan Higher Secondary School (JKHSS). JKHSS is a government school in Kapilbastu district, in Nepal's Tarai, the plains adjoining India. The school is located in the middle of a Tharu village.⁴ At the time the fieldwork was undertaken, there were a total of 1,048 students in JKHSS, of which 304 students in

---

3   By bad words, he meant the rude words (*gāli*) and forms that denote a less respectful way of addressing people (*tu* instead of *aap*).

4   Tharus are classified as an indigenous nationality (ādivāsi *janajāti*) by the Government of Nepal. According to the Census of Nepal 2011, there are 1,737,470 Tharus in Nepal, making up 6.6% of its total population.

the primary grades were the direct beneficiaries of the MLE project, 90 per cent of whom are Tharus according to school statistics. As part of the MLE program, JKHSS had published textbooks in Dangaura Tharu and Awadhi that were used in JKHSS and its five 'feeder' primary schools. During my fieldwork, I researched how 'mother-tongue' was understood and what was actually happening when the local language was officially introduced in the school. For this purpose, I spent time interacting with students, parents and teachers, observing classroom teaching and staff meetings, studying school textbooks, and participating in the everyday life of the schools. By drawing attention to the Tharu textbook development process, this chapter discusses the ways in which local textbook authors are transforming a primarily oral language such as Tharu into a written script and, through this, claiming linguistic authority.

This chapter argues that by 'performing' a language in a particular way in a particular situation, people assert the legitimate authority of that language and seek to shift power relations between languages. I will elaborate on this by, first, discussing the ways in which local languages are being reconfigured by their supposed sanitization. Second, I will discuss how standardization and correction played a role in the writing of Dangaura Tharu, thus ensuring its claim as 'language' as opposed to 'dialect'. Third, I will show how local languages were transformed in new ways via linguistic standardization. In doing so, I will discuss the ways in which local language authors sought authority through the process of publishing textbooks within the national education framework. This chapter aims to add to the existing scholarship on language contact by highlighting the implications language contact has for the negotiation of linguistic authority, and by drawing attention to the often overlooked dynamics of written language contact and the legitimization of specific regimes of authority. This analysis may help us to appreciate the inherently constructed nature of language.

Linguistic Authority Through Language Contact

In Nepal, the institutional space for the use of minority languages for the purpose of education opened up in a context in which language had become a highly politicized issue. During the 1990s, Nepal witnessed persistent ethno-linguistic activism that raised voices against the 'one nation, one language' policy of an earlier era. Gellner (2007) identifies the post-1990 period as a time of 'ethnicity-building' (distinct from the period of nation-building before 1990) where different ethnic groups made demands for mother-tongue education and the use of local language in public offices, in addition to various other claims for territorial autonomy and recognition. In such a context, language has served as an important tool for promoting and challenging varying visions of Nepal. In response, the Constitution of Nepal (1990) declared Nepal a multi-ethnic (*bahu jātiya*) and multilingual (*bahu bhāsik*) country, with all the languages spoken as mother tongues duly recognized as 'national languages' (*rāstriya bhāsā*). The constitution also granted citizens the fundamental right to primary education in their own mother tongue, a provision that was carried over to the subsequent Constitution of 2015. This official adoption of minority languages for the purpose of education in Nepal is often portrayed as a radical departure from a historical context in which the use of languages other than the one former national language, Nepali, was considered divisive and therefore against the law.

One of the key features of the language movement in Nepal has been its effort to normalize minority languages in public arenas such as education, media, and state institutions. At the time of writing in 2018, there is now a five-minute news broadcast on Radio Nepal, the state-run radio station, in a number of 'languages of the nation' and a weekly page in *Gorakhapatra*, the state-run newspaper, in a number of languages other than Nepali. The Royal Nepal Academy has included research on ethnic languages in its programs since the 1990s. Similarly, Nepal National Plan of Action (GoN 2003:47) has created space in the existing policies that focus on the inclusion of ethnic, minority, Dalit and women and girls on the development and use of local languages. This was further taken up by the School Sector Reform Plan 2009–2015, which set a target of 7,500 schools using the mother tongue as a medium of instruction in grades one to three. In line with this goal, the Government of Nepal piloted multilingual education in seven primary schools in 2009 (mother tongues, Nepali and English as mediums of instruction).[5]

---

5   In 2009, the government of Nepal piloted multilingual education in seven primary schools: Sharada Primary School, Sunsari (Tharu and Uraw), Rastriya Ekta Primary School, Jhapa (Rajbanshi, Santhal, and Nepali), Bhimsen School, Thulo Balkhu, Rasuwa District (Tamang), Rastriya Lower Secondary School, Saraswati Lower Secondary Schools, Thade, Rasuwa (Tamang), and Deurali Lower Secondary School, Dhankuta (Athppahariya Rai) (UNESCO 2011). This research was not conducted in any of these schools.

While such actions have not been enough to bring about significant changes, they have nonetheless opened up spaces for more minority language education, while at the same time demonstrating the Nepali state's commitment to embrace the linguistic diversity of its population.

It is within this constitutional context that JKHSS started implementing multilingual education, and introduced Tharu and Awadhi as languages of instruction. Multi-Lingual Education in Nepal describes a model that involves starting education in the medium of the language that a student already speaks, i.e., the mother tongue. Inside a classroom this means learning school subjects like math, science and social studies in the student's first language (usually the mother tongue, or L1), then introducing a second (Nepali, L2) and third (English, L3) language as 'subjects', and gradually transitioning to L2 and L3 as media of instruction as needed. Multi-Lingual Education is based on the principle of 'first-language-first' in order to help children make a better start, and they go on to perform better than those who begin their education in a language they don't understand (UNESCO 2011). In addition, Multi-Lingual Education also operationalizes provisions in the Constitution of Nepal that recognize the multi-ethnic and multilingual nature of the country. The idea and practice of mother-tongue education thus played out in changing discourses of social inclusion and multi-ethnicity.

In the socio-political context of Kapilbastu, where Nepali is the dominant language of education, multilingual schools such as JKHSS are also spaces where different minority languages come into close contact with dominant languages. Scholars such as Pratt (1991) describes these overlapping spaces as 'zones of contact' or the areas in which two or more cultures communicate and negotiate shared histories and power relations. These are also the spaces where 'cultures meet, clash and grapple with each other' (Pratt 1991: 34). Given that different groups in the contact zones enjoy different power positions, Bourdieu's work on language and power is also instructive here. Bourdieu notes that language symbolizes relation to power, and therefore that no one acquires a language without acquiring a relation to that language (Bourdieu 1977). In this context, what counts as an authoritative performance of language and who is deemed to be a legitimate speaker reveal how social boundaries are constructed.

Multilingual school spaces, therefore, provide an ideal site for exploring the dynamics of language contact in education. They not only bring ethno-linguistic groups together but also provide a context to examine how various actors negotiate a 'complex network of historical power relations between the speakers as well as between the respective groups to which they belong' (Bourdieu 1991: 118). Further, Bourdieu argues that the production and reproduction of relations of power are legitimized through ideologies of language (Bourdieu 1977) and accomplished through social and discursive practices in a number of institutional sites, one of the most important being educational institutions (Bourdieu and Passeron 1970). Through the process of endorsing a particular language as an official language, using it for the purposes of schooling, and providing accreditation, education institutions legitimize the use of languages. Schools thus serve as important institutional spaces for conferring social authority and legitimacy on the use of a specific language in society.

Precisely because of the power-laden dimensions of education, the issue of language in education can become important to the social and political struggles of a country. The choice of language in education can play a critical role in the construction of modes of participation in, and legitimation of, activities controlled by the state. Many studies on language education around the world have discussed how the introduction of a minority language in school education can allow for the possibility of revaluing languages within the same institutions (Gal 1995; Heller 1996; Martin-Jones and Heller 1996). This growing body of research illustrates how particular social groups organize themselves to claim space in these educational institutions. These researchers argue that discursive negotiation in educational institutions can offer insights about the specific kinds of language practices that are legitimized, thereby illustrating the ways in which particular practices help to advance or marginalize the interests of different groups, and in the process alter the relations of power between these groups.

In Nepal, even as mother tongues, in principle, are accepted as the language of education, the 'under-developed' nature of various languages is perceived to pose practical challenges for the successful implementation of mother-tongue education. More mainstream languages, such as Nepali, are regarded as well-developed in terms of their grammar, phonology, vocabulary, standardized form and written tradition, and therefore deemed to be more suitable for use in public domains. Many minority languages in Nepal do not have standard orthographies, grammar, or written traditions. This perceived linguistic 'under-development' assigns minority languages low status, thereby rendering them undesirable for use in public spaces and for the purpose of education. Turin (2006) notes that Nepal's National Language Policy Recommendations Commission presented a four-fold stratification of languages spoken in Nepal, ranked on the basis of having a written form. Written languages were accorded higher status than solely spoken ones. Accordingly, many ethnic and language activists seek to transform spoken languages into written languages as a way to seek linguistic authority. In this chapter, I discuss the ways in which the speakers of minority languages seek to enhance their sociolinguistic status through various mechanisms such as claims of 'authenticity' (Woolard 2016; Jaffe 2001), 'correction' (Bilanuik 2006), 'acceptability' (Gal and Woolard 2001) and 'legitimacy' (Bourdieu 1977).

By analyzing how language is performed in multilingual school spaces, we may be able to discern the process through which linguistic standards and linguistic ideologies are strengthened. Categories such as linguistic standards and authority are produced by expert knowledge as well as linguistic ideologies shared more widely among speakers. By 'doing things with words', as Austin (1962) explains, language performance constitutes social action. When people struggle to elevate and legitimize their identity through language, they reaffirm a system that links linguistic forms with social status. As Heller argues, it is most fruitful to analyze language performances as discursive spaces within which 'social actors, whatever else they may be doing, also define (again and again, or anew) what counts as legitimate language' (2010: 278). Since the minority languages often start out at a relatively less powerful position, these ways of negotiating linguistic authority by adhering to linguistic standards are important methods for minority languages to be legitimized in an educational context. In the following sections, this chapter outlines how language contact in educational institutions has implications for the production, legitimization and distribution of linguistic authority.

Writing Language, Claiming "Authenticity"

When JKHSS joined the MLE program, local teachers in the school commenced an important project of publishing textbooks in Tharu. As Guneratne (1998, 2002) notes, the category 'Tharu' is used to denote several disparate groups of people living in the southern areas of Nepal, often referred to as the Tarai. Although they share the same name — Tharu — the members may belong to many communities with very different languages and cultural practices living across the Tarai.[6] Nonetheless, the Tharu encounter with Hill people has sharpened the sense of Tharu being a distinct group of people, even though different Tharu groups might speak different languages (Guneratne 2002). Several national and local social Tharu organizations such as the Tharu Welfare Society and the Backward Society Education (BASE) have been working on various development projects for the welfare of the Tharu population (Krauskopff 2008; Guneratne 2002). McDonaugh (1989: 200) records the establishment of 'the association for the improvement of Tharu language and literature in the west of Nepal' in the 1970s. Many of these organizations relied on cultural and language activities to organize the various Tharu communities. However, these are primarily oral languages, with very limited written literature, with the result that none of the Tharu languages have been used for education purposes, either in the school or for higher education.

In this context, the textbook writers had the challenging task of not only transforming the oral language into a written one, but also ensuring that it represented "authentic" Tharuness that would be acceptable both at the local and national level. This was important, especially given that the set of mother-tongue textbooks developed by the Nepal Government's Curriculum Development Centre (CDC) in nineteen different languages had not been accepted by the various schools across the country. Since most of the mother-tongue textbooks were centrally published by the CDC in Kathmandu, school administrators and teachers were dissatisfied that books were translations from Nepali textbooks and the contents were disconnected from local realities. In addition, the form of language used in the book did not match with the local variant of that language, and since the printing and distribution of

---

6   At least five distinct groups are popularly known: Rana Tharu in the far western region, Kathariya Tharu to their east, Dangaura Thari near the Dang valley, Chitwaniya Tharu in the Central Tarai and Kochila Tharu in the eastern region of Nepal's Tarai. Teachers in the school listed nine different varieties of Tharu language: Dangaura Tharu, Desauri Tharu, Rana Tharu, Saptaria Tharu, Chitwaniya Tharu, Deukhariya Tharu, Bhaurahia Tharu, Nawalpuria Tharu and Sunsariya Tharu.

these books were coordinated centrally, schools always faced problems in their timely distribution, resulting in availability problems and shortages. Because of these ongoing issues, both the CDC and JKHSS felt that the local publication of the Tharu language curriculum was both relevant and practical.

The books were introduced as 'local' subjects as per the government of Nepal's 2003 (2060 BS) provision for a 'local subject' in the primary school curriculum. In addition, the guidelines for primary education set aside twenty per cent of the curriculum for subjects like social studies and health and hygiene to be based on locally-relevant material (CDC 2007). The Curriculum Development Centre (CDC) outlines the minimum skills and competence to be delivered by textbooks in all languages in its Model Curriculum for Mother Tongue and Textbook Guidelines 2007 (2064 BS). According to the guidelines, the subject material should be prepared in coordination with the local resource center and district curriculum coordination committee. However, in order to be approved by the Curriculum Development Centre (CDC), the school materials needed to adhere to the age-grade objectives and competence level mentioned in the guidelines.

Table 3.1. List of mother-tongue textbooks used in the Jana Kalyan Higher Secondary School (JKHSS).

Name of Textbook	Subject	Class	Language
Apane Bhasa, Apane Sikhi	Tharu	I, II, and III	Tharu
Aapan Bhasa, Apanen Shikhav	Awadhi	I, II, and III	Awadhi
Bighyan Sikhi	Science	I, II, and III	Tharu, Awadhi, and Nepali
Sahajey Sikhi Hisab	Math	I, II, and III	Tharu, Awadhi, and Nepali
Hausille Sikhi, Samajik	Social Studies	I, II, and III	Tharu, Awadhi, and Nepali

Source: Published jointly by JKHSS, the United Mission to Nepal (UMN) and the government of Nepal

Within this state-sanctioned space, JKHSS introduced a series of textbooks in 2010. This series included Tharu language textbooks called *Apane Bhasa, Apane Sikhi* and Awadhi language textbooks called *Aapan Bhasa, Apanen Shikhau* ('let us learn our language') for students in grades 1, 2 and 3. These language textbooks were introduced with the objective of teaching these languages both as a subject and as a medium of instruction. The textbooks included a collection of poems, stories, essays, letters and plays. Each lesson was followed by a list of questions and exercises to ensure that the students had learned the appropriate language skills for that age grade. The textbook writers ensured that the various lessons in the textbook met reading, writing, and comprehension skills as per the guidelines of the Curriculum Development Centre (CDC).

Fig. 3.1. Mother-tongue textbooks in Tharu and Awadi. Photograph supplied by the author with the consent of the textbook publishers, CC BY.

3. Transforming Language to Script

Fig. 3.2. Math textbook, lesson 5, page 5. Photograph supplied by the author with the consent of the textbook publishers, CC BY.

For subjects like science, mathematics and social studies, the books were prepared using three languages — Nepali, Tharu and Awadhi — simultaneously on every page. In the textbook extract above, presented on the right, the mathematics chapter on geometry is printed with Tharu on the top, followed by Awadhi and Nepali. Each line in the textbook is written in three different languages. The school teachers explained that although 90 per cent of JKHSS students speak Tharu as their first language, they also have students who speak Awadhi and Nepali as their first languages. All three languages — Tharu, Awadhi, and Nepali — belong to the Indo-Aryan language family, and are shown in Figure 3.1. The three languages are recognized as distinct, considered to be mother tongues by different linguistic communities, and have varied literary traditions (as will be outlined in the following sections).

Therefore, in order to facilitate the mother-tongue education of this multilingual student population, the textbook was written using different languages. Moreover, Devanagari script was used for all three languages to facilitate easy readability. The choice of script will be discussed further below.

These books were written and printed locally, and their chapters made reference to various objects and activities that were considered 'authentic' representations of the locality. The textbook writers made a particular effort to include local stories, names, contexts, and pictures while designing the contents of each book. This space occupied by 'the local' (*sthaniya*) in the textbooks enabled the textbook writers to reproduce more 'authentic' language and to establish mother-tongue education as legitimate pedagogy. This process of textbook publication was not without conflict and contestation. The national guidelines also required the school-level bodies such as the School Management Committee (SMC) and the Parent Teacher Association (PTA), as responsible bodies, to support and sign off on the textbook production. In case of any disagreement between the textbook writers and the committees, the final decision was reached on the basis of the most 'authentic' and 'local' representation, in addition to an adherence to the guidelines provided by the government of Nepal.

These textbooks included local knowledge for educational purposes within the national curriculum framework, and often presented overtly essentialized notions of ethnicity as the 'authentic' identity of Tharu and Awadhi language speakers. Through this process, more 'traditional' representations of Tharu and Awadhi culture and artifacts influenced final decisions on the subject matter, pictures, and the presentation of the book. As other studies on minority languages around the world have also pointed out, the idea of 'authenticity' serves an important function in reconstructing the public form of a language and negotiating its authority. Stroud (2003) points out that using the notion of authenticity, local languages are articulated as the social identities of their speakers. Authenticity, Woolard (2016) explains, is more concerned with who one is rather than what one says, i.e., with social indexicality rather than referential function.

Mother-tongue education was therefore not just about getting marginalized groups into and through schools successfully, but also

Fig. 3.3. Class 2 Tharu textbook, lesson 10, page 33. Photograph supplied by the author with the consent of the textbook publishers, CC BY.

about changing the nature of education itself, in both its organization and in its curriculum. Comparing his efforts in contributing to textbooks with his early experience of publishing Tharu newspapers, the chief editor of the Tharu textbooks reasoned: 'Writing a school textbook is more meaningful. Once approved, it is printed in thousands of copies and the younger generation read it and learn about it' (Interview, 15

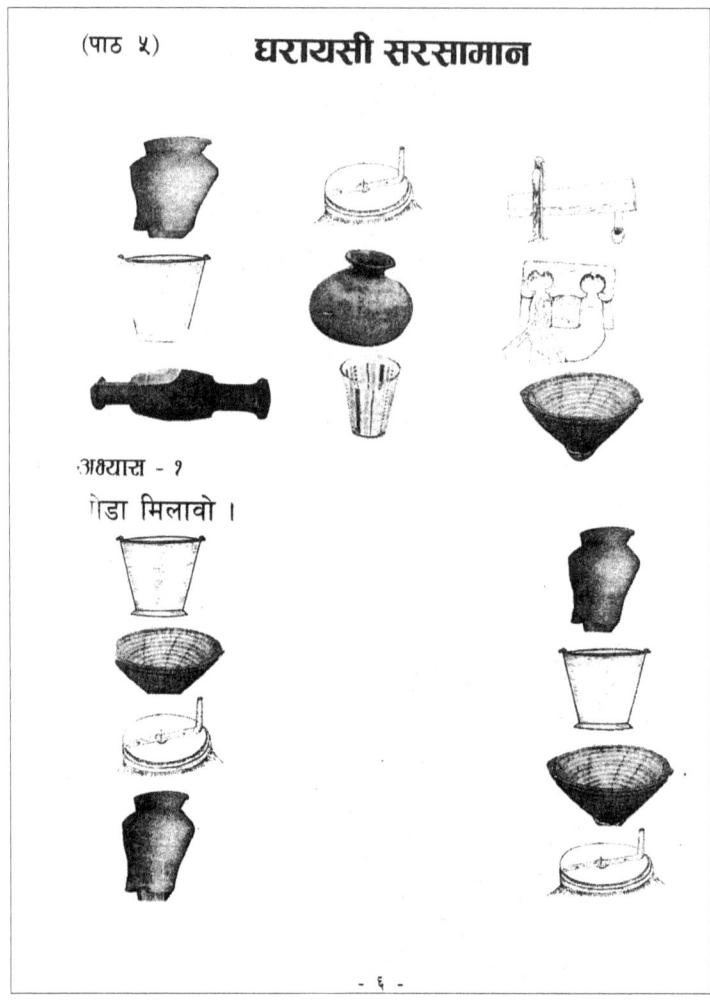

Fig. 3.4. Class 2 Awadhi textbook, lesson 3, page 68. Photograph supplied by the author with the consent of the textbook publishers, CC BY.

Jan 2014). Teaching language to the younger generation in the schools was seen as an important way to keep a language alive, especially in the context of Nepal where studies have shown that younger people are increasingly ceasing to speak their mother tongues (Pettigrew 2000; Turin 2013). In order to combat this and to reformulate the grounds on which demands for the language could be made, the school actively engaged in publishing textbooks in local languages and seeking recognition. This was also seen as an important way to overcome the designation of their language as a 'dialect.'

Language, Dialect, and Making "Corrections"

According to the introductory section of the textbooks, one of their objectives was to strengthen students' competence in speaking, reading, writing and understanding the language. The emphasis on various aspects of language competence, including reading and writing in addition to speaking and understanding, meant that these languages required a systematic written tradition. In a context where the languages did not have a well-developed written tradition, the process of writing books transformed the languages in ways that would impute 'rationality to intelligible utterances' (Burghart, 1993: 763). This meant developing an internal process to set phonological rules and grammatical structures, and to develop age-grade appropriate literary vocabulary. The teachers and the school administration in JKHSS thus sought to 'refine' their languages through textbooks. Weinberg (2015) also documents a similar process of publishing school textbooks in order to facilitate education in the Dhimal language — a language spoken by the Dhimal community, primarily located in the Jhapa and Morang districts of southern Nepal.

This emphasis on various aspects of language competence, including reading and writing in addition to speaking and understanding, meant that each language required the development of a writing system and an agreed orthography. Therefore, as Turin (2006: 66) points out 'the lexicalization of a language and the development, or resurrection, of a suitable script or set of orthographical conventions have become prerequisites for introducing a language into education as the medium of instruction.' Explaining the situation of different languages in Nepal, Noonan (2006: 179) argues that for languages such as Gurung, Magar, and Tamang, the differences between dialects will have to be resolved before a standard can emerge if these languages are ever to serve as vehicles of education or administration. A similar thought animated the Nepal National Language Policy Commission when they presented a four-fold stratification of language on the basis of having a written form. The written tradition has gradually become the basis for a 'caste-system of language' (Turin 2006).

Many studies on the Tharu language have shown that Tharu is a highly contested linguistic category (Sonntag 1995; Guneratne 1998). Scholars have also noted the difficulty in distinguishing it from its regional Indo-Aryan variants such as Awadhi, Maithili and Bhojpuri. However, since Tharu is often perceived as a language mainly spoken in Nepal, as opposed to Awadhi, Maithili and Bhojpuri which are also spoken in India, Tharu has often been prioritized in the Nepali state's language policy (Sonntag 1995). This perception was echoed by the chief editor of the textbooks who stated, 'Awadhi and Tharu are very different languages. In addition to the use of a distinct set of adjectives and a grammatical structure, one of the distinctive features is that Awadhi is closer to Hindi whereas Tharu is closer to Nepali' (Interview, 3 Jan 2014). In his MA thesis on Tharu and English adverbs, he had made this case when arguing for the position of Tharu as a distinct language. In his thesis, he also annexed a collection of Awadhi adverbs used in his locality. This list clearly listed that the Tharu and Awadhi had very different words used as adverbs; thus showing that Tharu and Awadhi are different languages. As Burghart (1984) points out 'mutual unintelligibility with other languages' is not necessarily the main criteria for determining a language. The difference between *bhasa* (language) and *bhashika* (dialect) is determined by its social and political status. *Bhasika* is by definition local and spoken (*sthaniya boli*). A *bhasa* exists in a formal sense (dignified by grammatical description) and possesses written literature, making schooling in that language possible.

The writing of textbooks in JKHSS also facilitated a larger project of developing grammatical descriptions for the purposes of written literature. However, this process also transformed these languages into new forms. The legitimacy of a language as an acceptable tool for education is often linked to 'correct' use of the linguistic code. The constant process of 'correction' of the Tharu and Awadhi languages served a dual function: first, to ensure distinctiveness and, second, to gain acceptance as a formal language. This also allowed these languages to find a space within state institutions, as languages with fully-developed writing systems and codified grammar. For Tharu, which is primarily a spoken language with limited written traditions, this process was also seen as a way to demarcate the linguistic identity of one language from that of the other. For languages like Awadhi, which has a written tradition, the process of textbook writing enabled it to be presented as a more formal language.

'Writing' therefore became a way to prevent a language from being labelled as a dialect of another language. It also helped to standardize the language, thereby granting it the status of a developed language in which schooling would be possible. Though Dangaura Tharu had a written tradition, it had not been systematized earlier. Drawing mainly from the oral traditions and limited written material available, Tharu textbooks were prepared. In the case of the Awadhi language, though it had a fairly well-developed written grammar, there were disagreements regarding the use of some vowels. In spoken Awadhi, the vowel *'ya'* is more commonly used, instead of *'ai'* used in Nepali. The first set of text books printed in Awadhi therefore used the vowel *'ya'* in the text, e.g., *padhaya* (to read), *banakaya* (in the forest). However, in the later versions, they decided to use the vowel *'ai'* instead of *'ya'* e.g., *padhai* (to read), *banakai* (in the forest). This rewriting of Awadhi, resembling the Nepali system, was considered more practical because was would facilitate easy reading in schools.

This process of correction works to maintain patterns linked with the language of power, which in turn become more visible in the form of judgements about the language. Scholars studying the development of the Nepali language have repeatedly illustrated similar dynamics in the language standardization that occurred in the 1900s. In the early 1900s, Nepali had a very limited literary role compared to many other languages used in India such as Hindi and Bengali. Nepali was characterized, as Chalmers (2003: 144) points out, by a lack of uniformity in spelling, grammar, and style. In addition, it was not the only language spoken by people of Nepali origin residing in India. Disappointed by the state of their language, the Nepali-educated middle class living in Banaras and Darjeeling spearheaded a language revival movement. The process to standardize Nepali also brought Nepali writers from different places to agree on the most acceptable form of literary Nepali (Hutt, 1988). Chalmers (2003) notes that the idea of the *unnati* (progress) of the Nepali population was the key driver of much of the work on developing the Nepali language in Benaras. These early Nepali literary scholars regularly published journals for the purpose of *'bhasonnati'* (language progress) to mitigate a perceived sense of backwardness in relation to other communities in India.

साफ पीढ़ा पर धइकय घुघुरी अँव लावा चढ़ावत हिन ।

जानत हैव यह दिन सब के सब सज-बज कय अपने-अपने इच्छा अनुसार केय खेल खेलय, फलुवा फूलय अँव आल्हा सुनय जात हयँ । लेकिन यह दिने सब से बडा होत हय बिटियन केय फलुवा । बिटियय नवा-नवा कपडा पहिर केय फुण्ड केय फुण्ड बगियामें फलुवा फूलय जात हिन । फलुवा फूलत केय समय कजरी गावत हिन । यह तिउहार के खास कइकय बिटियन केय ससुरारि से नइहरे बोलावा जात हय । नाग देवतक पूजा खतम होयक बादमें सन्झक जूने लड़के लोग बासेक कइन से गुड्डीन पीटत हयँ ।

यहिक नाते नाग पञ्चमी केय गुडियक तिउहार फिर कहा जात हय । यहि किसिम से नाग पञ्चमी केय तिउहार धार्मिक अँव सामाजिक दूनौं दृष्टि से बहुत महत्वपूर्ण हय ।

५४

Fig. 3.5. Class 2 Awadhi textbook, lesson 16, page 54. Photograph supplied by the author with the consent of the textbook publishers, CC BY.

The legitimacy of a language as an acceptable tool for education is often linked to 'correct' use of the linguistic code. This constant process of 'correction' of the language serves a dual function: firstly to ensure distinctiveness and secondly to gain acceptance. This practice of language 'correction,' as Bilaniuk (2005) points out in her study of Ukrainian language politics, is an important way to claim language

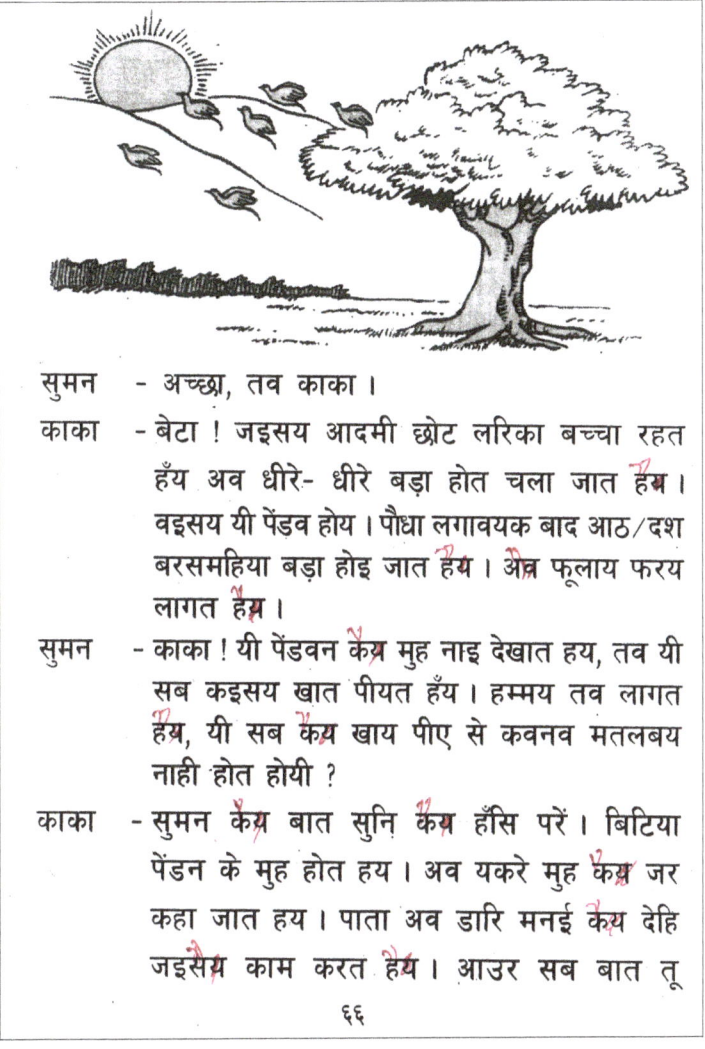

Fig. 3.6. Class 2 Awadhi textbook, lesson 3 page 66. Photograph supplied by the author with the consent of the textbook publishers, CC BY.

authority. She argues that the legitimacy of a language as a discrete entity is often linked to linguistic correctness, and points out that a locally-spoken hybrid language, known as *surzhik*, was stigmatized as a substandard form of speech. This cleansing of language has also been defined by Deborah Cameron (1995) as linguistic 'hygiene', a normative practice that represents a symbolic attempt to impose a particular order on linguistic practice. It is for this reason that Bourdieu (1991: 60) defines 'legitimate language' as a semi-artificial language that has to be sustained by a permanent effort of correction.

By striving to refine their language, the textbook writers were altering it from the multiplicity of oral forms to the singularity of a written form. In addition, this process helped to stabilize and standardize the language. Such corrections show that the professional linguist's insistence on objectivity and scientific inquiry appears to arise partly from the neglect of the sociological use and importance of language. Historical studies of language show that standard languages have often been superimposed on dialects (Milroy and Milroy 1985). As Bourdieu reminds us, it is important to appreciate that 'disagreements over merit or demerit of specific forms, whether particular pronunciation, lexical items, or syntactic forms, mask the fact that in their disagreement people are agreeing to the rules of the game by which the legitimacy is defined' (1991: 58). By carefully constructing what speaking the 'authentic' language means, the textbook writers and teachers also reveal the value attached to certain linguistic rules and the ways these rules determine people's choices towards correction and purification in anticipation of social acceptability.

Language, Script, and Social Acceptability

As the language activists and JKHSS school administration began to systematize the language for the purpose of schooling, they also engaged in the process of standardization. Transforming oral language to written form also meant that many variations of the same word or many words for the same objects had to be presented in a uniform manner. Sheshram Chaudhury, the chief editor of the Tharu textbooks, said 'In cases where different names were used to denote the same thing, we chose the one that was closer to Nepali.' Similar language dynamics have been documented by Hutt (1986) in his analysis of the Nepali language standardization process, where Nepali intellectuals deliberately chose Sanskrit words that were different from the Hindi words, in order to establish Nepali as a distinct language. This ensured that the local languages had wider readability, mediated potential conflicts, and enabled them to engage more meaningfully with the state.

Fig. 3.7. Class II social studies textbook, lesson 2, page 40, written in Tharu, Awadhi and Nepali, using Devanagari script. Photograph supplied by the author with the consent of the textbook publishers, CC BY.

Moreover, all the books were in written in the Devanagari script, the same writing system used for the Nepali language. The teachers in JKHSS explained that the use of a common script makes it easier for all the various people involved: the writers and the teachers can follow it easily, and the students learn it faster as the same script is used in most of their other school subjects. Since many languages either do not have a separate script or have more than one script associated with their language, it is easier for language workers to use Devanagari. Using a common script was seen as a way to make the language legible to the state and to other people who were literate in Nepali. According to the recommendations presented in a Report on Primary Education in Mother Tongue (GoN 1997):

> Devanagari script must be used when using mother tongue as a language of instruction, while protecting the authenticity of the language (*niji visheshta*). If different languages are used, the students will face difficulties when they graduate to higher grades. This might hinder the overall development of education in Nepal. In order to avoid this problem, a common script i.e., Devanagari, must be used. Historically, we have seen that languages such as Maithili and Newari have used Devanagari script. This will serve many purposes: it will strengthen the unity of the country, the students will not be overburdened with the additional script, and it will also facilitate easier learning of Nepali texts.[7]

Various other book-writing instruction manuals recommended similar positions. The Support Material for Implementation of Multilingual Education Program (Kadel 2010: 83) cautions mother-tongue textbook writers against placing emphasis on the language rather than the script. It urges writers to follow the phonetic pronunciation of the word in the mother tongue and use Devanagari script to codify it in writing. If there are any popular ways of writing any words in the mother tongue, Nepali or English language, the book suggests a similar convention must be used in writing them in the mother tongue, e.g., the English word 'computer' should be written phonetically in Devanagari. Similarly, a Report on Primary Education in Mother Tongue (GoN 1997: 12) recommends that every language should collect at least 5,000 basic words so that it could be used for the purpose of primary education. In addition, every subject, such as science, social studies, mathematics, health, literature etc. should include an additional 1,000 subject-specific words to the textbook vocabulary. If some (technical) words are not available in local languages, these words can be taken from other languages.

The emphasis on having a standard script for different languages serves multiple functions. First, different languages that do not have a

---

7   Translation by the authors.

standard script may seek to develop their language into written form. Second, it mediates potential internal tensions within the language group that may arise if there were more than one script that were commonly used. Third, the use of a standard script facilitates the wider recognition of the language. This particular way of constructing the social 'acceptability' of language highlights a deep-rooted social hierarchy, as well as its manifestation in language. This creation of an apparently naturalized link between language and its social value, often referred to as language ideology, is a judgement based on the existing social order (Gal and Irvine 1995). It is through an adherence to these widely accepted forms that people seek to either confer or deny social legitimacy.

While there are many minority languages in Nepal that have been advocating for their own distinct scripts (e.g., *prachalit lipi* for Nepal Bhasha, *sirijunga* script for the Limbu language), it has been difficult for language activists to garner wider social acceptance at the national level. Language activists often see a unique script as an embodiment of an 'authentic' language and as an important milestone in gaining higher status on the national stage, especially with the Language Commission (Shneiderman and Turin 2006). In JKHSS, however, the textbook writers paradoxically saw the unique script as posing a challenge in making the language more accessible to the students and more acceptable to the Nepali government. These overall frameworks that shape linguistic practices are invariably manifestations of linguistic ideologies, and indicate the practices in the making of political authority (Gal and Woolard 2001).

It is also important to note that the schools at no point sought to establish themselves as separate from the state. On the contrary, their efforts were geared towards engaging with the state more effectively. For the schools, strong engagement with the state was essential for gaining its recognition of mother-tongue education and strengthening their relationship with the state. This emphasis on working with the state is also prominent in the Diamond Jubilee souvenir book from 2011, published by JKHSS, which begins with a letter of commendation from the then Prime Minister, Dr Baburam Bhattarai. In the souvenir book, written in Nepali, the Prime Minister commends the school for its 'exemplary' work and hopes that this inspires other schools to follow the same path. The school magazine also includes letters of appreciation from the Minister for Education, Mr Dinanath Sharma, Minister for

Women, Children and Social Welfare, Mr Dan Bahadur Chaudhary, Secretary of Education, Mr Kishor Thapa, and the District Education Officer, Mr Shankar Bahadur Gautam.

Language, Education and Frames of "Legitimacy"

Textbook writing was an important way to engage with the state effectively via its curriculum development framework. As I came to know later, the Curriculum Development Centre rejected the first set of books written at JKHSS when they were reviewed against the criteria for school textbooks and learning objectives specified for each school year. Sharing his experiences, Bikram Tripathy, a writer in Awadhi and one of the trainers for book-writing workshops, said, 'The school had misunderstood the local textbook guidelines. If the schools publish their own textbooks, they need to abide by the criteria set out in the curriculum development guidelines and apply for approval from the Ministry of Education.'

The curriculum framework demarcated the boundaries of what is considered appropriate school knowledge. The curriculum evaluation proforma, used by the government of Nepal to evaluate the additional school textbooks, lists several criteria for the evaluation of the textbooks. One important criterion for approval is adherence to the guidelines on the subject matter of the textbook. This includes questions such as: Do the lessons comply with the topic mentioned in the curriculum guideline? Do the contents respect national values and integrity, respect *janajati* identity, and preserve the languages of the nation? Does it portray a balance of traditional and modern skills, technology, and employment? Do the books pay attention to localization and pay attention to the inclusiveness of various identities? The CDC also mandates that textbooks present a balanced collection of different genres, including local stories, essays and poems (CDC 2007).

Through this process of selecting, classifying and distributing school knowledge, the Nepali state delineated the boundaries of the ways in which certain stories and representations could be expressed as public knowledge. The Mother Tongue Textbook Guidelines also notes that one of the important objectives of primary education is to build the moral character of the student by instilling the values of national unity and democratic culture (CDC 2007). This usually translates into demonstrating that the contents of the school textbook respect ethnic identities and national identity. However, the possibility of pitting an ethnic identity against the national identity is completely ruled out. Vigilance on such issues of national sovereignty and integrity was evident from the guidelines published by the government, and in the school textbook that was finally published.

This textbook creation process also transformed language in different ways. As listed in the evaluation criteria, local language was reshaped to include not only words and concepts that are appropriate for the purpose of school education, but the reorganization of the language through the rules of grammar and standardization. For example, the curriculum evaluation proforma also had a section on linguistic evaluation: the richness of vocabulary, appropriateness of grammar, clarity of language, age-grade appropriateness of the subject matter, and appeal of the presentation. This required the textbook's writing team to transform the spoken language into written language, thereby limiting various forms of expression. This process also shaped an understanding of which form of a language is considered to be appropriate by its formal acceptance in school textbooks.

After the first set of textbooks was rejected, the textbook team in the school revised them systematically. JKHSS also held several rounds of training and workshops for all the authors in order to communicate the process of writing school textbooks. The writers and editors of these books carefully followed the existing curriculum guidelines while designing the textbooks. In JKHSS, I was often told by the teachers that it was important to have Tharu textbooks if they wanted to teach the MLE program properly. Moreover, the official approval of the publication of these textbooks meant that the approach of the school was endorsed by the state, thus making it a form of legitimate knowledge. In JKHSS, the textbooks were approved on the second application. The result was three different seals on the textbook: those of the government of Nepal, the United Mission to Nepal (UMN), and the School itself.

This wider acceptance from the state is important in Nepal, where programs like MLE face multiple challenges. Since it was supported by a Christian faith-based NGO in UMN, both JKHSS and UMN were careful in presenting MLE as a non-political initiative. At the time of this fieldwork, another faith-based organization — the Summer Institute of Linguistics (SIL) — was under scrutiny due to alleged proselytizing while implementing mother-tongue education. In this context, UMN was cautious about this issue and presented MLE as a technical project to facilitate access and quality of education. There was a conscious effort not to stir up any potentially controversial issues such as religious conversion, ethnic politics, or political demands for a separate *Tharuhat* region. The schools negotiated this legitimacy by, firstly, holding the state accountable to the provisions made in the constitution, and secondly, by adhering to legitimate and widely-accepted frameworks for language education. The textbook authors also sought to mitigate deep-rooted tensions around issues of ethnicity and language in Nepal, emphasizing MLE as an education program rather than a politically charged issue.

State officials also readily accepted the discourse of legal and constitutional provisions. As one high-ranking official in the Ministry of Education stated,

> These days in Nepal there is national-level political consensus around diverse languages [...] there is an inclusive discourse. It has become the foundation of our constitution (*sambidhān-ko* ādhar). Even in the popular media, such as TV and radio, we can hear advertisements in different languages. So it is impossible to say no to mother-tongue education (Interview, November 2013).

The constitution provides a widely endorsed framework that serves to bring various conflicting groups into alignment. In my interviews with various NGO personnel, language activists, government officials, and teachers, I was often told that the demand for mother-tongue education is a demand to make the state accountable to provisions guaranteed in the constitution, and implementing the rights guaranteed in international covenants such as the Universal Declaration of Human Rights 1948 and the United Nations Declaration on the Rights of Indigenous People 2007. Based on these provisions, the Government of Nepal also oriented its education policies towards mother-tongue education in the National Education Committee 1992, the Higher Education Commission 2000, the Basic Primary Education Program 1991–2004, and School Sector Reform Program 2010–2015 (UNESCO 2011: 28).

The endorsement from the state was central to claiming legitimacy in national education. In one of the conversations in JKHSS, a teacher said, 'We realized that we could impart education in the Tharu language only after our school officially started MLE and we started using these new books.' This was quite an odd realization because JKHSS had been using Tharu in the classroom as a medium of informal instruction before the program officially started in 2010. Nonetheless, it was only after the introduction of the state-supported initiative that teachers acknowledged it as acceptable pedagogy. The official introduction of mother-tongue education provided it with institutional visibility and much-needed legitimacy.

Conclusion

This contribution illustrates the process by which linguistic authority is negotiated in the context of language contact in mother-tongue schools. As discussed in this chapter, this context created a productive space where a complex negotiation of linguistic legitimacy could take place, albeit in a limited way, sanctioned by the state. In JKHSS, students were fluent in Tharu and used it as the main language of communication. However, this competence and the local relevance did not legitimize these languages as the language of education. Though the language hierarchy has been increasingly questioned in contemporary Nepal, it still plays an important role in the context of education. In this context, the school used language standardization as a key strategy to negotiate the position of the mother tongue as the language of education within a state-sanctioned space of multilingual education. By analyzing the construction of apparently neutral grammatical and lexical forms, this chapter draws attention to the sociocultural process that shapes the socially charged life of language (Ahearn 2017).

What emerges strongly from the practices in these schools is a process of claiming language authority that, paradoxically, conforms to the existing systems of education. In this process, different ethno-linguistic communities have sought to define and redefine their languages in order to claim linguistic authority and gain recognition from the state. The discussion presented in this chapter also points out that the negotiation of linguistic authority is inevitably framed, and constrained, by wider historical and social relations. The analysis of the process of linguistic authority construction serves as a lens to understand the ways in which such legitimizing ideologies and their authority are redefined and reimagined. In such contexts, education offers a symbolic space where, as Levinson et al. describe, 'new relations, new representations, and new knowledge can be formed, sometimes against, sometimes tangential to, sometimes coincident with the interests of those holding power' (1996: 22). And while there might be no cohesion or consensus, dynamics in a mother-tongue school generated a process where the production of textbooks in a minority language was seen to be viable for school education.

Acknowledgements

I am deeply indebted to the teachers, parents and students of Jana Kalyan Higher Secondary School for allowing me to be part of their lives during my PhD fieldwork. I am also grateful to United Mission to Nepal (UMN) team. This research would not have been possible without their logistical support and countless insightful discussions with the United Mission to Nepal (UMN) team. I would like especially to thank Khitiz Raj Prasai (UMN), Sheshram Chaudhary (JKHSS), and Nanda Kumar Giri (JKHSS) for their time and support. This paper has benefitted enormously from feedback from and discussions with David Gellner, Nandini Gooptu and David Mills at the University of Oxford. I cannot thank enough the editors of this volume, Selma Sonntag and Mark Turin, for their very detailed feedback and the opportunity to publish this chapter. All errors remain my own.

References

Ahearn, L. 2017. *Living Language: An Introduction to Linguistic Anthropology*, (Oxford: Wiley Blackwell).

Austin, J. L. 1962. *How to Do Things With Words: The William James Lectures Delivered at Harvard University in 1955* (London: Oxford University Press).

Bilaniuk, L. 2005. *Contested Tongues: Language Politics and Cultural Correction in Ukraine* (Ithaca, NY: Cornell University Press).

Bourdieu, P. and Passeron, J. C. 1970. *Reproduction in Education, Society and Culture* (Beverly Hills, CA: Sage).

Bourdieu, P. Transl. G. Raymond and M. Adamson 1991. *Language and Symbolic Power* (Cambridge, MA: Harvard University Press).

Bourdieu, P. 1977, 'The Economics of Linguistic Exchanges', *Social Science Information* XVI: 645–68.

Burghart, R. 1993. 'Quarrels in the Language Family: Agency and Representations of Speech in Mithila', *Modern Asian Studies* 27: 761–804.

Burghart, R. 1984. 'The Formation of the Concept of Nation-State in Nepal', *Journal of Asian Studies* 44: 1–25.

Cameron, D. 1995. *Verbal Hygiene* (London New York: Routledge).

Chalmers, R. 2003. *Language, Literature, and the Formation of a Nepali Public Sphere in India, 1914–1940* (PhD Dissertation, School of Oriental and Asian Studies (SOAS), University of London).

Gal, S. and Irvine, J. 1995. 'The Boundaries of Languages and Disciplines: How Ideologies Construct Differences', *Social Research* 62: 967–1001.

Gal, S. and Woolard, K. 2001. *Languages and Publics: The Making of Authority* (Oxon, NY: Routledge).

Gellner, D. N. 2007, 'Caste, Ethnicity and Inequality in Nepal', *Economic and Political Weekly* 42: 1823–28.

Government of Nepal (GoN), *Guideline for Development of Mother-Tongue Textbook and Curriculum. Ministry of Education* (Sanothimi Bhaktapur: Curriculum Development Centre, Ministry of Education, 2007 (2064 BS.)).

Government of Nepal (GoN), *Guidelines for Local Subject in Primary Education* (Sanothimi Bhaktapur: Curriculum Development Centre, Ministry of Education, 2003 (2060 BS)).

Government of Nepal (GoN), *Report on Primary Education in Mother Tongue* (Sanothimi Bhaktapur: Curriculum Development Centre, Ministry of Education, 1997).

Guneratne, A. 2002. *Many Tongues, One People* (Ithaca and London: Cornell University Press).

Guneratne, A. 1998. 'Modernization, the State, and the Construction of a Tharu Identity in Nepal', *The Journal of Asian Studies* 57: 749–73.

Heller, M. 1996. 'Legitimate Language in a Multilingual School', *Linguistics and Education* 8, 139–57.

Heller, M. 2010. *Media, The State, and Linguistic Authority*, in *Language Ideologies and Media Discourse: Texts, Practices, Politics*, ed. by Sally Johnson and Tommaso M. Milani (London: Continuum).

Hutt, M. 1986. 'Diversity and Change in the Languages of Highland Nepal', *Contributions to Nepalese Studies* 14: 1–24.

Hutt, M. 1988. *Nepali: A National Language and its Literature* (New Delhi and London: Sterling Publishers).

Kadel, P. 2010. *The Support Material for Implementation of Multilingual Education Program* (Kathmandu: Language Development Centre).

Krauskopff, G. 2008. 'An "Indigenous Minority" in a Border Area: Tharu Ethnic Associations, NGOs, and the Nepalese State, in *Resistance and the State: Nepalese Experience*, ed. by David N. Gellner (New Delhi: Social Science Press), pp. 199–243.

Martin-Jones, M. and Heller, M. 1996, 'Language and Social Reproduction in Multilingual Settings, *Linguistics and Education* 8: 127–37.

McDonaugh, C. 1989. 'The Mythology of the Tharu: Aspects of Cultural Identity in Dang, West Nepal', *Kailash* 15: 191–206.

Noonan, M. 2006. 'The Rise of Ethnic Consciousness and the Politicization of Language in West-Central Nepal', in *Lesser Known Languages in Nepal: Status and Policies, Case Studies and Applications of Information Technology*, ed. by Anju Saxena and Lars Borin (Berlin and New York: Mouton de Gruyter), pp. 161–74.

Pettigrew, J. 2000. 'Gurkhas in the Town: Migration, Language and Healing', *European Bulletin of Himalayan Research* 19: 7–40.

Pratt, M. L. 1991. 'Arts of the Contact Zone', *Profession* 33–40.

Shneiderman, S. and Turin, M. 2006. 'Seeking the Tribe: Ethno-politics in Darjeeling and Sikkim', *Himal Southasia* (March-April): 54–58.

Stroud, S. 2003. 'Postmodernist Perspectives on Local Languages: African Mother-Tongue Education in Times of Globalization', *International Journal of Bilingual Education and Bilingualism* 6: 17–36.

Sonntag, S. K. 1995. 'Ethnolinguistic Identity and Language Policy in Nepal', *Nationalism and Ethnic Politics* 1 (4): 108–12.

Turin, M. 2006. *Minority Language Policies and Politics in Nepal, in Lesser Known Languages in Nepal: Status and Policies, Case Studies and Applications of Information Technology*, ed. by Anju Saxena and Lars Borin (Berlin and New York: Mouton de Gruyter), pp. 161–74.

Turin, M. 2007. 'My Tongue or Yours?', *Nepali Times* 16–22 February.

Turin, M. 2012. 'Our Language in Your Hands', BBC Radio, 4 December, http://www.bbc.co.uk/programmes/b01p3hnv

UNESCO. 2011. *Multilingual Education in Nepal: Hearsay and Reality? A Report* (Kathmandu: UNESCO).

Weinberg, M. 2015. 'Schooling Languages: Investigating Language-in-Education Policies in Kathmandu and Jhapa District', Paper presented in Annual Kathmandu Conference on Nepal and the Himalayas, 22–24 June.

Woolard, K. A. 2016. *Singular and Plural: Ideologies of Linguistic Authority in 21st Century Catalonia* (New York: Oxford University Press).

4. The Significance of Place in Ethnolinguistic Vitality

Spatial Variations Across the Kaike-Speaking Diaspora of Nepal

Maya Daurio

Group vitality has long been a framework for the inquiry into language maintenance and the sustainability of ethnolinguistic communities (Smith et al. 2017). Giles et al. (1977) conceptualized the vitality of an ethnolinguistic community 'as that which makes a group likely to behave as a distinctive and active collective entity in intergroup situations' (308). They outlined three objective 'structural variables' which together may 'permit an ethnolinguistic community to survive as a viable group' (308): demographics, institutional support, and status. Bourhis et al. (1981) introduced the concept of subjective vitality, the idea that a group's own perception of its ethnolinguistic vitality and position relative to other ethnolinguistic groups also influences its viability. To better describe how vitality is used in language maintenance studies, Ehala (2015: 1) proposes a new definition, which posits that 'ethnolinguistic vitality is a group's ability to maintain and protect its existence in time as a collective entity with a distinctive identity and language.' Roche characterizes this idea of vitality as the 'relationship between a language, its speakers, and its wider linguistic, social, and political context' (2017: 193). Ehala's conceptualization comprises four key indicators: 'continuing intergenerational transmission of a group's language and cultural practices, sustainable demography and active social institutions, social cohesion, and emotional attachment to its collective identity' (Ehala 2015: 1).

Following Ehala's framework, I examine the ethnolinguistic vitality of an endangered language community in Nepal over a four-decade period: the Kaike speakers from Tichurong Valley in Dolpa. I engage with both existing scholarship around vitality, identity, and language maintenance, as well as with ethnographies of the Kaike-speaking diaspora, to assess the variability and uniformity of ethnolinguistic vitality across the diaspora. I suggest that ethnolinguistic vitality among Kaike speakers can be differentiated both geographically and generationally, and is affected by fluctuations in the status and power of the language and its speakers. Building upon existing scholarship on negative demographic shifts and power disparities among language communities, I also argue that another indicator of ethnolinguistic vitality is the ability of the group to maintain and protect its existence — not only in time, but also in place (Landweer (2000), and Hildebrandt and Hu (2017) explicitly address spatial factors in the context of vitality). Memory of, and language about, place is a form of cultural knowledge which is site-specific, processual (Pearce and Louis 2008: 110), and shapes a group's understanding of itself and its collective history.

Kaike Speakers

Kaike is a Tibeto-Burman language spoken by a group of people originating in the Tichurong Valley in Dolpa, Nepal (see Fig. 4.1). Dolpa is one of Nepal's largest, least populated, and most remote districts. It is bounded by the Tibet Autonomous Region and Nepal's districts of Mugu, Jumla, Jajarkot, Rukum, Myagdi, and Mustang, located in Karnali Zone. As of the 2011 Census, Dolpa had a total population of 36,700 people (Central Bureau of Statistics (CBS), 2014: 278) and actually saw a population increase of 2.17% between 2001 and 2011 (CBS 2014: 24). Dolpa has among the fewest number of outmigrants, with less than 10% of the population in that category (CBS 2014: 256). It is also not a high inmigration district.

Kaike speakers are often called *Tarali*, which in fact refers to any inhabitant of the Tichurong Valley, or *Tichurongba* in Tibetan. Throughout this chapter, I use the term 'Tarali' interchangeably with 'Kaike-speaking Tarali'. Kaike speakers predominantly occupy three villages in the Tichurong Valley, referred to here as Tarang,[1] Tupatara and Tarakot. Members of the Kaike-speaking Tarali community also reside elsewhere, with the largest populations outside the Tichurong Valley in Kathmandu and in Dunai, the headquarters of Dolpa district. I conducted research during the course of two separate stays over a span of nine years in Tarang, Dunai, and Kathmandu, as well as virtually. This research is based on informal interviews conducted in Nepali and correspondence over social media and via email in English.

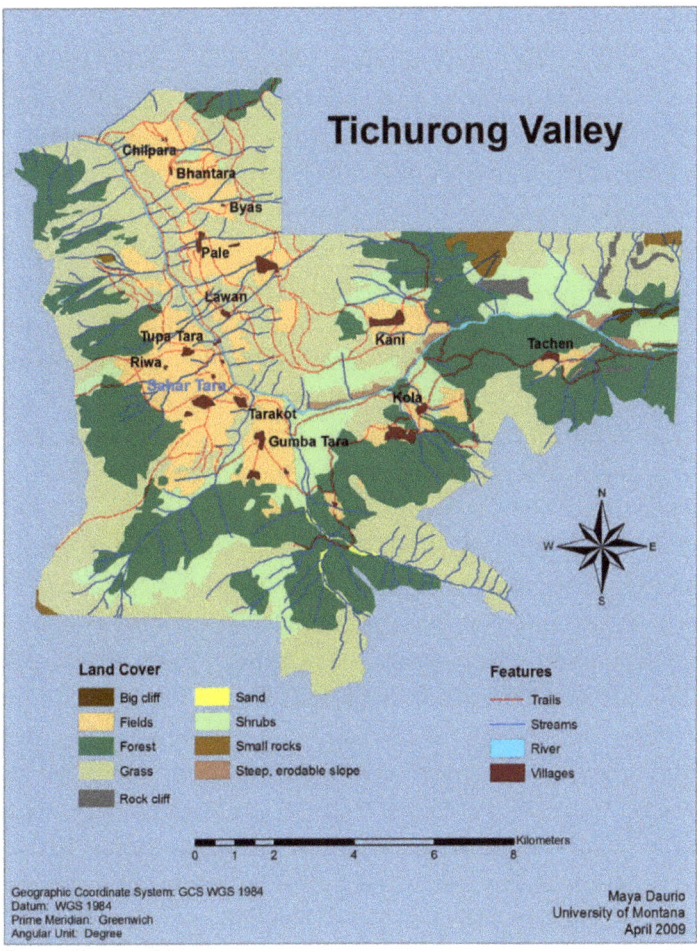

Fig. 4.1. Tichurong Valley. Map provided by the author, CC BY.

---

1   Tarang is the Kaike name for the village referred to as Sahartara in Nepali.

There are currently no roads connecting the Dolpa district with other districts, and Tarang is a 5–7 hour walk from Dunai, which is several hours walk from Juphal, the main airstrip for the district. There is a marginal road between Juphal and Dunai, with jeeps running regularly between the two locales carrying passengers. As of May 2017, villagers needed to walk several hours from Dunai to a point blocked by road construction except to foot traffic. From here, a single jeep takes passengers as far as a large rock slide, from which point they make their own way on foot to Tarang, crossing the Bheri River and ascending switchbacks to the village.

Tarang is the largest of thirteen villages in the Tichurong Valley (see Fig. 4.2), with seventy to eighty houses (Daurio 2012) out of 780 households (Central Bureau of Statistics 2014 [Dolpa]: 10) in the Kaike *Gaunpalika* (Rural Municipality), formerly the Sahartara Village Development Committee (VDC). Prior to March 2017, Tichurong was divided into two VDCs, Sahartara and Lawan, each respectively named after the largest village on either side of the Bheri River in the valley. Both former VDCs have been combined into the Kaike Rural Municipality as a result of local elections, a change which will be addressed in detail below. People largely practice subsistence agriculture in Tarang, growing several varieties of millet, sweet and sour buckwheat, amaranth, corn, potatoes, and a few other vegetables. Household incomes are heavily supplemented by harvesting *yarsagumba* (Ophiocordyceps sinensis), a highly prized fungus sold primarily to China that grows at around 4,000 meters and is used medicinally and as an aphrodisiac.

Each village in Dolpa near these high-altitude areas has its own identified harvesting grounds for Ophiocordyceps sinensis, and people who come from outside the village are required to apply for access. Some harvesting grounds are more lucrative than others, but one Tarang villager estimated that an entire family can make between Rs. 100,000–300,000 (USD $960–2,800) during the approximately month-long harvesting season. Other people make money from selling goods to people at the harvesting grounds. The income generated by activities related to *yarsagumba* harvesting constitutes the main source of income for most Tarang villagers and has also led to a decline in agricultural production with greater reliance on purchased grains and goods (Budha 2015).

Of the thirteen villages in Tichurong, Tarang is the only village with a lower secondary school with classes up to the eighth grade, whereas all the other government schools only go up to the fifth grade. Of the eight or nine teachers, only one is from Tarang. All but two are male. In 2017, a female teacher was hired from Gumbatara, a village an hour's walk away but visible from Tarang. The other teachers are from outside the district.

Tarang exerts greater political and economic influence than other villages in the valley. For instance, the majority of forests in the vicinity belong to the village of Tarang. Tansa, the oldest and most important Buddhist monastery in Tichurong, is in the village of Gumbatara but half under Tarang jurisdiction and half under the shared jurisdiction of Gumbatara and Tupatara. A lama and his family from Tarang take up residence in Tansa Monastery every two years and assume all the religious responsibilities that go along with that position. In addition, his family cultivates and reaps the benefits from the land associated with the monastery during this time. A lama from Gumbatara, on the other hand, will alternate residency every other two years with a lama from Tupatara, a village, about an hour's walk from Gumbatara through Tarang, which is halfway between the two. Tarang is a land-rich village, as most of the lands in the former Sahartara VDC belong to the village of Tarang. There is also a larger number of shop-owners from Tarang in the district headquarters of Dunai compared to the other villages in Tichurong. Taralis from Tarang, in particular, as well as from other Tichurong villages, wield disproportionate political power in the district. There have been three MPs and four district chairmen representing the district of Dolpa who came from Tichurong, including the current MP, Dhan Bahadur Budha, who is originally from Tarang.

There are an estimated fifty adults from Tarang living in Kathmandu, and an estimated 100 children from Tichurong as a whole who have been sent to boarding schools in Kathmandu, fifty to sixty of whom hail from Tarang. Approximately ninety Taralis from the three Kaike-speaking villages in Tichurong live in Dunai, and a number of children study in boarding schools in Dunai, although the exact number is unknown. Taralis are spread out across Nepal in several other locations besides Kathmandu and Dunai, with the next largest concentration of people living in Pokhara (around sixteen individuals), and up to several

Fig. 4.2. Tarang in the upper right; Tarakot in the lower left; Tupatara is to the right of Tarang out of the picture. November 2008. Photo courtesy of the author, CC BY.

individuals in smaller locales such as Bhaktapur, Bhentara, and Maikot, in addition to at least four individuals in Tachen, another village in Tichurong. Additionally, there are a handful of Taralis spread out across the world in India, Australia, Belgium, and the United States, who emigrated in the pursuit of employment, education, or marriage. For the purposes of this chapter, I am concerned with the Kaike-speaking Tarali, predominantly from Tarang, who live in Tichurong, Dunai, and Kathmandu.

Kaike-speaking Taralis residing in Dunai are employed primarily as shopkeepers, and some also engage in *yarsagumba* trading. Kaike speakers are a sizable minority in Dunai, trailing Chhetris, Kamis, Thakuris, Brahmins, and Magars (see discussion below regarding Magars) in numbers, but more populous than various other ethnic and caste groups residing in Dunai (CBS 2014: 15).

Among the Kaike-speaking Taralis who live in Kathmandu, there are many who travel back and forth between Kathmandu and Tarang throughout the year. These Taralis primarily reside in Kathmandu during the cold winter months and return to Tarang in the summer to engage in agricultural production and activities related to the harvesting of *yarsagumba*. The livelihoods of these Taralis remain primarily tied to Tichurong, but they have the financial capacity to travel to and live in Kathmandu for part of the year. The other Taralis who live in Kathmandu have businesses there, with a number of different families owning carpet-manufacturing and export businesses (Fisher 2017: 32) supplemented by trading in *yarsagumba*, either from Kathmandu or Dunai. Nearly all of the Taralis who reside in Kathmandu at least part of the year raise their children in Kathmandu and send them to English-medium schools, including those Taralis who spend months at a time in Tichurong. The children of Kathmandu-based Taralis rarely travel to Tichurong and do not grow up speaking Kaike, although they hear their parents speaking it. There is a generational divide among Kathmandu Taralis in which those who were born and raised primarily in Tichurong maintain their language, cultural practices such as celebrating indigenous festivals, and an emotional attachment to the Tichurong Valley. Their children, however, do not learn Kaike, rarely visit Tichurong, and in the course of their urban lives, observe celebrations of deities residing in particular trees and glaciers in Tichurong they have likely never seen.

It is within the context of these divided and at once specific experiences of Kaike-speaking Taralis living in Tichurong, Dunai, and Kathmandu that I explore the uniformity and differentiation of ethnolinguistic vitality.

Language and Identity

In addition to speaking Kaike, Kaike-speaking Taralis identify as (Tarali) Magar, one of Nepal's most prominent and numerous ethnic groups. According to James Fisher, this identification as Magar 'is simply a convenient status summation which can be readily and incontestably claimed by anyone (except untouchables) who wants it' (Fisher 1986: 3). Similarly, Michael Noonan attributes the appeal of this alignment with the Magar ethnic/caste group to the fact that Magars belong to a caste which cannot be enslaved to higher castes (Noonan 2005).

This self-affiliation with a particular ethnic group or caste is not exclusive to the Magars of Tichurong and has in fact been recorded as a common practice throughout South Asia since medieval times (Turin 2011; Whelpton 2005: 11). In the nineteenth century when the caste system was codified in Nepal, the Magars, Gurungs, and some of the other Tibeto-Burman groups were 'allocated a position clearly below the high, twice-born castes but were not regarded as ritually unclean' (Whelpton 2005: 31). Additionally, until the eighteenth century, there had also existed a flexible relationship sometimes resulting in intermarriage between Magars and Khasas, the Nepali-speaking ruling elite of the western middle hills (Whelpton 2005: 32). Later, after the establishment of Gorkhali rule in the eighteenth century, the western hills of Nepal served as a predominant source of slaves (Whelpton 2005: 28), and the Magars were able to remain unenslaved by paying an additional tax for this privilege (Whelpton 2005: 53).

It is not known when Kaike speakers or other inhabitants of Tichurong — who speak a dialect of Tibetan[2] (*Pöke*) but also identify as Magar (Fisher 2017: 39) — chose to affiliate themselves with the larger Magar group. The Magars of Tichurong have no particular connection with other Magars in Dolpa outside of Tichurong other than identifying as Magar. Kaike, although recognized as one of three Magar languages, has no relation with the other two Magar languages, other than also belonging to the Tibeto-Burman language family. All of the languages within the Magar group are distinct from each other (Whelpton 2005: 14). In contrast to the Taralis in Tichurong, there is an effort among some Kathmandu Taralis to situate themselves within the larger Magar ethnic community in Kathmandu through active participation in Magar associations. One Tarali businessman, for example, is the vice-president of the Nepal Magar Sangh (Magar Society of Nepal), which promotes the interests of the three different Magar groups in Nepal (Fisher 2017: 39).

Magars constitute the largest indigenous group in Nepal, with a population of 1,622,399, totaling 7.4 per cent of the country's entire population (Rana 2005). As in other parts of the world, understanding of the word indigenous in Nepal is complicated and fractured. Generally speaking, and in common with most definitions of indigeneity, tenure

---

2 Two different Tibetan dialects are spoken in Tichurong and in Upper Dolpa, respectively, but they can be understood by speakers of the other. One man from Gumbatara said that the Tibetan spoken in Tichurong is to the Tibetan in Upper Dolpa as Nepali is to Hindi. He also said that the Tibetan spoken in Tibet is unintelligible to him (personal correspondence, March 2018).

on the land and a distinct written or oral history are important criteria in Nepal, along with, more uniquely, a group's cultural traditions separate from that of ruling high castes, according to The National Foundation for Uplift of Adivasi/Janajati Act (Cultural Survival 2017). While addressing the extensive history and subsequent scholarship specific to Nepali ethnic politics (see Lawoti 2008; Shneiderman 2014; and Gellner 2017, among others) is beyond the purview of this chapter, it is necessary to frame Magar self-identification among Taralis within the context of the *adivasi janajati* (indigenous nationalities) rights movement in Nepal, which has been burgeoning since the People's Movement of 1990 overthrew the Panchayat system and restored multi-party democracy (Rai 2008: 7). In 2006, the government officially recognized fifty-nine indigenous nationalities and formed the National Foundation for the Development of Indigenous Nationalities (NFDIN) to address and deal with indigenous issues (Muan 2007). The issue of indigenous rights was also pushed to the forefront during the Maoist insurgency and subsequent rule by the CPN(M) party, which in 2009 assembled a list of ethnic and indigenous groups for which quotas in government jobs should be reserved (Nepal News 2009). The practice of establishing quotas for ethnic and indigenous groups in government positions continues today, with varying levels of success.

Ethnic identity is an ongoing social and political process (Bucholz and Hall 2004; Gellner 2016), which helps people to locate themselves within a particular social, economic, and political context (Chettri 2017: 22). Mona Chettri sums up ethnic politics in the Eastern Himalaya as follows: 'the political nature of ethnic groups can be explained in terms of their aims to better facilitate access to or control over resources that are controlled by the state' (2017: 29). Given the size of Nepal's Magar population, it is clearly a socio-economic and political advantage for Taralis not only to continue to identify as Magar but to seek active and participatory membership of that group, particularly in Kathmandu, where there is greater competition for political and social capital. In Tichurong and Dunai, access to political and social capital associated with Magar ethnicity is more closely related to the position of Magars within the caste system, discussed above, which allows Taralis to situate themselves in positions of power relative to lower caste Dalits and casteless Tibetans or the ethnolinguistically related *Bhotiyā*, who are of Tibetan descent. Interestingly, identifying as Magar simultaneously allows Kaike-speaking Tarali access to the political and social clout of the larger Magar ethnic group while also distinguishing them among Magars by their unique Kaike language.

Kaike is a language firmly rooted in the Tichurong Valley, encapsulated in the origin story of the language. This story tells of a lake of milk in Gumbatara — a village which can be seen from Tarang — where three goddesses[3] who were sisters bathed every day. One day a boy, the only inhabitant of Tichurong along with his mother, kidnapped one of the sisters and eventually married her. She only spoke Kaike, which the boy and his mother also learned to speak. The descendants of the boy and the goddess are the Kaike-speaking Tarali people (Fisher 1986; Daurio 2012). The Kaike-speaking Taralis of Tarang are multilingual in Kaike, Nepali, and Pöke, but Kaike is the language in which they conduct their daily lives.

Like other indigenous language communities, through the longevity of their relationship with a particular place, Taralis have developed detailed and adaptive knowledge about their environment, which is manifested in livelihood systems and expressed and encoded in language (Nettle and Romaine 2000). Similarly, the transmission of cultural knowledge across generations is facilitated largely through oral and performative traditions situated in a particular landscape, which lose their relevance when language speakers no longer reside in that landscape (Harrison 2007; Turin 2013).

The successful and highly adaptive system of agricultural production (see Fisher 1986 for a broader discussion) is contextualized through oral histories, as is the origin of the Kaike language itself. Taralis 'situate themselves in their landscape in culturally specific and linguistically coded experiences. Their worlds are strongly delineated, and these boundaries are both named and imbued with spiritual significance' (Daurio 2012: 17–18). There are, for example, more than twenty Kaike names for areas encompassing different fields, twenty-four names for different areas of forest, and twenty names for different areas of the village of Tarang itself (Daurio 2012: 12). This kind of intimate, place-based knowledge of livelihood systems encoded in

---

3   Fisher was told a version of the story in which there were seven goddesses. See Fisher (1986: 36).

the Kaike language is inaccessible to younger, Kathmandu-raised Tarali and is indicative of the centrality of place within the context of ethnolinguistic vitality.

The actual number of Kaike speakers is difficult to discern. As Ambika Regmi notes, the 2001 Central Bureau of Statistics (CBS) reports 794 speakers (2013: 1), which was improbably reduced to fifty speakers in the 2011 Census (CBS 2012). Despite the lack of an accurate count of active speakers, it is considered a seriously endangered language (Yadava 2004). Kaike-speaking Taralis speak Kaike exclusively among themselves, although as previously mentioned, they are also fluent in Pöke and Nepali. Nepal is a country of multiple languages and identities, and multilingualism is the norm. As the other authors in this volume demonstrate, language contact produces multilingualism which is inherently mitigated by the power relations that exist between the language groups in contact. David Gellner (2016: 19) characterizes multilingualism in Nepal this way:

> There is a hierarchy, with different forms of language, or even different languages, being spoken at different niches and levels, both by different people and by the same person in different contexts.

The majority of Kaike speakers live in Tarang, Tupatara, and Tarakot, and of the ten other villages in Tichurong, Pöke is spoken in all but Riwa. In Riwa, which is less than a half hour's walk from Tarang, Nepali is both the lingua franca and mother tongue of the Dalits who perform manual labor such as house building, grinding grain into flour, or tilling fields for the Taralis in Tarang and Tupatara. The Dalits in Riwa migrated to the Tichurong Valley over 165 years ago, and families in Riwa have inherited patron-client relationships with certain families in Tarang and other Tichurong villages (Fisher 1986: 181). A Tarali woman who is separated from her husband and who splits her time between Kathmandu — where her son attends an English-medium school — and Tarang recently gave all of her inherited fields to a family of Dalits from Riwa, in exchange for them providing her with a percentage of the grain they produce on those fields. The people of Riwa also speak Kaike fluently. There is some intermarriage between people from different villages (though not between the inhabitants of Riwa and other Tichurong villages), especially between people from the Kaike-speaking villages and nearby Gumbatara. Interestingly, although both the Taralis and the Dalits speak Nepali and Kaike fluently, Taralis choose to speak with Riwa villagers in Kaike rather than Nepali. Landweer (2000) writes about language choice as a function of group identity and cohesion, and conversely points out that a strong ethnic identity can also influence language choice. Although Taralis are mostly practicing Buddhists, they adhere to the Hindu caste system, and the Dalits of Riwa belong to the lowest caste, untouchables. This, combined with the patron-client relationship outlined above, is indicative that the decision to use Kaike instead of Nepali with the Dalits of Riwa appears to be an assertion of status and power. Given the longevity of the relationship between the Taralis and the people of Riwa, it would be interesting to know whether this has fluctuated over time.

In addition to the people of Riwa, some people from Upper Dolpa (Dolpo) also reportedly speak Kaike. The anthropologist James Fisher lived in Tarang from 1968–1970, and he recorded that many Tibetans and people from Dolpo stayed in Tarang during the cold months, escaping the harsher winter in Dolpo and bringing salt from Tibet to trade (1986: 92). The salt trade is largely no longer active, as salt is now conveyed from India via the road system in the Tarai, although Fisher reports that remnants of the salt-for-grain trading circuits persist to some extent (2017: 10). The number of people from Dolpo staying in Tarang in the winter has decreased, but there are a few who still come and occupy the houses of those who go to Kathmandu for the winter or stay with families with whom they have developed relationships over time. There is a long tradition of established business partnerships (*netsang*) between Dolpo pastoralists and people in each village where they conduct trade (Bauer 2004: 108). These *netsang* relationships have long existed between Dolpo people and Tichurongba (Budha 2015: 6). Fisher described Taralis in the late 1960s conducting trade with people from Dolpo and Tibetans in Tibetan, and with people from lowland Nepal in Nepali. 'The Tarangpur trader must endeavor to be all things to all men' (Fisher 1986: 94).[4] This portrayal implies that it

---

4   Interestingly, a participant originally from Upper Dolpa at the Himalayan Studies Conference in Colorado in September 2017 informed me that he had once stayed in Tarang for three months, learned Kaike during that time, and that most interactions between Taralis and Dolpo-pa occurred in Kaike, not Pöke.

was Taralis who were expected to accommodate the dominant language in a particular setting, whether it be Pöke or Nepali. In a more recent observation, Fisher describes listening to a discussion between two political leaders from Tarap, in Upper Dolpa, and the MP for Dolpa District from Tarang, about a dispute over the collection of *yarsagumba* (2017: 54). The discussion took place in Kathmandu and was conducted entirely in Nepali, instead of in Pöke, which all discussants also speak. Nepali is not the mother tongue for either of the parties. Contact among the various peoples from different geographic regions in Dolpa has resulted in multilingual relationships between individuals from these regions, and language choice appears to be moderated by power and status in addition to location.

It may be that spatiality is a factor in determining which language is used in interactions between Kaike speakers and people from Dolpo and Tibet. The higher status of Taralis in the caste system relative to the casteless people from Dolpo and Tibetans alike might also influence language choice, as may the fluctuating positions of power and prestige occupied by different groups of people at different times. These fluctuations occur both in terms of how Kaike speakers experience their own language and how Kaike speakers intersect with other speech communities (Pugh 1999). Such interactions and experiences serve to formulate Tarali identity within a 'flexible system of identities' (Chandrahasan 2015: 15) situated in changing group boundaries (Chettri 2017; Turin 2014) and informed by power dynamics. As previously referenced, Kaike speakers and Tichurongba enjoy greater political representation at the national and district levels compared to the more remotely located people from Dolpo. Because Kaike-speaking Taralis are multilingual, their interactions with other speech communities that speak Kaike, Nepali, Pöke, or all three, involve a calculated choice about which language to use. This choice is informed by complex understandings of relative occupations of power and status (see Roche et al., this volume) which may confer upon the language the contemporaneous prestige of its speakers. Perceptions of power and its associated characteristics, such as prestige, status, and economic and political dominance, define the dynamics of language contact between groups speaking different languages, regardless of the size of the language group or some intrinsic quality of the language itself (Ehala 2010: 208). 'Languages do not exist as mere languages. Instead, they reveal affiliations to certain class and socio-ethnic groups that choose to include and exclude elements' (Ibrahim 2015: 190) of a particular language. Annamalai (2002) refers to this pattern of language choice as the 'multilingual networking' of languages, which is based on the functional relationship between the languages in both public and private domains and reflects the social and political dynamics between them. A language's vitality is higher if it is used in all domains (Hildebrandt and Hu 2017) and depends not only on the number of speakers and the exertion of external forces on the community but also on the attitudes and practices of the speech community itself (Ehala 2010: 204; Hildebrandt and Hu 2017: 154).

The attitudes of Taralis toward their language have changed over time. In the late 1960s, Taralis thought of Kaike as unsophisticated and primitive (Fisher 2017: 41). Now, Taralis in Tichurong, Dunai, and Kathmandu alike embrace the Kaike language as important and valued. Those Taralis who live in Tarang, who move through their daily lives speaking almost exclusively in Kaike, have no sense that Kaike is an endangered language. Fisher (2017) also observes that the perception of Kaike among Taralis is largely positive and that they possess a sense of pride regarding their language. A young man from Samtiling, a cluster of houses directly above Tarang, is studying to be a monk and also trying to write a Kaike dictionary, an act which would have been unimaginable four decades ago (Fisher 2017: 41).

For Taralis across the Nepal diaspora, speaking Kaike may hold important symbolic value in defining themselves as a distinctive 'collective entity in intergroup situations' (Giles et al. 1977: 308). As Fisher aptly observes about Tichurong, it is not a 'homogeneous area inhabited by ethnically identical people' (1986: 25), and language choice among Kaike speakers may be an exertion of group solidarity.

For those Kaike speakers who live outside Tichurong, the continued use of Kaike is a cultural expression, a means of creating social cohesion beyond the geographic borders of Tichurong Valley. Mark Turin refers to the 'emotive power of linguistic attachment' (2014: 372) and to language heritage facilitating a sense of belonging. Compared to the late 1960s, when Fisher lived in Tarang, many Kaike speakers have migrated out of Tichurong. The Taralis who primarily live in Tarang have no sense of the impending loss of their language because they are surrounded by it. In contrast, those who primarily live in Kathmandu are more invested in promoting Tarali culture, participating in Magar or Tarali social groups, and the continuation of the Kaike language, even while they send their children to English-medium schools and while the generation of those Taralis not born in Tichurong lack fluency in Kaike and certainly in the situated knowledge associated with that language. The preference among Taralis to educate their children in the dominant language of English is typical of marginalized (marginalized within the national and global context) speech communities. 'They want their languages to appear to have power, but they in practice want to have their personal power enhanced through the dominant language(s)' (Annamalai 2002: n.p.).

Kathmandu-based Taralis continue to celebrate important cultural rituals, such as Chaigo, the Tarali New Year, as well as Choputa *puja*, a two-month long celebration of a major deity (Fisher 2017: 36). There are also two cultural organizations founded by Kathmandu-based Kaike speakers to promote and preserve Tarali culture, part of which involves organizing the observance of Chaigo (Fisher 2017). The effort to preserve Tarali culture among Kathmandu-based Taralis precludes the maintenance of the Kaike language among the younger generations living in Kathmandu. Among the generation of Taralis raised outside of Tichurong, Kaike is passively understood but not actively used (Fisher 2017: 42). In contrast to the Kaike-speaking Taralis in Tichurong, whose language use intersects with both the public and private domain, language use among the Kaike-speaking Taralis in Kathmandu occurs solely in the private domain, such as at home and at social events, an expression of cultural identification and of belonging to a group (Annamalai 2002; Chandrahasan 2015; Landweer 2000; Turin 2014).

The Taralis in Dunai occupy a unique space. Only a day's walk away from Tichurong and several hours walk (or an hour-long jeep ride) away from the airstrip in Juphal, they have relatively easy access to their childhood homes as well as to urban centers outside of Dolpa, cost notwithstanding. Kaike-speaking Taralis in Dunai, the majority of whom are shopkeepers, exist within a relatively tight-knit community of other Kaike speakers and Tichurongba, who share the town with a variety of other ethnic groups, a number of whom are more populous than the Kaike-speaking Taralis. While I was speaking with a shopkeeper from the village of Tachen, which is in Tichurong, a man in his forties originally from Tarang joined our conversation. He was sent to Kathmandu as a boy to study and subsequently forgot the Kaike language. However, he moved back to Dunai to open a shop and eventually learned Kaike again. A Tarali woman born in Tichurong but raised in Dunai, now working as a teacher, likewise speaks Kaike with her fellow Kaike-speaking Taralis in Dunai. Turin, like Landweer (2000), posits that 'speech communities maintain and manage their borders to create a sense of cohesion or group belonging' (2014: 375), and the tendency of Kaike-speaking Taralis in Dunai to interact with one another in Kaike serves to differentiate them from others, and also to form a sort of solidarity among Kaike speakers within the town of Dunai. Language, in a sense, becomes a representation of identity (Samuelson and Freedman 2010: 197). In the process of emphasizing distinctions between social groups as expressed in the ascription of ethnic identity, language is one of the 'most flexible and pervasive symbolic resources available for the cultural production' of this identity (Bucholtz and Hall 2004: 371).

Additionally, among the Taralis I have met living outside of Tarang, many have spoken of the sweet *hāwā-pāni* (an expression in Nepali literally meaning 'air and water') in Tarang and how much they prefer it to that of Dunai or Kathmandu. The man who returned to Dunai and learned Kaike after living there spoke fondly of the food in Tarang, which is grown, harvested, and processed locally. Among those in Tarang with whom I spoke who either live in Tarang full-time or spend part of the year there and part of the year in Kathmandu, there were a variety of opinions about whether they prefer Tarang or Kathmandu. An elderly couple who had been in Kathmandu for several years without returning to Tarang because of illness contrasted the traffic and dust in Kathmandu with the serenity and clean air of Tarang, while a middle-aged woman who splits her time between Tarang and Kathmandu spoke of preferring her lifestyle in Kathmandu, perhaps because her life there requires less manual labor. Although not all among those Taralis who left Tarang continue to return there — often because the initial part of the journey involves expensive air travel, and the latter part of the journey on foot is long and strenuous — most retain a nostalgia for Tichurong. Fisher recently observed 'those who have settled in urban areas continue to feel as much at home in their ancestral villages as they do in the urban environments where they spend most of their time. Rather than flee their past or deny it, they seem to want to nourish and strengthen it' (2017: 58).

In addition to a positive perception of the Kaike language, celebration of Tarali festivals, and active engagement in Tarali cultural organizations, there are other signs of an elevated regard for Tarali culture, the Kaike language, and an attachment to place compared to how Taralis perceived themselves and their language four decades ago, particularly among those who left Tarang as adults to pursue economic opportunities in Dunai or Kathmandu. Not least was a referendum in the May 2017 elections — the first local elections held in twenty years — to combine Sahartara and Lawan Village Development Committees (VDCs) into the Kaike Gaupalika (Rural Municipality), a symbol of both the clout of those from the largest village in Tichurong in Dolpa politics and an indication of the high regard in which Kaike is held. No other *gaupalika* in Dolpa was designated by the language spoken. This change was promulgated by the current MP from Dolpa, who is originally from Tarang and was recently nominated the Culture, Tourism and Civil Aviation State Minister. One community member from Gumbatara is personally dissatisfied with the name and has been lobbying to change it to 'Tichurong Kaike Gaupalika.' This man said that among those Tichurongba with whom he has spoken, there is general discontent about the name because the majority of Tichurongba do not speak Kaike but Pöke (personal correspondence, March 2018). In contrast, among the Kaike-speaking Tarali with whom I spoke, both in Kathmandu and in Tarang, the name is a source of pride. The ascription of the name of the Kaike language to a political entity is historically meaningful and culturally significant and memorializes the language in a particular geography (Pine and Turin 2017).

The use of Kaike by Taralis persists in the foundational social domain of the home (Landweer 2000), across geographic boundaries and, in Tichurong, across generations. The intergenerational transmission of the Kaike language does not occur among those Taralis born and raised in Kathmandu. However, the preference of Taralis in Tichurong, Dunai, and Kathmandu to use Kaike among themselves in spite of the availability of other language choices is an expression of cultural identification with the language itself as well as with other users who have the same preference (Annamalai 2002). The decision to speak in Kaike or not in the public domain, the zone of power where speech communities compete, is more variable depending on whether one lives in Tichurong, Dunai, or Kathmandu, and on the nature of intergroup contact.

Intergenerational Transmission

As Fisher (1986) describes Tichurong in 1969, the Taralis of Tarang utilized mobility as an adaptive strategy for expanding economic capacity. At the time, Taralis were transporting salt from Tibet to the Tarai and needed supplies in the reverse direction. Multilingualism was important in navigating between the cultural zones in the Tarai and Tibet, both areas with which Taralis maintained interdependent economic relationships (Fisher 1986: 184). Mobility in its current form is multiple. There are, as mentioned before, around fifty adults from Tarang who live in Kathmandu, some of whom split their time residing in Kathmandu and Tarang, or Kathmandu and Dunai. Those that live entirely in Kathmandu do so because their business enterprises (e.g., carpet manufacturing and export) keep them there; some of them engage in trade with yarsagumba, which requires them to spend several weeks each summer in Dunai, where they buy recently harvested yarsagumba and then sell it in Kathmandu to another buyer. Those that return to Tarang for part of the year also do so primarily for economic reasons: to tend to their fields and to harvest yarsagumba or sell goods to those harvesting yarsagumba.

Another kind of mobility is recorded among more privileged Taralis who choose to send their children to school in Dunai, Kathmandu, and sometimes even farther afield. The reasons for this are clear: formal education is limited in Tarang and across all of the Tichurong Valley, and access to a good education — particularly in an English-medium curriculum — is highly valued and viewed as a pathway to greater opportunity (Fisher 2017). Therefore, those families who can afford to send their children to Dunai, Kathmandu, or, more rarely, to India, Europe, Australia, or the United States, may choose to do so. Many from Tichurong send their children to study at an English-medium school run by a lama near Budhanilkhanta outside of Kathmandu. Parents are required to pay Rs. 80,000 (USD $820) up front, and then the rest of tuition is paid for by foreign donors who support the school.

Most of the children sent to Kathmandu, India, or further abroad do not grow up speaking Kaike, do not learn about traditional agricultural practices, and do not return to the village to live. There are a few exceptions. I met two men who returned after studying in Kathmandu: the aforementioned man in his forties who returned to Dunai to open a shop and a man in his twenties who couldn't find a job in Kathmandu and returned to Tarang to start a family. Revealingly, when I asked people if they were worried about the loss of the Kaike language due to the outmigration of children from the village to study, the common response was that if they returned, they would likely relearn Kaike quickly. When I followed up with a question about whether children who are sent to Kathmandu to study generally return to the village, the usual answer is that they do not. Indeed, it would be difficult to imagine children raised in Kathmandu to adulthood returning to a village, a provincial way of life filled with backbreaking manual labor, and returning to speak a language in which they have not conversed for most of their lives. For example, I traveled to Tarang from Kathmandu with a twenty-two-year-old nursing student whose elderly parents had recently returned to Tarang for the warmer months. She hadn't been to Tarang in ten years and had moved away when she was seven. She lived with her brother and his family in Kathmandu and was sent for a short visit to Tarang. She was in most ways a typical young, middle class, Kathmandu urbanite and was wholly out of place, uncomfortable, and unfamiliar with Tarang, its rusticity, and its customs. She could understand a little Kaike but largely spoke and was spoken to in Nepali. She left Tichurong to return to Kathmandu as soon as she was allowed. Her much older brother, by contrast, who was raised in Tarang, is one of the most active Kathmandu-based Taralis in terms of promoting Tarali culture and pride through his leadership in Tarali cultural organizations. He also visits Tarang once every one or two years, speaks Kaike exclusively with his wife and other Taralis in Kathmandu, and maintains an emotional attachment to Tichurong. This fondness for and continued familiarity with Tichurong, with the Kaike language, and with Tarali cultural traditions is exclusive to those Taralis who were born and raised in Tichurong and left as adults, and does not characterize the experience of their children or siblings born outside of Tichurong.

As previously noted, knowledge about the environment among Taralis in Tarang is extensive and expressed in language. This kind of knowledge is often referred to as traditional ecological knowledge (TEK). Formal education has been associated with the erosion of TEK (Benz et al. 2000; Cruz Garcia 2006; Kuyakanon et al. 2017; McCarter and Gavin 2011; McKinley and Castagno 2009; Ruiz-Mallen et al. 2009; Saynes-Vásquez et al. 2013) and the decline of language vitality (Landweer 2000; Turin 2008 and 2014; Botha 2010; McCarter and Gavin 2011; Reyes-Garcia et al. 2005; Zent 1999). There are many reasons for this. Most environmental knowledge is acquired at an early age and is based on direct experience and interaction with cultural traditions, beliefs, and rituals. Formal education systems often remove children from these place-based and linguistically coded traditional knowledge systems (McCarter and Gavin 2011) or do not account for nor value local knowledge and traditions (La Belle 1982; Ruiz-Mallen et al. 2009). In Nepal, in spite of multiple laws and acts in recent years that adopt policies to provide primary level education in mother tongues (i.e., with mother tongues as the medium of instruction) (Phyak 2015; Singh et al. 2012), these have yet to be implemented on a country-wide scale or for all of the mother-tongue languages that exist. Challenges to mother-tongue-based multilingual education (MTB-MLE) are multifold, including, among others, lack of a writing practice in most mother tongues, lack of involvement of affected stakeholders at the policy level, and lack of community management of mother-tongue teachers (Phyak 2015; see also Pradhan, this volume). Furthermore, although children taught in their mother tongue from an early age tend to perform better and exhibit higher cognitive, linguistic, and social skills compared to their peers educated in the dominant language (Coleman 2015; Pinnock 2015; UNESCO 2003), English-language education in Nepal is still highly valued and heavily invested in (Phyak 2015; Singh et al. 2012) because of its association with greater cultural and economic dominance.

Ironically, those who seem to hold Tarali customs and traditions, including the Kaike language, in the highest regard — those Taralis who were raised in but who now live outside the Tichurong Valley — are also those who are most invested in educating their children in

English-medium schools. They are also more likely to have the financial means to do so. Speakers of marginalized languages around the world often do not prefer the use of their language as the medium of formal education (Annamalai 2002; Coleman 2015; Turin 2014). The English language is associated with economic opportunity as well as the possibility of mobility outside the borders of Nepal. As much as Kathmandu-based Taralis strive to preserve their culture, the prospect of providing better opportunities to their children through an English-medium education trumps the perceived benefits of attempting to preserve their own language from generation to generation by pursuing a mother-tongue-based education, which is currently unavailable in Kaike.

Those Teralis who reside in Tarang, even without necessarily believing their language to be under threat, are presented with poor choices regarding the educational opportunities they are able to provide to their children, a common experience of smaller language communities (UNESCO 2003: 15). Formal education consists of subdomains where language choices are made, including the language of instruction, of study, the language allowed in recreation, and the language used by teachers to communicate to parents (Landweer 2000). The momentum toward linguistic and cultural erosion in Tarang is not so much a result of the Nepali-medium language instruction and a culturally irrelevant curriculum at the local school as it is the outright removal of children from the social-ecological landscape into which they are born. In the case of Tarang, providing children with a good education and with a strong foundation of traditional knowledge are mutually exclusive endeavors. The fact that only an eighth-grade education is achievable without leaving the valley means that either children are denied access to a full education or they are forced to seek higher education away from family and are denied access to their language, and to the culturally and linguistically transmitted knowledge associated with landscape, livelihood systems, and sacred spaces and practices.

The Kaike language situates the Taralis of Tarang in a particular landscape and facilitates the transmission of knowledge about that landscape. The pursuit of better education and opportunities for children outside the socio-ecological landscape associated with the Kaike language serves to lower the practical transmission and retention of that language among younger generations, even while the regard for Kaike and the knowledge with which it is imbued continue to rise among older generations, particularly those residing in Kathmandu.

Conclusion

Language can serve as a marker of ethnic identity (Landweer 2000). In Nepal, among most indigenous speech communities, mother-tongue language competence is a key indicator of ethnic identity (Turin 2014). Across the Kaike-speaking diaspora, the choice to speak in Kaike among Taralis solidifies group cohesion and a sense of belonging. The decision about when to speak in Kaike is dependent upon relative positions of status and power among speech communities. Kaike speakers in Tarang occupy a politically dominant position both within Dolpa and Tichurong, which confers greater status on the Kaike language itself.

Taralis everywhere ascribe a higher value to their language now as compared to the late 1960s, when Fisher described a perception among Taralis that the Kaike language was unsophisticated (see Bendi Tso and Turin, this volume, for a comparable discussion about Chone Tibetan). Positive perceptions of the Kaike language signify greater emotional attachment to both the language and the collective identity it affords its speakers, and is an important indicator of ethnolinguistic vitality (Ehala 2015). Greater emotional attachment to Kaike does not equate with successful intergenerational transmission of the language itself across all Tarali communities, specifically among those who reside outside of Tichurong. The perpetuation of the Kaike language across generations requires situatedness in the landscape in which the language continues to be relevant. Within Tarang itself, Kaike continues to serve as the primary language, and its transmission across generations is facilitated by linguistically encoded and place-based cultural and ecological knowledge.

Kaike-speaking Taralis persist as a socially cohesive group across multiple locations and operate within a variable and dynamic system of identities, articulated through language and negotiated through economic and political positioning.

Active participation in social institutions, demonstrable connection to a shared identity, and a capacity to protect one's existence are indicators of ethnolinguistic vitality (Ehala 2015). In addition, I argue that spatiality is another important factor in the vitality framework, particularly with regard to intergenerational transmission of language and cultural knowledge.

References

2018. 'Reclassification of Indigenous People in Nepal', *Cultural Survival*, https://www.culturalsurvival.org/news/reclassification-indigenous-people-nepal

2009 (3 March). 'Government to Come Up With Separate List of Indigenous Groups', *Nepalnews.com*.

Annamalai, E. 2002. 'Language Policy for Multilingualism', Keynote in *World Congress on Language Policies* (Barcelona: Linguapax IX, 2002).

Bauer, Kenneth M. 2004. *High Frontiers: Dolpo and the Changing World of Himalayan Pastoralists* (New York: Columbia University Press).

Bruce Benz, Judith Cevallos E., Francisco Santana M., Jesus Rosales A. and S. Graf M. 2000. 'Losing Knowledge About Plant Use in the Sierra de Manantlan Biosphere Reserve, Mexico', *Economic Botany* 54 (20): 183–91, https://doi.org/10.1007/BF02907821

Botha, Louis R. 2010. 'Indigenous knowledge as culturally-centered education in South Africa', *Africa Education Review* 7 (1): 34–50, https://doi.org/10.1080/18146627.2010.485804

Bourhis, Richard, Howard Giles and Doreen Rosenthal. 1981. 'Notes on the construction of a "Subjective Vitality Questionnaire" for ethnolinguistic groups', *Journal of Multilingual and Multicultural Development* 2 (2): 145–55, https://doi.org/10.1080/01434632.1981.9994047

Bucholtz, Mary and Kira Hall, 'Language and Identity', in *A Companion to Linguistic Anthropology*, ed. by Alessandro Duranti (Malden: Blackwell Publishing Ltd., 2004), pp. 369–94.

Budha, Jag Bahadur. 2015. *Yarsagumba and Emerging Consumption Culture Among Tarali Magar People in Dolpa District* (Master's thesis, Tri-Chandra Multiple Campus, Kathmandu).

Nepali Government, Central Bureau of Statistics. 2012. *National Population and Housing Census 2011: National Report* (Kathmandu: Federal Democratic Republic of Nepal).

Nepali Government, Central Bureau of Statistics National Planning Commission Secretariat. 2014. *National Population and Housing Census 2011 (Village Development Committee/Municipality): Dolpa* (Kathmandu: Federal Democratic Republic of Nepal).

Nepali Government, Central Bureau of Statistics National Planning Commission Secretariat. 2014. *Population Monograph of Nepal: Population Dynamics Volume 1* (Kathmandu: Federal Democratic Republic of Nepal).

Chandrahasan, Nirmala. 2015. 'Monolingualism, Bilingualism and Multilingualism: The Human Rights Perspective', in *Language and Social Cohesion in the Developing World: Selected Proceedings of the Ninth Language and Development Conference*, ed. by Hywel Coleman (Colombo: British Council and Deutsche Gesellschaft für Internationale Zusammenarbeit (GIZ) GmbH), pp. 15–21.

Chettri, Mona. 2017. *Ethnicity and Democracy in the Eastern Himalayan Borderland: Constructing Democracy* (Amsterdam: Amsterdam University Press).

Coleman, Hywel, ed. 2015. *Language and Social Cohesion in the Developing World: Selected Proceedings of the Ninth Language and Development Conference* (Colombo: British Council and Deutsche Gesellschaft für Internationale Zusammenarbeit (GIZ) GmbH).

Cruz García, Gisella S. 2006. 'The Mother-child Nexus: Knowledge and Valuation of Wild Food Plants in Wayanad, Western Ghats, India', *Journal of Ethnobiology and Ethnomedicine* 2 (39), https://doi.org/10.1186/1746-4269-2-39

Daurio, Maya. 2012. 'The Fairy Language: Language Maintenance and Social-Ecological Resilience Among the Tarali of Tichurong, Nepal', *Himalaya, the Journal of the Association for Nepal and Himalayan Studies* 31 (1), Article 8, https://digitalcommons.macalester.edu/himalaya/vol31/iss1/8/

Ehala, Martin. 2010. 'Ethnolinguistic Vitality and Intergroup Processes', *Multilingua* 29 (2010): 203–21, https://doi.org/10.1515/mult.2010.009

Ehala, Martin. 2015. 'Ethnolinguistic Vitality', in *The International Encyclopedia of Language and Social Interaction* (London: John Wiley & Sons), https://doi.org/10.1002/9781118611463.wbielsi046

Fisher, James F. 1986. *Trans-Himalayan Traders* (Berkeley and Los Angeles: University of California Press).

Fisher, James F. 2017. *Trans-Himalayan Traders Transformed: Return to Tarang*, (Bangkok: Orchid Press).

Gellner, David N. 2016. *The Idea of Nepal, The Mahesh Chandra Regmi Lecture 2016*, (Kathmandu: Himal Books for Social Science Baha), http://soscbaha.org/mcrl-2016/

Giles, Howard, Richard Y. Bourhis and Donald M. Taylor. 1977. 'Towards a theory of language in ethnic group relations', in *Language, ethnicity and intergroup relations*, ed. by Howard Giles (London: Academic Press), pp. 307–48.

Harrison, K. D. 2007. *When Languages Die: The Extinctions of the World's Languages and the Erosion of Human Knowledge* (New York: Oxford University Press).

Hildebrandt, Kristine A. and Hu, Shunfu. 2017. 'Areal Analysis of Language Attitudes and Practices: A Case Study from Nepal', in *Documenting Variation in Endangered Languages. Language Documentation & Conservation Special Publication no. 13*, ed. by Kristine A. Hildebrandt, Carmen Jany, and Wilson Silva (Honolulu: University of Hawai'i Press), pp. 152–79, http://hdl.handle.net/10125/24753

Ibrahim, Rukshaan. 2015. 'The Role of the Standard Variety in Defining Sub-Varieties: A Study Based on Teaching English and Tamil', in *Language and Social Cohesion in the Developing World: Selected Proceedings of the Ninth Language and Development Conference*, ed. by Hywel Coleman (Colombo: British Council and Deutsche Gesellschaft für Internationale Zusammenarbeit (GIZ) GmbH), pp. 186–94.

Kuyakanon, Riamsara and Gyeltshen, Dorji. 2017. 'Propitiating the Tsen, Sealing the Mountain: Community Mountain-closure Ritual and Practice in Eastern Bhutan', *HIMALAYA, the Journal of the Association for Nepal and Himalayan Studies* 37: 8–25.

La Belle, Thomas J. 1982. 'Formal, Nonformal, and Informal Education: A Holistic Perspective on Lifelong Learning', *International Review of Education* 28 (2): 159–75.

Landweer, Lynn. 2000. 'Indicators of Ethnolinguistic Vitality', *Notes on Sociolinguistics* 5 (1): 5–22.

Lawoti, Mahendra. 2008. 'Exclusionary Democratization in Nepal, 1990–2002', *Democratization* 15 (2): 363–85, https://doi.org/10.1080/13510340701846434

McCarter, Joe and Gavin, Michael C. 2011. 'Perceptions of the Value of Traditional Ecological Knowledge to Formal School Curricula: Opportunities and Challenges from Malekula Island, Vanuatu', *Journal of Ethnobiology and Ethnomedicine* 7 (38), https://doi.org/10.1186/1746-4269-7-38

McKinley Jones Brayboy, Bryan and Castagno, Angelina E. 2009. 'Self-determination through self-education: culturally responsive schooling for Indigenous students in the USA', *Teaching Education* 20 (1): 31–53, https://doi.org/10.1080/10476210802681709

Muan, G. Chin Khan. 2007. *'Indigenous Peoples' Human Rights Report, Nepal* (Chiangmai: Asia Indigenous Peoples Pact Foundation).

Nettle, Daniel, and Romaine, Suzanne. 2000. *Vanishing Voices: The Extinction of the World's Languages* (New York: Oxford University Press).

Noonan, Michael. 2005. 'Language Documentation and Language Endangerment in Nepal', Lecture at the University of Iceland, Dialogue of Cultures (14 April).

Pearce, Margaret Wickens and Louis, Renee Pualani. 2008. 'Mapping Indigenous Depths of Place', *American Indian Culture and Research* 32 (3): 107–26.

Phyak, Prem. 2015. 'Multilingual Education, Social Transformation and Development in Nepal', in *Language and Social Cohesion in the Developing World: Selected Proceedings of the Ninth Language and Development Conference*, ed. by Hywel Coleman (Colombo: British Council and Deutsche Gesellschaft für Internationale Zusammenarbeit (GIZ) GmbH), pp. 128–43.

Pine, Aidan, and Turin, Mark. 2017. 'Language Revitalization', in *Oxford Research Encyclopedia of Linguistics*, ed. by Mark Aronoff (New York: Oxford University Press), https://doi.org/10.1093/acrefore/9780199384655.013.8

Pinnock, Helen. 2015. 'Multilingual Education: From "Why" to "How"', in *Language and Social Cohesion in the Developing World: Selected Proceedings of the Ninth Language and Development Conference*, ed. by Hywel Coleman (Colombo: British Council and Deutsche Gesellschaft für Internationale Zusammenarbeit (GIZ) GmbH), pp. 36–43.

Pugh, Stefan M. 1999. 'Language and Identity', in *Handbook of Language and Identity*, ed. by Joshua A. Fishman (Oxford and New York: Oxford University Press).

Rai, Shiv Kumar. 2008. 'Nepalmā Ādibāsi Janajati, Swāsthya Adhikār Ra Swāsthya Pesāma Unihariko Upasthiti', *Nepal Indigenous Journal* 1: 1–19.

Rana, B.K, 2005. 'Recent Change in Language Communities of Nepal', *OGMIOS Newsletter* 3.02.26, https://www.ogmios.org/ogmios_files/265.htm

Regmi, Ambika. 2013. 'A Sociolinguistic Survey of Magar Kaike: A Tibeto-Burman Language, *A Report Submitted to Linguistic Survey of Nepal* (*LinSuN*) (Central Department of Linguistics. Tribhuvan University, Kathmandu, Nepal).

Reyes-Garcia, V., Vincent Vadez, Elizabeth Byron, Lilian Apaza, William R. Leonard, Eddy Perez and David Wilkie. 2005. 'Market Economy and the Loss of Folk Knowledge of Plant Uses: Estimates from the Tsimane' of the Bolivian Amazon', *Current Anthropology* 46 (4): 651–56, https://doi.org/10.1086/432777

Roche, Gerald. 2017. 'Linguistic Vitality, Endangerment, and Resilience', *Language Documentation & Conservation* 11: 190–223.

Ruiz-Mallen, I., Laura Barraza, Barbara Bodenhorn, Maria de la Paz Ceja-Adame, and Victoria Reyes-García. 2009. 'Contextualizing Learning through the Participatory Construction of an Environmental Education Program', *International Journal of Science Education* 32 (13): 1755–70, https://doi.org/10.1080/09500690903203135

Samuelson, Beth L. and Freedman, Sarah W. 2010. 'Language Policy, Multilingual Education, and Power in Rwanda', *Language Policy* 9: 191–215.

Saynes-Vásquez, A., J. Caballero, J. A. Meave, and F. Chiang. 2013. 'Cultural Change and Loss of Ethnoecological Knowledge among the Isthmus Zapotecs of Mexico', *Journal of Ethnobiology and Ethnomedicine* 9 (40), n. p., https://doi.org/10.1186/1746-4269-9-40

Shneiderman, Sara, 2014, 'Reframing Ethnicity: Academic Tropes, Recognition Beyond Politics, and Ritualized Action between Nepal and India', *American Anthropologist* 116 (2): 279–95.

Singh, Navin Kumar, Shaoan Zhang, and Parwez Besmel. 2012. 'Globalization and Language Policies of Multilingual Societies: Some Case Studies of South East Asia', *Revista Brasileira de Linguística Aplicada* 12 (2): 349–80, https://doi.org/10.1590/S1984-63982012000200007

Smith, Benjamin King, Martin Ehala, and Howard Giles. 2017. 'Vitality Theory', in *Oxford Research Encyclopedia of Communication*, ed. by J. F. Nussbaum (Oxford: Oxford University Press), pp. 1–22.

Turin, Mark. 2008. 'Living Languages and Troubled Tongues: Linguistic Diversity and Endangerment in the Himalayas', *Jetwork* (October): 58–63.

Turin, Mark. 2011. *Languages of the Greater Himalayan Region, Vol. 6: A Grammar of the Thangmi Language* (Leiden: Brill's Tibetan Studies Library, 2011), https://doi.org/10.1163/9789004223769

Turin, Mark. 2014. 'Mother Tongues and Language Competence: The Shifting Politics of Linguistic Belonging in the Himalayas', in *Facing Globalization in the Himalayas: Belonging and the Politics of the Self: Governance, Conflict, and Civic Action*, ed. by G. Toffin and J. Pfaff-Czarnecka, Vol. 5 (Delhi: Sage Publications), pp. 371–96.

UNESCO. 2003. 'Language Vitality and Endangerment', *UNESCO Ad Hoc Expert Group on Endangered Languages*. Document submitted to the International Expert Meeting on UNESCO Program Safeguarding of Endangered Languages, Paris, 10–12 March 2003, http://www.unesco.org/new/fileadmin/MULTIMEDIA/HQ/CLT/pdf/Language_vitality_and_endangerment_EN.pdf

Whelpton, John. 2005. *A History of Nepal* (Cambridge, UK: Cambridge University Press, 2005).

Yadava, Yogendra P. 2004. 'Pattern of Language Endangerment in Nepal: An Approximation', Linguistic Society of Nepal Silver Jubilee Conference (Kathmandu: Linguistic Society of Nepal).

Zent, Stanford. 1999. 'The Quandary of Conserving Ethnoecological Knowledge: A Piaroa Example', in *Ethnoecology: Knowledge, Resources and Rights*, ed. by T. Gragson and B. Blount (Athens, GA: The University of Georgia Press).

5. Speaking Chone, Speaking 'Shallow'
Dual Linguistic Hegemonies in China's Tibetan Frontier

Bendi Tso and Mark Turin

The People's Republic of China (henceforth, PRC) is firmly committed to a language policy of promoting the Chinese language among ethnic minority groups and encouraging ethnic minorities to construct a Chinese national identity through linguistic and cultural assimilation. Running parallel to such assimilationist policies are standardization projects that recognize China's heterogeneity, and preserve and promote ethnic minority languages that are sponsored by the PRC government and maintained by ethnic minorities. The state has succeeded in both of these ideological and strategic endeavors. The Chinese language and associated cultural norms have been widely adopted and ethnic minority languages have effectively been standardized. However, as a collateral byproduct of these processes, non-standard dialects of ethnic minority languages have been marginalized and begun to disappear.

This chapter examines official language policy as it is played out in Chone County, located in the Kanlho Tibetan Autonomous Prefecture (TAP) of Gansu Province, and explores how state policy interacts with locally-held language ideologies among Chone Tibetans. Using the concept of hegemony, we argue that China's language policy and Chone Tibetans' willingness to adopt new languages serve to generate both coercion and consent. These two forces work together to contribute to a three-tiered linguistic hierarchy that has emerged from an intensification of language contact since the 1900s, if not earlier. This three-tier linguistic hierarchy, with Chinese and Amdo Tibetan as the dominant languages — albeit with Chinese firmly situated above Amdo Tibetan — and Chone Tibetan as the subordinate language, has accelerated the loss of Chone Tibetan through the dual oppression from two linguistic hegemonies that have exerted complex pressures on the speech community of Chone.

In this chapter, we first present the theoretical framework of our study and discuss how forces of coercion and consent work together to secure and maintain the dual linguistic hegemonies. We then proceed to sketch out the context of our research and our methodology. Next, we illustrate how literacy campaigns and educational policies in Chone function to coercively establish the linguistic hierarchy. We then discuss the apparent willingness of Chone Tibetans to internalize this linguistic hierarchy and to adopt new languages, and how this helps to generate a sense of consent that in turn legitimizes the hierarchically superior positions enjoyed by Chinese and Amdo Tibetan. Our goal, throughout this chapter, is to contribute to an emerging and critical conversation about linguistic diversity within cultural Tibet.

The Shape of Linguistic Hegemony: Coercion and Consent

Building on Woolard's (1985) and Wiley's (1996) notions of hegemony, for the purpose of this study we define linguistic hegemony as the position and power that the dominant language enjoys in legitimating and reproducing prevailing ideologies and practices. The hegemony to which we refer here is linguistic and cultural rather than political. The adoption of a particular language by a group of speakers is never random nor is it accidental (Carlucci 2013; Ives 2004; Suarez 2002; Wiley 1996). Instead, it is assisted, shaped and promoted by coercive forces. And the consent displayed by speakers in turn justifies and secures the existence and practice of coercion. Consent and coercion work together in powerful and socially effective ways to establish and secure the superior position enjoyed by the dominant language or languages.

To better understand how linguistic hegemony is created and reproduced in the context of Chone, we examine two interactive aspects of hegemony: coercion and consent. The first point of analysis is located within the powerful nature of hegemony itself and explores how state institutions and policies enable and maintain linguistic domination. Social institutions, including but not limited to law and language policy, shed light on the politics of language by producing expectations of 'standard' language and by taming diverse language ideologies held by the people so that only a standard language appears to be natural and proper (Eriksen 1992; Wiley 1996). Through powerful social institutions, the linguistic hierarchy is established. Language norms are shaped and then take hold. Furthermore, linguistic hierarchy is produced and reinforced by social institutions that lead to speakers of minority languages and varieties eventually accepting an ideology that defines their heritage language as inferior, ultimately leading to its abandonment (Eriksen 1992).

Yet, at the same time, we acknowledge that 'authority and hegemony cannot be mechanically read out from institutional dominance' (Woolard 1985: 743) since the successful normalization of a linguistic hegemony relies on the extent to which 'linguistic minorities will believe in and participate in the subjugation of the minority language to the dominant, to the point where just the dominant language remains' (Suarez 2002: 514). In other words, institutions alone cannot fully sustain the power of a dominant language. The consent of speakers of minority languages, and their willingness to adopt a dominant language, is another key aspect of hegemony, and one that grants the coercive force important legitimacy. In contrast to coercion, consent is achieved through the apparently willing participation of minority language speakers in promoting, accepting and appreciating the dominant language (Ives 2004; Suarez 2002; Wiley 1996). In the context of consent, minority language speakers' adoption of a dominant language is not an 'accommodative behavior' (Woolard 1985: 741) that conceals their true and deep feelings of value towards their heritage language and thus accommodates to the coercive force. Rather, their internalized language ideology becomes part of the 'collaborative consciousness' (Woolard 1985: 741) and is naturalized, thus working to shape their daily language practice and reproduce the linguistic and cultural hegemony. It is, then, through their language ideologies that minority language speakers participate in the social reproduction of consent, and the cultural and linguistic domination over them is justified, secured and sustained.

To summarize, the superior position enjoyed by a dominant language cannot be established without a combination of institutional coercion and the consent of minority language speakers. With the support of institutional powers, a dominant language becomes the yardstick for establishing a linguistic hierarchy, which in turn makes minority language speakers accord it high value (Turin 2018). Through the participation of minority language speakers, language ideologies that offer the dominant language prestige, pride of place and authority are given legitimacy. This iterative process secures and reinforces the position of the dominant language.

Situating Chone County in Time and Place

Chone County is located on the Sino-Tibetan border. It was incorporated into Kanlho Tibetan Autonomous Prefecture (henceforth, Kanlho TAP) of Gansu Province, China, in 1953. Ethnolinguistically speaking, Chone is located in Amdo, one of three cultural-linguistic regions of cultural Tibet.

According to Choephel (1978), Chone was an ancient border outpost of the Tibetan empire. The earliest definitive evidence showing the settlement of Tibetans in this area dates to the seventh century, when Songtsen Gampo — the famed King of Tibet — sent his troops to Chone. Chone is also home to several other ethnic groups, including but not limited to Chinese, Hui Muslims, Mongols and Monguors. Chone County is closely interlocked with Batse County of Kanlho TAP, the majority of whose residents are Hui Muslims and Chinese. In broad strokes, Chone shares its northern, western, and southern borders with Tibetan communities and its eastern border with Chinese communities.

As a multi-ethnic border zone, the political and linguistic history of Chone is rich and complex. Chone is marked by 600 years of governance by a Tibetan chieftain family who maintained religious connections with Lhasa in Central Tibet while winning political recognition from Chinese courts (Rock 1933; Yang 1990). Also noteworthy is the massive Chinese immigration into Chone that began in the early twentieth century due to

5. Speaking Chone, Speaking 'Shallow' 141

Fig. 5.1. Map of Chone County as situated within Amdo, within China. Adapted from Kolås and Thowsen (2005: 2), CC BY-NC-ND.

the Hui Muslim revolt in 1928 in He Zhou — which came to be referred to as the He-Huang Incident — located in what is today the Linxia Hui Autonomous Prefecture,[1] adjacent to Kanlho TAP (Chone Gazetteer Compilation Committee 1994: 166). Since the 1950s, the PRC's national language policy has promoted Chinese in Chone. Also, since the late 1980s, the Amdo Tibetan standardization movement — encouraged by the Chinese state to preserve and develop the Tibetan language, and later instigated by Tibetan political and cultural elites to safeguard the survival of the Tibetan language and assert Tibetans' Tibetanness — has further complicated the already complex ethnolinguistic landscape of Chone.

Broadly speaking, there are three identifiable Tibetan linguistic groups within Chone County, according to their geographical location and complex histories of migration: 1) the group of nomads who live in the western and northern pastoral regions of Chone and whose spoken language is close to Amdo Tibetan; 2) the group of farmers who live in the eastern enclave of Chone and whose spoken language shares linguistic feature with both Kham and Lhasa Tibetan; and 3) riverside Tibetans who live along the Luchu River and its tributaries, and whose spoken language is closer to Lhasa Tibetan (Chone Gazetteer Compilation Committee 1994: 164, 699). Our research site is located in the riverside Tibetan community. Within the official PRC discourse, 'riverside Tibetans' are recognized to be Chone Tibetans and the ethnonym has been accepted by locals. For the purpose of this study, then, we refer to the riverside Tibetan community as 'Chone Tibetans' and to their spoken tongue as the Chone Tibetan language. The Chone Tibetan language is only intelligible to speakers living alongside the Luchu River and its tributaries, making its linguistic ecology somewhat unfavorable. By this we mean that Chone Tibetans live in a traditional Amdo Tibetan-speaking area, but speak a form of Tibetan that is, if anything, closer to Lhasa Tibetan.[2] Due to their frequent, intensive and

---

1 The 'He-Huang Incident' was a Hui Muslim revolt against the Feng Yuxiang's administration and Kuominjun Army of Hezhou that occurred in May 1928. This conflict quickly swung against the Chinese and lasted for six years, causing over half a million casualties in Gansu and Qinghai (see also Jonathan N. Lipman 1997; Woser, Interview, 21 July 2013; Bendi Gyal, Interview, 19 June 2017). Due to the He-Huang Incident, many Chinese fled to Chone and settled there.

2 We are aware that linguists critically challenge the notion that Amdo, Lhasa and Kham are three dialects of the 'same' Tibetan language, and that they highlight the linguistic diversity and complexity that exists within these three dialects (Suzuki

prolonged contact with the Chinese language over time, Chone Tibetans have increasingly been exposed to strong assimilationist forces from mainstream Chinese culture, and have adopted many Chinese loan words into their language.

Our principle research site was Yarru village, a settlement located along the northern side of the Luchu River. According to oral histories passed down through the generations and augmented by interviews with Chone Tibetans in Yarru village, Tibetans from Central Tibet settled in the area thanks to its hospitable and fertile environment. There are currently sixty-four households in Yarru village, of which at least twelve are Chinese. The Chinese settlement can be accounted for in two ways: some Chinese were hired by Chone Tibetans as farm laborers in the early twentieth century,[3] while others were refugees who suffered during the Hui Muslim revolt in the 1920s and fled to Chone. The cumulative result of this Chinese immigration is that, since the early twentieth century at least, Chone Tibetans have been gradually exposed to both written and spoken Chinese language and culture. According to the interviews with Chone Tibetans in this village, during the earlier period of Chinese settlement, language shift did not occur because Chone Tibetans significantly outnumbered ethnic Chinese. Later, when a series of political and cultural events provided strong incentives for Chone Tibetans to incorporate Chinese loanwords into their language and to learn to speak, read and write Chinese, this triggered widespread language shift which further promoted the belief that the Chone language was a 'low-status' Tibetan language. As a result of these interconnected factors, many Chone Tibetans are now experiencing a growing sense of what may be described as linguistic and cultural anxiety and alienation.

2016; Tournadre 2014). However, we use these terms in order to emphasize the cultural hegemony associated with these languages instead of their linguistic distinctiveness *per se*. Meanwhile, there is a disparity between speakers' locally conceptualized linguistic categorization and those defined by linguists. Based on the data collected from interviews, local Chone Tibetans tend to believe that their language is similar to Lhasa Tibetan.

3   This labor force later developed into the Small Households, which refers to the shelters that some long-term laborers and refugees built at the outskirts of Tibetan villages along the Luchu River (Chone Historical Accounts Compilation Committee 1984: 10; Lhamo, Interview, 23 May, 2017).

Research Methods and Subject Position

This research is based on interviews and observations conducted with community members between May and August in Yarru village in 2013, a series of follow-up interviews with Chone Tibetans in Yarru village between October and December 2016, and ethnographic fieldwork conducted between mid-May and late June 2017 in Yarru village and the neighboring villages. Our research questions focused on language practice, shift and ideology among Chone Tibetans in the context of China's wider language policy.

In the field, the lead author's identity as an ethnic Chone Tibetan with distant relatives living in Yarru village facilitated her acceptance within the community. Participant observation served as her primary research method, which — when combined with familiar contact and continual encounters with community members — opened up many spaces for designing and honing complex research questions. Semi-structured interviews with county, township and village officials helped her to explore the role played by institutions and bureaucrats in shaping Chone Tibetan language ideologies. We also used semi-structured interviews to explore Chone Tibetans' language proficiency and attitudes towards their heritage language, as well as towards the more dominant Amdo Tibetan and Chinese languages. Semi-structured interviews with parents, children and village school teachers helped us understand their experiences of language acquisition, while life story interviews with elder Chone Tibetans were particularly useful in documenting shifting experiences of and changing attitudes towards language acquisition. All of these methodological techniques were used to assess the processes of consent and coercion that are integral to the formation and normalization of dual linguistic hegemonies.

Interviews were conducted in the local Chinese dialect, which is known as the Taozhou Chinese dialect. It belongs to the Northwest subdialect of the Northern dialect of Chinese (Wang 2013), and it has now become the lingua franca of Chone and Batse Counties. It was necessary to use the local Chinese dialect to conduct interviews because the majority of Chone Tibetans under the age of forty are now monolingual in Chinese, and generally speak the local Chinese dialect amongst themselves. Second, the lead author's imperfect proficiency in Tibetan limited her ability to conduct interviews in her ancestral language. In this chapter, we use pseudonyms for research partners and locations to mitigate any unwanted and unwelcome repercussions.

Coercion as an Aspect of Linguistic Hegemony

The adoption of a dominant language by minority language speakers and the establishment of a linguistic hierarchy are not processes that occur in a vacuum. Instead, these actions are supported by the policy contexts in which they occur. The national language policy of China plays a central role in constructing and maintaining the linguistic hierarchy and triggering language shift from ethnic minority languages to Chinese. To date, there have been two dominant discourses within the PRC's language policy. First has been the promotion of Chinese in almost all domains, including education, the workplace, and the media, at both national and community levels (Spolsky 2014; Rohsenow 2004; Wang and Yuan 2013). Second, the state has offered incentives and some resources to encourage the preservation, standardization and development of minority languages (Harrell 1993; Zhou 2004; Li and Huang 2004; Li and He 2014). Laws and regulations have been implemented by both central and local governments that enshrine and guarantee minorities' rights to use and develop their own heritage languages. Within the Kanlho TAP, the rights to use, learn, preserve, standardize, and develop Tibetan are enshrined in the *Autonomy Statute of Kanlho Tibetan Autonomous Prefecture of Gansu Province*, which was passed in 1989 and amended in 2010 (Articles 24, 28, 60, 63, 64, and 74).

Even though these two distinct discourses are emphasized within the PRC's language policy, they do not guarantee that minority languages have a linguistic position equal to Chinese or that minority languages can access the same range of discursive and financial resources that Chinese does (Zhou 2012). The government — through the state's language policies and associated ideology — decides which language can be used in which context, with the result that languages are accessed to differing degrees, forming a language order or hierarchy (Zhou 2012). As Arienne Dwyer (1998) observes, a five-tiered linguistic hierarchy has been established in the PRC. This hierarchy positions Mandarin Chinese at the top and situates standardized minority languages over 'primary minority languages, secondary minority languages and unrecognized languages' (Dwyer 1998: 71–72). The niche that a language occupies within this five-tiered linguistic hierarchy is highly dependent upon the prestige and political influence of the language, and the number of speakers (Dwyer 1998). The state, in turn, offers various levels of support to different languages depending on their position along and within this hierarchy (Dwyer 2005). In the case of Tibetan, the three main vernaculars (Lhasa, Kham and Amdo Tibetan) have become the most prestigious Tibetan language varieties in their respective regions. Amdo Tibetan — the dominant language in Amdo region (Roche 2017) — has been promoted over local Tibetan varieties because its pronunciation is closer to literary Tibetan (Prins 2002). In addition, the nomadic pronunciation of Amdo Tibetan adds extra prestige to the language since nomadic life is often imagined as the key aspect of Tibetan identity (Prins 2002).

In this section, by examining literacy campaigns and educational policies implemented in Yarru village from the 1950s onwards, we argue that the PRC's coercive language policies are powerful forces for the establishment and maintenance of hegemonies. These influences have prompted language shift from Chone Tibetan to Chinese, and have helped to establish Amdo Tibetan as the effective standard Tibetan language for this region.

The Role of Literacy Campaigns

Following the foundation of the PRC, on account of the powerful symbolic connection between literacy and the imagining of the nation-state, the government set out to address illiteracy in Chinese as well as in other regionally-dominant ethnic minority languages through national and local policies (Spolsky 2014; Zhou 2005). At the national level, ethnic communities were encouraged to improve their literacy in ethnic minority languages in the early period of the PRC, especially during the 1950s (Zhou 2005). Article 6 of the *Regulations on the Eradication of Illiteracy*, which was passed in 1988 and which was later amended in 1993, states that the medium of instruction for literacy campaigns should ideally be Mandarin Chinese, but that in ethnic minority areas, either the ethnic minority language or the language most commonly used by all of the ethnic minorities in a community could be the medium for literacy education. At the Prefectural level, Article 9 of the *Regulations on Tibetan Language Use in Kanlho TAP* (1996) stated that the campaign to improve Tibetan literacy among Tibetans should be systematically implemented. At the County level in Chone, Tibetan learning materials were distributed in 2005 in certain villages where the Tibetan language has been used as the medium of education to combat Tibetan illiteracy (Chone Education Bureau 2011: 82). In Yarru village and other villages where Chone Tibetans reside, however, the seven-decade-long literacy campaign was focused on increasing Chone Tibetans' literacy in *Chinese* rather than Tibetan. This has resulted not only in Chone Tibetans learning to read and write in Chinese, but has also accorded high value to Chinese since 'literacy is a primary vehicle for maintaining and transmitting cultural values and beliefs' (Zhou 2005: 117–18).

In Yarru village, the shape taken by literacy campaigns has changed over time, but their purpose — namely exposing Chone Tibetans to the Chinese language — has remained the same for seven decades. In the early years, from 1953 to the mid 1960s, literacy classes were the major expressions of literacy campaigns (Chone Education Bureau 2011: 20; Chone Gazetteer Compilation Committee 1994: 550). These literacy classes were not only classroom-based, but were also held in informal locations throughout the village. Teachers, students and cadres who were literate in Chinese participated in teaching Chinese characters to illiterate Chone Tibetans. Lhamo, a grandmother now in her mid-eighties, recalled that in the 1960s, after a day of hard work on the farm, Chone Tibetans would gather together to learn Chinese. Lhamo spoke of how local Chinese cadres and Tibetan students who had received education in the Chinese language taught basic vocabulary such as numbers and commodities, introducing her to new terms. Even though the classes were held only intermittently, Lhamo reported that after several years of learning, she could write her name in Chinese and had learned basic vocabulary. Along with acquiring rudimentary Chinese, Lhamo was also taught that old Tibetan kinship terms should be replaced with Chinese ones: '*Ama* (mother in Chone Tibetan) should be *muqin* (mother in Chinese); *Ape* (father in Chone Tibetan) should be *fuqin* (father in Chinese)'. Through the erosion and belittling of traditional Tibetan terminology — even in the domain of kinship — the supremacy of the Chinese language and cultural hegemony with which it was associated began to be established.

During the Cultural Revolution (1966–1976), literacy campaigns were escalated. Alongside literacy classes, villagers were expected to memorize *Quotations from Chairman Mao* as a foundational Chinese language-learning resource. Chinese language learning was evaluated by reading quotes out loud from blackboards, which were even mounted outside the communal dining hall of Yarru village and the ferry pier along the Luchu River. Bendi Gyal, a grandfather now in his mid-seventies, recalled that two students from a local school usually stood beside the blackboard and would ask villagers to read the quotes aloud. If they were unable to read the quotes correctly, they would not be permitted to eat or take the ferry, and students would offer instruction in the quotes until villagers could read them. When the policy was tightened further, blackboards were mounted at the entrance of villages. Every time villagers passed by the gateway, they were required to read the quotes on the blackboards. Although we cannot say to what extent this literacy campaign helped Chone Tibetans acquire Chinese, such practices certainly changed Chone Tibetans' attitudes towards the Chinese language in which Chinese was positioned as a resource that could bolster status and garner prestige. As Lhamo said, 'when we were young, those who could speak and write Chinese were [thought to be] the talented ones.'

After 1976, each household received a radio from the government. News from China National Radio and Chone County Radio were broadcast in Mandarin Chinese at 7pm every day, introducing Mandarin Chinese to the community in a more systematic way. Since the 1990s, literacy campaigns in Yarru village have become increasingly diverse and multimodal, including — but not limited to — meetings, songs, TV, blackboards, posters, and job trainings. In 2005, the literacy campaign strategy gradually shifted its focus from teaching Chinese characters to receiving skills training in the Chinese medium (Chone Education Bureau 2011: 83). Literate Chone Tibetans were told that they would become more competitive in the labor market through reinforcing the Chinese characters that they had learned. Courses introducing skills in vegetable cultivation, animal husbandry, construction, noodle making and using sewing machines have been offered to people in Yarru village through the medium of Chinese, all on the understanding that this will make them more competitive in the labor force.

Even though specific statistics on changes in Chone Tibetan literacy rates as a result of this seven-decades-long campaign are still lacking,[4] overall literacy rate changes in Chone County are available. While the illiteracy rate was above 90% before the foundation of the PRC in Chone (Chone Gazetteer Compilation Committee 1994: 165), by the end of 2010, the illiteracy rate in Chone had dropped to 3.14% (Chone Education Bureau 2011: 84). Through the waves of successive literacy campaigns, Chone Tibetans now not only know how to speak and write Chinese, but have also internalized the prevailing linguistic order. The strong and sustained position taken by the government has helped to establish the linguistic domination of Chinese.

Changing Educational Policies

While the national literacy campaign outlined above introduced the Chinese language to Chone Tibetans and helped to establish a linguistic hierarchy with Chinese as the superior language, educational policies worked to further complicate the linguistic hierarchy by having Chone Tibetans learn both Chinese and Amdo Tibetan in a structured and formal way, speeding up the loss of the Chone Tibetan language. As widely documented (cf. Aronowitz 2002; Macedo, Dendrinos and Gounari 2003; Wiley 1996), schools are important sites for a dominant language and its associated culture to be asserted, justified and reinforced. Schools are also important locations where people's consent is acquired and linguistic hegemony is reproduced. In China, the stated aim of bilingual education is to introduce the Chinese language to ethnic minorities and have ethnic minorities develop Chinese language proficiency in order to better assimilate them into Chinese society (Dwyer 2005). At the same time, as an intended or unintended byproduct, bilingual education helps to establish the superior and authoritative position of standardized minority languages over local varieties, as the standardized local language is chosen as the medium of instruction in school settings. In the case of Yarru village, educational policy has legitimized Chinese

---

4   Chone Tibetans (riverside Tibetans) are also recognized as Tibetans. Therefore, the statistics about their literacy are not separated from other Tibetan groups in Chone.

and elevated Amdo Tibetan as the regional standard, which in turn has encouraged Chone Tibetans to view their heritage language as inferior and less formal. The dual hegemonies engendered by this bilingual education policy have contributed to the rapid loss of Chone Tibetan and to a growing sense of linguistic anxiety among its former speakers.

The primary school in Yarru village was founded in the 1950s at the same time as the establishment of the People's Commune; because of political campaigns, classes were not regularly offered until the mid-1970s. Chone Tibetans recall that since the founding of the school, the medium of instruction has always been Chinese, and that Tibetan classes were not offered until 1987. The only opportunity for Chone Tibetans in Yarru village to learn a Tibetan language in school before 1987 was to enroll in the Town Center Middle School where both Tibetan and English were taught as school subjects. Pema, aged forty-seven, was educated in the Town Center Middle school, and confirmed that standardized Amdo Tibetan was taught there twice a week. When asked about his experience of learning Amdo Tibetan in a school setting, he answered, 'our [Chone Tibetan] language is different from the spoken language taught in school, which is taught by teachers from regular school.' From Pema's point of view, the major difference between Amdo Tibetan and Chone Tibetan was formality. He further added, 'Ironically, the Tibetan language class was later cancelled in the second year while the English class was never cancelled in all of my three years. Just as in English, we are dabblers in Tibetan.' Pema is an ethnic Tibetan whose native language is Chone Tibetan. However, the standard form of the language taught in school has changed his understanding of the Tibetan language. Having described himself as a dabbler in Tibetan, he further perceives Chone Tibetan to be linguistically deficient, inauthentic, and subordinate when compared to Amdo Tibetan.

In 1987, when the Tibetan language was finally offered for instruction in Yarru village twice a week under Model Two of China's bilingual education policy,[5] it was the standardized Amdo Tibetan language

---

5   Currently, two bilingual models have been implemented in the Tibetan areas of China. The first, known as 'Model One', refers to an approach where the medium of instruction is Tibetan and all textbooks are written in Tibetan, except for those used in Chinese and English classes. The second, known as 'Model Two', refers to an approach where the medium of instruction is Chinese and all textbooks are written in Chinese, except for those used in Tibetan and English classes

that was selected to be taught. The first Tibetan language teacher, Dorje Men, is an ethnic Chone Tibetan born in Yarru village. She was stationed in Yarru village immediately after graduating from Kanlho Minorities' School in 1987 where she first learned to write Tibetan using standardized Amdo Tibetan over the course of three years. She recalled that back then, most of her students could speak Chone Tibetan but they did not know how to read or write in any Tibetan language. She therefore corrected their pronunciation and taught the Tibetan script in standardized Amdo Tibetan form, so that both standardized vocabulary and pronunciation would be imparted to the students. Through such approaches, a linguistic hierarchy was established within schools with the Chinese language as dominant and Amdo Tibetan as secondary and subordinate, and this hierarchy was maintained through the medium of instruction. However, two years later, Dorje Men was transferred to a primary school in the Chone County seat to teach math and music. When villagers were unhappy with her departure and asked the principal of the Town Center School to assign a new Tibetan teacher to the village school, their request was not honored due to a shortage of recognized Tibetan language teachers. Later, several Tibetan language teachers were stationed in Yarru village school but none of them stayed long. As a result, the educational model of Yarru village school was finally switched from Model Two to Model Three, and Tibetan classes were permanently canceled (see n.5 for more information on the different educational 'Models'). This situation lasted until the Yarru village primary school was permanently shuttered in 2013.

(Yang 2017). In addition to these two bilingual models, 'Model Three' refers to an approach where the medium of instruction is Chinese, and all textbooks are written in Chinese except for the ones used in English class. 'Model Three' does not include the provision of a Tibetan class. These three models were implemented based on both geographical location and the modes of production on which people have relied (Personal communication with cadres). 'Model One' was implemented in the pastoral region of Chone. 'Model Two' was implemented in farming-pastoral regions, where most Chone Tibetans, including Tibetans in Yarru village and some Chinese, reside. Nowadays, apart from one primary school in a village where Chone Tibetans reside that still follows 'Model Two', the rest of the schools that Chone Tibetans attend, including the primary school in Yarru village, have gradually shifted to 'Model Three' due to the lack of Tibetan language teachers and at the insistence of parents. Such a policy has its own limitations since Tibetan classes were offered based on the modes of production of the community rather than students' ethnicities, thereby arguably not meeting the real needs of Tibetans who wish to learn their Tibetan language.

From 2013 to the present, children in Yarru village either attend the Town Center Boarding School or Chinese schools in the Chone County seat. No matter which school they choose, the medium of instruction and all of their textbooks are in Chinese, and Tibetan has increasingly become a foreign and distant language for them. At the same time, Mandarin Chinese is being robustly promoted in school. Teenagers have described a Language Commission Office that was set up in the Chinese high school in the Chone County seat, with two teachers in the office taking charge of promoting Mandarin Chinese. Also, because most teachers working in the Chone High School were not local and spoke only Mandarin Chinese, the local Chinese dialect was not widely tolerated in school and teachers strongly encouraged teenagers to use Mandarin Chinese for all communication. The same process occurred in the Town Center Boarding School. Slogans such as 'please speak Mandarin Chinese, please write standardized Chinese characters' were displayed and conveyed the prevailing belief that only Mandarin Chinese in standardized Chinese characters was a legitimate language within the school setting. Children's extensive exposure to Chinese in school made parents believe that it was the children's Chinese learning that triggered language shift within the family. During fieldwork, the principal author noted that the sentiment that 'ever since the children were sent to school, the transmission of the (Chone) Tibetan language is over' was heard time and again.

This review of seven decades of educational policy changes in Yarru village illustrates how policies have shifted back and forth between promoting Chinese, on the one hand, and supporting Chone Tibetans to learn Amdo Tibetan on the other. This oscillation can be explained by understanding how China's language policy is tightly connected to its policy relating to ethnic minorities and nation-state building, both of which have been subjected to changes in response to state-ethnic minority relations over the years (Zhou 2003). Dwyer categorizes such dramatic policy pivots as 'ideologically and pragmatically chaotic' (2005: 22). A consequence of such frequent changes is the creation not only of 'generation gaps' in terms of language learning and literacy development, but also 'gaps in historical knowledge' (Beckett and Postiglione 2012:14). In the case of the Chone Tibetans of Yarru village, frequent educational policy changes not only deprived them of their right to learn the Tibetan language, but also resulted in most generations being fully exposed to Chinese language and culture, thereby speeding up the production and reproduction of Chinese linguistic and cultural hegemony and the assimilation of Tibetans.

In today's Chone, following the cancelation of Tibetan classes, Chinese has become the single most prioritized language in the school setting. However, this has not resulted in Amdo Tibetan losing its considerable influence in Chone County. Chone Tibetans are still under the linguistic and cultural influence of the Amdo Tibetan language, an influence which at times can feel oppressive. Recently, guided by the Regulations on Tibetan Language Use in Kanlho TAP of Gansu Province (1996), the Article 24 of the Autonomy Statute of Kanlho TAP of Gansu Province (2010), and the Implementation Rules for the Regulations on Tibetan Language Use in Kanlho TAP of Gansu Province (2006), Tibetan language and its use, development and promotion within Kanlho TAP has been strongly encouraged in both letter and spirit. In Chone, the Tibetan Language Committee was formed in 2010, and consists of five staff of whom four majored in Tibetan Language and Literature. The Committee is tasked with implementing six goals, one of which is to promote Tibetan language standardization and the use of Tibetan in Chone. Even though it is nowhere explicitly stipulated which form or variety of Tibetan should be regarded as the standard language in Chone, the lead author of this chapter was informed that the unwritten rule is that it be Amdo Tibetan. Consequently, Amdo Tibetan is widely used in formal linguistic contexts in Chone when Tibetan is called for. For example, shop signs and road signs are written in Amdo Tibetan; the Chone Television Station broadcasts in Amdo Tibetan; and the medium of instruction in Tibetan class at the Tibetan High School of Chone County is Amdo Tibetan, with accommodations made for different teachers' accents. Supported by the state, then, Amdo Tibetan is now encroaching into every domain in which Chone Tibetan was once used, and is even expanding into new domains.

As is clear from the above description, educational language policies implemented by the central and local governments are also hegemonic projects. These policies not only inscribe and reinforce a linguistic hierarchy — which gives priority to Chinese and Amdo Tibetan through the medium of instruction, textbooks and public signage and media — but also serve to create a sense of language deficit and linguistic alienation, whereby Tibetans in Yarru village lose the opportunity to learn their own heritage language.

The Role of Consent in Shaping Linguistic Hegemony

As noted by Peter Ives, 'language is spread predominantly not by government or state coercion, military or police action, but by speakers accepting the prestige and utility of new languages, phrases or terms' (2004: 7). By this we understand that the willingness of minority language speakers to adopt a dominant language leads to the reproduction of a linguistic hegemony, thereby offering the dominant language further legitimacy. The rationale behind people's attitudes and choices about the languages they adopt is socio-political, economic and cultural (Kroskrity 2000). In the context of Chone, we argue that Chone Tibetans have internalized the dominant belief that Chinese is a more modern and useful language than their variety of Tibetan, leading to pronounced language shift. At the same time, Chone Tibetans have also internalized a related if different language ideology: that Amdo Tibetan should be thought of and promoted as the standardized Tibetan language in formal and public contexts. The internalization of a three-tiered language hierarchy with Chone Tibetan at the bottom of the stack has resulted in Chone Tibetans voluntarily participating in the legitimization and reproduction of dual linguistic hegemonies.

Tracking Language Shift from Chone Tibetan to Chinese

Supported by China's language policy and nation-state building, Chinese is the language associated with notions of science and modernity (Dwyer 2005; Prins 2002). Minority languages, including Tibetan languages, have borrowed new words from Chinese in order to engage in new technologies and domains of use. Such linguistic processes have made Chone Tibetans feel that Tibetan languages, and in particular their own form of Chone Tibetan, are not as useful, modern or advanced as Chinese. Tashi, a grandfather in his late sixties, said: 'I always think that Tibetan is shallow. For example, in Chinese we can say the government constructs this or that thing, that it makes an airplane or cannon. Can we say these things in Tibetan?' When compared with Chinese, then, Tibetan languages — especially Chone Tibetan — do not have an indigenous vocabulary for post-1949 innovations. This lack of a modern lexicon has worked to make local Tibetans undervalue their heritage language and imagine Chone Tibetan to be 'shallow,' accelerating the language shift from Chone Tibetan to Chinese.

Language shift and the sense of linguistic inferiority are further reinforced by the linguistic market. In China, Chinese is the lingua franca and is used in almost every domain with the support of both the state and the market. Chinese is also a language that people believe can provide them with economic security and upward mobility (Bulag 2003; de Varennes 2012; Harrell 1993; Prins 2002). Tibetan is not used in the same kinds of social interactions as Chinese is, leading Chone Tibetans to perceive it as having less value. Discussing which language was more useful, Dorje Men, the former Tibetan language teacher, said, 'Tibetan is of little use. If you go to Lanzhou (the provincial capital of Ganzu province), you have to speak Chinese, and Tibetan becomes useless. Without knowing Chinese, you cannot even find a bathroom or ask people where a bathroom is.' From Dorje Men's perspective, it is almost impossible to engage in any activities in today's China without resorting to the use of Chinese. At the same time, Chinese is also valued more highly in the labor market. For most Chone Tibetans, the labor market has become a major source of income due to their gradual abandonment of livestock farming since the 2000s. Currently, only two households in Yarru village still herd sheep. The remaining Chone Tibetans either grow cash crops and medicinal herbs or choose to work as migrant workers. However, as the forty-seven-year-old Pema, who took standard Tibetan classes in the Town Center Middle school, argued, the precondition of being a migrant worker in the labor force is that 'you have to be literate in Chinese.' Increasingly, Chone Tibetans are realizing that gaining proficiency in Chinese is a prerequisite for them to lead a better — or at least modern — life and have the chance of social mobility in the context of the nation that the PRC is building. In a tangible indication of the shift, in 2002, parents in a village near Yarru even demanded that the Chone Education Bureau cancel their children's weekly Tibetan class in order that their children learn Chinese intensively and have a better chance of being admitted to a good university.

Such parental requests reflect the success of a powerful linguistic hegemony among Chone Tibetans. As Suarez has noted, 'the results of successful linguistic hegemony are often language shift from the minority language to the majority language and, ultimately, language loss' (2002: 514). A strongly held language ideology, as the consent component of linguistic hegemony, can result in speakers of a minority language holding a negative view towards their heritage language and giving up opportunities to learn the heritage language. For example, an eighteen-year-old high school student, Khacho Men, stated firmly that Tibetan languages, especially Chone Tibetan, should not be used in formal contexts, such as meetings and conferences, because 'Tibetan is not a presentable language.' This growing sense of inferiority has bred a sense of linguistic fatalism in which local Tibetans believe that Tibetan languages will eventually cease to be used. Tashi, the grandfather in his late sixties, stated: 'not many years from now, Tibetan languages will be extinct. The influence of Chinese is so strong that it will leave no space for the development of Tibetan. Other than the monks learning Tibetan to study Buddhist scriptures, there is no use for farmers or herdsmen to learn Tibetan. [Famers and herdsmen] are incapable of strengthening the Tibetan language.' For Chone Tibetans, then, whereas Chinese is considered to be a useful language, Tibetan is perceived to be of little use on account of its low social status and slow response to new domains of use.

Establishing the Superiority of Amdo Tibetan over Chone Tibetan

Alongside perceiving Chinese to be the most useful language, Chone Tibetans also believe that standard Tibetan can necessarily only be Amdo Tibetan on account of a successful standardization movement and the use of Amdo Tibetan in formal contexts. Chone Tibetan is considered less prestigious, less useful, and less authentic than Amdo Tibetan due to its heavy reliance on loanwords from Chinese. The notion that the Chone Tibetan language has been more contaminated by Chinese at the lexical level is deeply rooted in Chone Tibetans' understandings, further contributing to Chone Tibetans' disparagement of their heritage language.

Even though in some contexts, linguistic purism can be seen as minority language speakers' resistance to a dominant language (Brunstad 2003, Turin 2014), linguistic purism can also jeopardize the maintenance of local linguistic varieties. This is because in the construction of an imagined linguistic purity, there is always a conception of what a good or standard language is. This in turn encourages people to accept and value the standard language given its support of institutional power. As a result, linguistic purism affects speakers' language ideologies and contributes to the linguistic and cultural hegemony of a standard language (Brunstad 2003). Compared to Amdo Tibetan — which is represented by institutional forces as the pure and standard Tibetan language — Chone Tibetan, with its heavy reliance on loan words from Chinese, has been belittled by its speakers as an impure and inauthentic local patois. As Woser, a man in his mid fifties, argued, 'the authentic Tibetan language should be the language spoken by Tibetans in Luchu, Machu, Labrang.[6] Their language is different from us in that we keep lots of Chinese words in our language, such as vinegar, pepper, matchstick, etc.' Loanwords from Chinese have made Chone Tibetans feel that their language is contaminated and therefore inauthentic, and they have further internalized this ideology to believe that even phonetically, Chone Tibetan is less *culturally* Tibetan than Amdo Tibetan. Dorje Men, the former Tibetan language teacher said, 'Amdo Tibetan is so delicate and sophisticated, while our language (Chone Tibetan) is a little bit coarse and crude.'

Chone Tibetan's heavy reliance on loanwords from Chinese, plus its low social prestige due to the lack of state support, has made its speakers, such as Pema Tso, look down on their heritage language and believe that: 'Chone Tibetan is just a local dialect, while Amdo Tibetan is a [more] standardized language.' Two teenagers who had equal proficiency in Chinese and Chone Tibetan also expressed their desire to learn Amdo Tibetan, indicating that the linguistic hierarchy has taken hold in the minds of young Chone Tibetans. This hierarchy reflects not only the limited material, educational and symbolic resources

---

6   Luchu, Machu, and Labrang (Sangchu) are three counties of Kanlho TAP that form the nomadic center of Kanlho TAP. Since Amdo Tibetan is based on the speech of nomads, Chone Tibetans attributed a high value to the Tibetan language spoken by Tibetans from the above-mentioned three counties and view it as the authentic Tibetan language.

to which the Chone Tibetan language and its speakers have access, but also indicates how local villagers unconsciously and voluntarily participate in and reinforce the reproduction of a linguistic hegemony by putting a favored regional language (Amdo Tibetan) ahead of their own heritage language.

When asked about the future of the Chone Tibetan language — from cadres to villagers, and from seniors in their eighties to teenagers — few people have an optimistic view. Woser, who received all of his education in Chinese, believes that the sidelining of Tibetan is unavoidable: 'the nature of Chinese society is Han Chauvinism. If you do not voluntarily assimilate yourself to Chinese society, you cannot go further.' Pema Tso said, 'preservation and promotion of Chone Tibetan is impossible. In the future, Chone Tibetan will only be spoken in the deep and remote valleys.' However, the majority of Chone Tibetans, including Pema Tso, are confident in the resilience and value of Amdo Tibetan. They believe that Amdo Tibetan, with the support of the state and its large number of speakers, will continue to be promoted widely. When asked if Tibetan classes would be offered in the future at the request of parents for the sake of preserving their ethnic and cultural identity in Yarru village, a government official replied, 'virtually impossible, since Chone Tibetans' linguistic environment has already become unfavorable. Nothing can be changed and Chone Tibetans are greatly Sinicized.'

What remains appears to be an almost hopeless situation for the historic language of Chone. Last year, with the equivalent of USD $8,000 of funding from the office of Cultural Affairs of Gansu Province, Chone Tibetans in Yarru village started to preserve their linguistic and cultural identity through the learning and preservation of Shépa, an important local oral tradition. However, because it was a voluntary activity, only those who understood Chone Tibetan participated in the cultural activities. Also, since almost all of the participants were illiterate in written Tibetan, they learned and documented the songs by writing the Tibetan lyrics in Chinese characters based only and incorrectly on their phonetic resemblance to Tibetan words. Therefore, to what extent and how effectively Chone Tibetans can revitalize their heritage language through the learning, preservation, and revitalization of Shépa remains an open question.

Conclusion

To conclude, the language policy of the People's Republic of China has shaped the Chone Tibetan language and ideologies around its use and future. Through examining the state's language policies as they have played out in Chone post-1953 and delineating Chone Tibetans' language practices and language ideologies, it is evident that the state's coercive language policies and the understandable willingness shown by Chone Tibetans to adopt new languages work together to contribute to a three-tiered linguistic hierarchy. This linguistic hierarchy positions Chinese and Amdo Tibetan above Chone Tibetan — albeit with Chinese firmly situated above Amdo Tibetan — with the result that Chone Tibetan faces a dual linguistic hegemony. This hierarchy has also shaped the language practices and beliefs of Chone Tibetans, and has led them to internalize a sense of linguistic fatalism towards their heritage language and reconcile themselves to its inevitable demise.

We hope that our research contributes to an emerging and necessary conversation about linguistic diversity within cultural Tibet, and helps to improve the visibility and viability of the varieties and dialects of Tibetan, each of which are distinct markers of identity and cultural expression. We also call for an approach to dialect documentation and preservation that is situated within the broader goal of minority language preservation in cultural Tibet. In the meantime, we hope that our work contributes methodological approaches and analytical advancements to research on minority language standardization processes, through our examination of the inherent tensions within such processes and through our discussion of how communities interact with minority language standardization projects.

References

Aronowitz, Stanley. 2002. 'Gramsci's Theory of Education: Schooling and Beyond', in *Gramsci and Education*, ed. by Carmel Borg, Joseph Buttigieg, and Peter Mayo (Lanham, MD: Rowman & Littlefield), pp. 109–20.

Beckett, Gulbahar H and Postiglione, Gerard A. 2012. 'China's Language Policy for Indigenous and Minority Education', in *China's Assimilationist Language Policy: The Impact on Indigenous/Minority Literacy and Social Harmony*, ed. by Gulbahar H. Beckett and Gerard A. Postiglione (London: Routledge), pp. 3–17.

Brunstad, Endre, 'Standard Language and Linguistic Purism', *Sociolinguistica* 17 (1) (2003): 52–70.

Bulag, Uradyn E. 2003. 'Mongolian Ethnicity and Linguistic Anxiety in China', *American Anthropologist* 105 (4): 753–63.

Carlucci, Alessandro. 2013. *Gramsci and Languages: Unification, Diversity, Hegemony* (Leiden: Brill).

Choephel Gedun, 1978. *The White Annals*, trans. by Samten Norboo (Dharamsala: Library of Tibetan Works and Archives).

Chone Education Bureau. 2011. *Zhuoni Xian Jiaoyuzhi* [*Chone Educational Gazetteer*] (Lanzhou: Beichen Printing House).

Chone Gazetteer Compilation Committee. 1994. *Zhuoni Xianzhi* [*Chone Gazetteer*] (Lanzhou: Gansu Nationalities Publishing House).

Chone Historical Accounts Compilation Committee. 1984. *Zhuoni Wenshi Ziliao Xuanji, Diyiji* [*Chone Historical Accounts, Vol. 1*] (Internal Materials).

de Varennes, Fernand. 2012. 'Language Rights and Tibetans in China: A Look at International Law', in *Minority Language in Today's Global Society*, ed. by Kunsang Gya, Andrea Snavely and Elliot Sperling (New York: Trace Foundation), pp. 14–61.

Dwyer, Arienne. 1998. 'The Texture of Tongues: Languages and Power in China', *Nationalism and Ethnic Politics* 4 (1–2): 68–85.

Dwyer, Arienne. 2005. *The Xinjiang Conflict: Uyghur Identity, Language Policy, and Political Discourse* (Washington, D.C.: East-West Center Washington).

Eriksen, Thomas Hylland. 1992. 'Linguistic Hegemony and Minority Resistance', *Journal of Peace Research* 29 (3): 313–32.

The Ethnic Affairs Commission of Gansu Province, 1996. *Gansusheng Gannan Zangzu Zizhizhou Zangyuyan Wenzi Gongzuo Tiaoli* [*Regulations on Tibetan Language Use in Kanlho Tibetan Autonomous Prefecture of Gansu Province*].

Harrell, Stevan. 1993. 'Linguistics and Hegemony in China', *International Journal of the Sociology of Language* 103: 97–114.

Ives, Peter. 2004. *Language and Hegemony in Gramsci* (London: Pluto Press).

Kolås, Åshild and Thowsen, Monika P. 2005. *On the Margins of Tibet: Cultural Survival on the Sino-Tibetan Frontier* (Seattle: University of Washington Press).

Kroskrity, Paul V. 2000. 'Regimenting Languages: Language Ideological Perspectives', in *Regimes of Language: Ideologies, Polities, and Identities*, ed. by Paul V. Kroskrity (Santa Fe: School of American Research Press), pp. 1–34.

Li, Xulian and Huang, Quanxi. 2004. 'The Introduction and Development of the Zhuang Writing System', in *Language Policy in the People's Republic of China: Theory and Practice since 1949*, ed. by Minglang Zhou and Hongkai Sun (Boston: Kluwer Academic Publishers), pp. 239–56.

Li, Xulian and He, Siyuan. 2014. 'An Overview of Ethnic Language Affairs', in *The Language Situation in China*, ed. by Yuming Li and Wei Li, Vol. 2 (Berlin: De Gruyter Mouton), pp. 25–31.

Lipman, Jonathan N. 1997. *Familiar Strangers: A History of Muslims in Northwest China* (Seattle: University of Washington Press).

Macedo, Donaldo, Bessie Dendrinos and Panayota Gounari. 2003. *The Hegemony of English* (Boulder: Paradigm Publishers).

The Ministry of Education of the People's Republic of China, 1993. *Saochu Wenmang Gongzuo Tiaoli* [*Regulations on the Eradication of Illiteracy*].

The People's Congress of Gansu Province. 2010. *Gansusheng Gannan Zangzu Zizhizhou Tiaoli (xiuding)* [*Autonomy Statute of Kanlho Tibetan Autonomous Prefecture of Gansu Province*].

Prins, Marielle. 2002. 'Toward a Tibetan Common Language: Amdo Perspective on Attempts at Language Standardisation', in *Amdo Tibetans in Transition: Society and Culture in the Post-Mao Era*, ed. by Toni Huber (Leiden: Brill), pp. 27–51.

Roche, Gerald. 2017. 'Introduction: Translanguaging in Song: Orature and Plurilingualism in Northeast Tibet', in *Long Narrative Songs from the Mongghul of Northeast Tibet: Texts in Mongghul, Chinese, and English*, trans. by Limusishiden and ed. by Gerald Roche (Cambridge, UK: Open Book Publishers), pp. 1–25, https://doi.org.10.11647/OBP.0124; https://www.openbookpublishers.com/product/638

Rock, Joseph F. 1933. 'The Land of the Tebbus', *The Geographical Journal* 81 (2): 108–27.

Rohsenow, John S. 2004. 'Fifty Years of Script and Written Language Reform in the PRC: The Genesis of the Language Law of 2001', in *Language Policy in the People's Republic of China: Theory and Practice Since 1949*, ed. by Minglang Zhou and Hongkai Sun (Boston: Kluwer Academic Publishers), pp. 21–43.

Spolsky, Bernard. 2014. 'Language Management in the People's Republic of China', *Language* 90 (4): e165-e179.

Suarez, Debra. 2002. 'The Paradox of Linguistic Hegemony and the Maintenance of Spanish as a Heritage Language in the United States', *Journal of Multilingual and Multilingual Development* 23 (6): 512–30.

Suzuki, Hiroyuki. 2016. 'Tibetan Dialectology and Linguistic Maps: How to Deal with "Khams Dialect"', *Journal of Ethnology* 7 (2): 1–13.

The Tibetan Language Committee of Kanlho Tibetan Autonomous Prefecture. 2006. *Gansusheng Gannan Zangzu Zizhizhou Zangyuyan Wenzi Gongzuo Tiaoli Shishi Xize* [*Implementation Rules for the Regulations on Tibetan Language Use in Kanlho Tibetan Autonomous Prefecture of Gansu Province*] (Internal Materials).

Tournadre, Nicolas. 2014. 'The Tibetic Languages and Their Classification', in *Trans-Himalayan Linguistics: Historical and Descriptive Linguistics of the*

Himalayan Area, ed. by Thomas Owen-Smith and Nathan W. Hill (Berlin: De Gruyter Mouton), pp. 105–30.

Turin, Mark 2014. 'Mother Tongues and Language Competence: The Shifting Politics of Linguistic Belonging in the Himalayas', in *Facing Globalization in the Himalayas: Belonging and the Politics of the Self: Governance, Conflict and Civic Action*, ed. by Gérard Toffin and Joanna Pfaff-Czarnecka, Vol. 5 (Delhi: Sage), pp. 372–96.

Turin, Mark. 2018. 'On Linguistic Borders: Official Language Policy in Settler-Colonial Nations', *Border Bites* 8: 1–10.

Wang, Hui and Zhongrui Yuan. 2013 'The Promotion of Putonghua (Mandarin Chinese): An Overview', in *The Language Situation in China*, ed. by Yuming Li and Wei Li, Vol. 1 (Berlin: De Gruyter Mouton), pp. 27–39.

Wang, Kefeng. 2013. 'Gansu Taozhou Fangyan Chengyin Tanxi. [Probing into the Formation of Taozhou Dialect of Gansu]', *Journal of Northwest University for Nationalities* 5: 158–62.

Wiley, Terrence G. 1996. 'Language Planning and Policy', in *Sociolinguistics and Language Teaching*, ed. by Sandra Lee Mckay and Nancy H. Hornberger (Cambridge: Cambridge University Press), pp. 103–47.

Woolard, Kathryn A. 1985. 'Language Variation and Cultural Hegemony: Toward an Integration of Sociolinguistic and Social Theory', *American Ethnologist* 12 (4): 738–48.

Yang, Miaoyan. 2017. *Learning to Be Tibetan: The Construction of Ethnic Identity at Minzu University of China* (Lanham, MD: Lexington Books).

Yang, Shihong. 1990. *Zhuoni Yang Tusi Zhuanlue* [*The Biographies of Chone Yang Chiefs*] (Sichuan: Sichuan Nationality Press).

Zhou, Maocao. 2004. 'The Use and Development of Tibetan in China', in *Language Policy in the People's Republic of China: Theory and Practice Since 1949*, ed. by Minglang Zhou and Hongkai Sun (Boston: Kluwer Academic Publishers), pp. 221–37.

Zhou, Minglang. 2003. *Multilingualism in China: The Politics of Writing Reforms for Minority Languages 1949–2002* (Berlin and New York: De Gruyter Mouton).

Zhou, Minglang. 2005. 'Legislating Literacy for Linguistic and Ethnic Minorities in Contemporary China', *Current Issues in Language Planning* 6(2): 102–21.

Zhou, Minglang. 2012. 'Historical Review of the PRC's Minority/Indigenous Language Policy and Practice: Nation-state Building and Identity Construction', in *China's Assimilationist Language Policy: The Impact on Indigenous/Minority Literacy and Social Harmony*, ed. by Gulbahar H. Beckett and Gerard A. Postiglione (London: Routledge), pp. 18–30.

6. Concluding Thoughts on Language Shift and Linguistic Diversity in the Himalaya
The Case of Nepal

Mark Turin

Location: The Greater Himalayan Region.
Topic: Language.
Status: It's complicated.

The process of building nations has involved the reimagining, recreating and repositioning of the language or languages that are spoken within, and sometimes across, national borders. Across the Himalaya, speech communities hailing from genetically unrelated languages have been in contact with one another across large periods of modern history — for reasons of trade, political alliance and interethnic ritual practice. However, prolonged language contact and even cohabitation did not historically result in large-scale language shift. Rather, the move from plurilingual spoken realities to more homogenous and increasingly monolingual linguistic identities is a central and even coercive feature of modern nation-building, and not an accidental byproduct of its success. Moreover, as the contributions in this volume show, the container of the 'nation-state' is not always the sole category to consider.

Nation-building projects can not only objectify languages through documentation, but may also inhibit the spread of some speech forms in the name of elevating a favored vernacular to the status of national or official language. We should recall that all projects involving ethnic categorization and linguistic classification are fraught with taxonomic, political and ideological problems, often compressing complex and highly local ethnolinguistic identities into standardized checkboxes. The tensions between competing frameworks of recognition are well-documented across the states that make up the Greater Himalayan Region (cf. Shneiderman 2015), and these intersect with ongoing national enumerative instruments such as decadal censuses and modern linguistic surveys in curious, and often complex, ways.

The Greater Himalayan Region extends for 3,500 km from Afghanistan in the west to Myanmar in the east, sustaining over 150 million people and is home to great linguistic diversity, including many of Asia's most endangered languages. Often described as one of the ten biodiversity 'mega centers' of the world, the area could also be thought of as a linguistic and cultural 'mega center', being home to one-sixth of all human languages (Turin 2007). Yet, despite this variety, many of the region's speech communities — variously understood as communities of subjects, citizens or even stateless individuals — are rapidly shifting from speaking traditionally unwritten and increasingly endangered vernaculars to regional, national and even international languages of prestige that carry with them the promise of economic benefit and political access. Communities that were once multilingual are becoming functionally bilingual and, in some cases, even monolingual, with the move from oral speech forms to written languages often that of replacement rather than of addition. At the same time, we must recognize that in hierarchically organized polities — whether these are stratified by caste, class or ethnicity — elites often have the privilege of remaining functionally and comfortably monolingual in the official, national language, while non-elite communities are more commonly and necessarily multilingual, switching register or shifting language entirely in order to access state services.

As we learn from the five contributions that together form this collection, language shift across the Himalaya is complex, uneven and highly specific, as attentive to grand historical processes as it is to granular local conditions. Language shift has been variously understood, but is commonly characterized as a process in which both *langue* and *parole* are systematically simplified. Individuals move from functioning as full speakers of a given language with complete grammatical and pragmatic command to being 'semi-speakers' with reduced verbal dexterity. Eventually, all competence drains away, leaving only a residual smattering of specialized vocabulary (often, but not always, food words, kinship terminology, or elements of ritual vocabulary), combined with a strong sense of attachment to a heritage identity as a former speaker.

For example, in the case of the Ahom in what is now Northeastern India, so insightfully outlined by Selma K. Sonntag in the second chapter, language shift from the Tai-Kadai language to Assamese, an Indo-Aryan language, occurred in the precolonial seventeenth century, creating a 'rupture in the language regime.' This move was both 'reified under the colonial language regime' and even helped to set 'the stage for post-colonial linguistic nationalism in Assam.' For contemporary self-identified Ahom who are now working to revitalize (and in the process, inevitably reimagine) their ancestral language, language shift is located in the past, and understood to be a historical rather than modern-day process. Similarly, language shift in Northern Pakistan is no recent phenomenon. Since the Pashtun invasion of Swat and Bajaur in the fifteenth century, Pashto has spread at the expense of more traditional languages, such as Domaakí and Gawri (Weinreich 2010).

By contrast, in the Tibetan cultural zone that extends across and beyond the borders of the People's Republic of China, Tibetan-speaking communities are responding to multiple and overlapping linguistic pressures that threaten the viability of the many regional Tibetan variants. Such processes include state-sponsored Sinification (within China at least) that positions Mandarin as the expected language of upward mobility and access; national language policies of India and Nepal that prioritize English, Hindi and Nepali respectively, where many Tibetan communities are resident and within which they have to operate; and current language standardization campaigns that position central, Lhasa Tibetan or other dominant regional variants as the optimal (and in some cases the only) acceptable form of the Tibetan language. As Tunzhi (Sonam Lhundrop), Hiroyuki Suzuki and Gerald Roche detail in their contribution, and as Bendi Tso and I document in the case of Chone, there is a pervading sense across the Tibetan-speaking realm that while all variants of Tibetan are putatively equal, some are more equal than others.

While the contributors all focus on communities who are visible to the state — sometimes, arguably, too legible — as co-editors of the volume, we have asked ourselves whether stateless peoples engage in or are swept up by language shift in the same way as state citizens are. We may spare a thought for the Rohingya in particular, 700,000 of whom have been forced to escape violence in Myanmar by fleeing to Bangladesh while thousands have been massacred in villages before they could flee. The Rohingya language, although part of the Indo-Aryan sub-branch of the greater Indo-European language family and related to the Chittagonian language spoken in the southern-most corner of Bangladesh, is not mutually intelligible with Bengali, and most Rohingya do not speak Burmese fluently, the *lingua franca* of Myanmar. Excluded from full participation in the Burmese state on the basis of ancestry, religion and culture, and not officially recognized as one of Burma's 'major national ethnic races', the plight of the Rohingya has given Myanmar the dubious honor of being the nation with the world's highest percentage of non-citizens in its population (cf. Bialystok 2011).

Other nations in the Himalayan region have also used culture and language as tools for social exclusion and political disenfranchisement. We need look no further than the case of the Lhotshampa of Bhutan — a nation missing from this edited collection and therefore worth noting in these concluding remarks — for a compelling illustration for how language became instrumentalized as a way to dispossess a people. In his powerfully titled *Unbecoming Citizens*, Michael Hutt documents Bhutan's demotion of the Nepali language that started in 1989. Until 1964, Hindi was the medium of instruction in schools across Bhutan, in part due to the absence of suitable curriculum in any other language, but also on account of a shortage of Bhutanese teachers. As a consequence, a large number of Hindi-speaking (and writing) Indian teachers were employed in Bhutan's government schools (Hutt 2003: 138). In 1964, English took the place of Hindi as the medium of instruction, and Bhutanese teachers were to trained to replace Indians as the pedagogical staff in the nation's schools. While Hutt is careful to describe Bhutan's language policy of the 1960s as 'pragmatic' (2003: 179), he draws attention to a growing sense of unease in Bhutan about the government's avowed, public and deepening commitment to Dzongkha on the one hand, and its chance of 'ever becoming a fully-fledged national language on the other' (2003: 180).

Over time, Hutt presents Bhutan's otherwise 'easy-going attitude to language matters' as becoming distinctly 'less compromising' (2003: 183), particularly as the prevalence of Nepali continued to rise. Even though the Bhutan Broadcasting Service (BBS) continues to this day to broadcast in Nepali, and *Kuensel*, the national newspaper, is still committed to printing a Nepali-language edition, the teaching of Nepali was discontinued at the beginning of the school year in 1989, and 'all curricular materials were removed from Bhutanese schools' at the same time (Hutt 2003: 183).[1] While linguist George van Driem does not dispute the fact that the Nepali language was eliminated from Bhutan's schools by 1990, he offers a very different interpretation of the intent and reasoning behind this change in national language policy, offering three reasons why the new measure was 'not directly connected with the southern problem' (1994: 101).[2] First, he argues, the use of Nepali in the south of Bhutan was 'counter-productive to the advancement of the national language'; second, Nepali was being unfairly privileged over other 'originally allochthonous' languages, a position not enjoyed by any other tongue and thus a situation which required balancing; and finally, given Bhutan's limited resources, the strategic priority for the nation had to be the development of modern curricula content in Dzongkha and English over Nepali, a process in which he himself participated (van Driem 1994: 101–2).

This period of modern Bhutanese history remains complex and contested, and the issue of whether Nepali was ever truly a medium of instruction or simply a subject in schools in Bhutan's southern belt remains unresolved. More germane to the current discussion, however, is that speaking Nepali, and a specific variant of Nepali in particular, became a diagnostic marker of identity and group membership for Lhotshampa. The vocabulary differences between modern Nepali as spoken in Nepal and the variant spoken in Bhutan were deemed to be significant enough that they served as the basis for a linguistic test

---

1   Hutt reports allegations of some schools disposing of their books by burning them in bonfires (2003: 185).
2   Euphemistically referred to as the 'southern problem', van Driem is referring the forced exodus and expulsion of tens of thousands of ethnic Nepalis from the primarily southern districts of Bhutan by the state in response to growing concerns about preserving the country's unique national, cultural, linguistic and religious identity.

to ascertain whether individuals claiming political asylum in Europe were indeed credible Lhotshampa from Bhutan (people of Nepalese ancestry who grew up in Bhutan) or citizens of Nepal dissembling as Bhutanese refugees in order to game the system and find safe passage to the European Union. Linguistic assessments — albeit of aptitude rather than critical examinations of dialect variation — are used by nations as part of their 'naturalization' test for aspiring citizens. In such instances, nation-states require that candidates demonstrate a communicative competence in the national language, with the ability to speak a certain language serving as a gatekeeping device to determine and grant membership of a nation.

Documenting, analyzing and historicizing patterns of language shift — alongside the changing linguistic identities that can result — are familiar territory for social scientists. Michael Noonan, writing about Chantyal-speaking villages in western Nepal, suggested that their 'relative isolation and poverty' might contribute to 'the retention of the language' (1996: 130). While outmigration may even prolong isolation for those left behind, inmigration brings individuals together in unexpected ways, sometimes creating new speech forms and often elevating regional tongues to the status of *lingua franca* or *Verkehrsprache*. As documented in Daurio's contribution to this volume, the entire Himalayan region is undergoing a period of profound social, economic and political upheaval — including but not limited to rapid urbanization, massive transformations in traditional livelihood practices and responses to ecological pressures and natural disasters. Languages and linguistic identities are also in flux, as 'language shifts are inextricably tied to shifts in the political economy in which speech situations are located' Urciuoli (1995: 530).

In a post-conflict era that has intersected with a national reconstruction project following the catastrophic earthquakes that rocked the country in April and May 2015, the newly minted Federal Democratic Republic of Nepal is grappling with the political complexity of contemporary language policy. Constitutions are powerful and aspirational framing documents, helping to 'constitute' the basis of the polity in which people live. The 2015 Constitution of Nepal recognizes all languages autochthonous to the nation as 'mother tongues' but elevates Nepali to the level of official language of the nation:

> All languages spoken as the mother tongues in Nepal are the languages of the nation, and the Nepali language in the Devanagari script shall be the official language of Nepal. In addition to the Nepali Language, a province shall select one or more additional languages that is spoken by the majority of people in that province as the language of official business, as provided for by provincial law.

We may ask what this really means. Is the framing of this foundational article of Nepal's constitution an example of fast footwork and intellectual agility on the part of the drafters of the document — an intentional and deliberately scripted ambiguity — or is it rather just a sign of muddled thinking, setting Nepal's citizens up for a prolonged period of confusion, contestation and legal wrangling about language? One inference is beyond doubt: in Nepal, Nepali remains firmly entrenched as the first among equals, paradoxically the same as — and yet substantively different to — the more than a hundred other languages spoken within Nepal's borders. This is a compelling demonstration of the 'tension' between language shift and language documentation and enumeration in this fast-changing nation, a tension that lies at the heart of all of the contributions to this volume.

Nepal needs a language to talk about language. Enumerating and then classifying people's mother tongues on a scale from *boli* to *bhasa*, spoken to written, or endangered to safe won't be enough. At both practical and theoretical levels, whether Nepal has 90 or 150 languages is at once beside the point and illustrative of the rigidity of officializing and recognizing frameworks. All Nepalis know that one language is dominant in politics, culture and media. Nepali — that supra-national language — functions as the lingua franca for much of the nation, and boasts millions of fluent speakers across northern India, most of Bhutan and even Cultural Tibet. Nepali is now a language with global reach: heard on the streets of London and the restaurants of New York, as well as in Lhasa and Manipur.

Over time, as language and belonging become reinscribed by each generation, communities may start thinking of their language as a *bhasa* rather than as a *boli*. An interesting example provided by the 2011 Census of Nepal is the 'emergence' of languages such as Doteli (at around 3.2% of the total population), Baitadeli (around 1%), Achhami and Bajhangi (around 0.1%), which were likely grouped together with Nepali in earlier decadal enumerations in response to the question of 'What is your primary language'. Indeed, these speech forms were entirely absent from prior censuses despite accounting for over 5% of the total population. A growing ethnolinguistic awareness of the political utility of distinct linguistic identities, combined with an emergent set of benefits that accord to diverse communities, are likely a major part of the explanation for the sharp increase in the number of languages reported as 'mother tongue' in more recent population censuses in Nepal. This newfound strategic visibility is yet another persuasive validation of how, over time, the relationship between language enumeration and language shift is changing. At present, languages such as Doteli, Baitadeli, Achhami and Bajhangi — to mention but a few — are not new additions to Nepal's already densely packed linguistic environment. Rather, these languages have long 'existed' but have only recently been visible to enumerators and strategically valuable to communities of speakers.

Interesting historical trends become apparent from a cursory look at the last three decadal population censuses, from 1991, 2001 and 2011. While the share of the population that report Nepali as their first language has dropped sharply from 51% to 44% between 2001 and 2011 (possibly because languages like Doteli have undergone an internal as well as external transformation from *boli* to *bhasa* and are now 'legible' to the state in ways that they were not before), the other major language-shares have remained largely stable. Despite the social anxiety and political panic about Hindi and English encroaching upon Nepali, the shares for both are stable or in decline: Hindi has decreased as a 'mother tongue' from 0.92% in 1991 to 0.29% in 2011, while English has remained stable at around 0.01%. The moral panic articulated by some over the perceived decline in the use of Nepali may not actually reflect less Nepali 'use' but rather a newfound visibility for historically underrepresented languages. National identity politics, then, is as vulnerable to existential and perceived threats as it is to tangible and real ones.

Globalization is regularly, and often uncritically, pilloried as a major threat to linguistic diversity. But in fact, globalization is as much process as it is ideology, certainly when it comes to language. The real forces behind cultural homogenization are unbending beliefs, exchanged through a globalized delivery system, reinforced by the historical monolingualism prevalent in much of the West and rolled out through imperial adventure and colonization. As a force, globalization is causing realignments in the relationship between language shift and language enumeration through documentary and classificatory projects. Just as there is a campaign to officialize and strengthen English in the United States, led by shrill and reactionary voices who perceive this most globalizing of languages to be under threat, so too the Nepali language has powerful advocates who declare the need to support it with additional protective legislation. And herein lies the irony: the worries of Nepali being eroded or diminished through the encroachment of English or Hindi echo the genuine alarm expressed by speakers of Nepal's Indigenous (and increasingly endangered) languages, who themselves fear being overwhelmed by Nepali. A language that appears to be vulnerable from one perspective is perceived as hegemonic from another, as is clear from the chapters in this volume that address the complexity of the Tibetan cultural area and its associated linguistic landscape.

As this volume was heading to the press, Nepal was at a pivotal political moment with regard to language. First, in whatever federal reconfiguration lies ahead following the decade-long civil war that raged from 1996–2006 and the catastrophic earthquakes that shattered large swathes of central Nepal in 2015, the polity will have to consider whether languages other than Nepali will be resourced and supported so that communities can live, work and represent themselves in their mother tongues. This question goes beyond the right of accessing legal representation in, for example, Maithili or Nepal Bhasa (Ojha 2017), and lies at the core of Nepal's understanding of itself as a nation. Will Tamang serve as the medium of instruction in schools in Province No. 3 or only a subject? Will airlines flying to Lukla make safety announcements in Sherpa alongside Nepali and English? Will government websites be translated into and made accessible in some of Nepal's most widely used native languages that have written traditions? Will ATMs offer users cash in Nepal Bhasa in Bhaktapur, in the same way that cash dispenser in Hawai'i offer an Ōlelo Hawai'i language option?

Second, as Nepal's Language Commission gains momentum in accordance with Article 287 of the Constitution, and exercises its mandate to recommend measures to be adopted for the protection, promotion and development of languages, it would be well advised to explore how similar processes have played out in New Zealand, Canada, Myanmar and India. Language Commissions and Language Authorities have a unique opportunity to reset language planning in a nation, but need to determine whether their mandate is proscriptive (citizens *must*...) or descriptive (citizens *already do*...). Is a one, two or three language formula appropriate and deliverable in Nepal, or are there other options as yet unexplored? Technology is an increasingly important element to consider, certainly for those Nepalis whose use of and interest in mobile and digital tools provides a huge opportunity for nurturing language diversity and supporting language mobilization.

Third, educational policy needs to embrace this digital turn, and focus not only on traditional textbook creation in Nepal's many mother tongues (as outlined in Pradhan's contribution) but on multimedia content that can be delivered through e-learning systems to schools in remote districts as so compellingly illustrated by the success of OLE Nepal.[3] Given that the penetration of mobile telephony has been a singular success story for Nepal over the last decade, now is an opportune time to create content to back it up. Nepal's infrastructure backbone is increasingly digital, and can be used to reflect the nation's diverse and vibrant multilingualism. Tools of globalization like the internet, so often blamed for homogenizing the world, are also enabling diverse and geographically dislocated language communities to connect across time and place.

Overall, Nepal — like many of regions and nations discussed in earlier chapters of this collection — needs to come to terms with its own multilingualism, both historic and contemporary, and find ways to recognize creative innovation even when these actions are not sanctioned by the state or explicitly contradict national policy. In her recent work on the Kumaun region of North India, Cynthia Groff explores the ways in which the lived multilingual reality quietly subverts national language

---

3   Open Learning Exchange Nepal (OLE Nepal) is a social benefit organization dedicated to enhancing education quality and access through the integration of technology in classrooms. Since its inception in 2007, OLE Nepal has pioneered the use of technology in schools and provided open and free access to quality education and innovative learning environments to children. Its education-focused free and open digital library, E-Pustakalaya, provides access to a collection of thousands of books and educational resources, course content and reference materials and has been installed in low power servers and deployed in schools and community libraries across the nation. See http://www.olenepal.org

policies, noting that the 'Kumauni example demonstrates how local ideologies and perspectives can preserve spaces for minoritized linguistic varieties regardless of official policy: spaces for unofficial mother tongue, unofficial media of instruction, and additive notions of multilingualism' (2018: 17). Language practice and mobilization in Nepal has long been similarly subversive, whether in the home, the community or the school, and Nepal has never been and likely will never be a monolingual nation in which one language is used exclusively for all interactions — whether in person, in print, online or on air.

Nepal's celebrated non-colonization by outside forces has helped lay the foundation for the extraordinary diversity of cultural and linguistic expressions to endure, although 100 years of Rana rule and more recent nation-building ideologies have done much to erode this very diversity and uniqueness. Nepal's multilingualism can help its citizens prepare to live in an ever more connected and interdependent world, particularly in the face of the inevitability of language change and ever-increasing language contact. Across the global north, parents anxiously encourage their children to learn another language in school because their daily lives are so deafeningly monolingual and they see tactical and intellectual benefit in speaking more than one language (Bialystok 2011). Multilingual and culturally diverse Nepal is already ahead of the curve on this, and well positioned to lead a global discussion on language, identity and belonging in education, administration and governance.

Although Nepal (a diverse nation state home to many ethnolinguistic communities) and Sikkim (India's least populous and second smallest state) differ massively in scale and in their historical trajectories, there is a certain utility in comparing the two because their populations continue to draw on similar narratives of belonging and linguistic association, in large part because of the common geographies and cultural histories that they share. One notable difference between Nepal and Sikkim, however, is in their experience of migration: Nepal has a tradition of 'sending' migrants, whereas Sikkim is a state that has accepted and 'received' them, even building itself on their labor. In Sikkim, the process of language shift is popularly presented as an unavoidable byproduct of the juggernaut of global progress and development, while in Nepal, the continued vibrancy of minority mother tongues has been associated with their remote and sequestered status. This opposition, at least in the popular imagination, is fleshed out to the extent that Sikkim is often imagined to be modern, literate, educated, and connected, whereas the ethnolinguistic homeland areas of Nepal — from which many contemporary Sikkimese residents derive their ancestry — are described as remote, backward, and traditional. My point here is not to endorse such descriptions, but to reflect on them for what they tell us about the different and changing language regimes that individuals and communities have been subjected to and participate in, and what these ideological formulations tell us about the different nation-building exercise in Nepal and India. As competence in Sikkim's traditional mother tongues has declined, their status has begun to shift from spoken vernaculars forming part of a lived ethnic identity to symbolic markers of an ancestral linguistic heritage. I would argue that in the language shift I observed in Sikkim, a growing attachment to the 'idea' of a mother tongue is directly related to its decline in use as a speech form.

Monolingualism — the condition of being able to speak only one language — is regularly accompanied by a deep-seated conviction in the value of that language over all others. Across the largest economies of the world, being monolingual is still often the norm, with multilingualism appearing unusual and even somewhat exotic (Turin 2013). This monolingual mindset stands in sharp contrast to the lived reality of most of the Greater Himalayan Region, which throughout its modern history and into the present has been more resolutely multilingual than unilingual. Through this collection of five essays, and Selma Sonntag's rich introduction, we learn that communities across the Greater Himalayan Region have complex and contingent linguistic identities that are rarely if ever predicated on a sole speech form, even if the states in which they live assume that ideal linguistic identities are homogenous and monolingual. The linguistic future of the Himalayan region is yet to be written, and only time tell whether its historic multilingualism will endure and outlive the narrow ruptures of nationalism.

Acknowledgements

My thinking in this contribution has been heavily influenced by substantive and stimulating conversation with my co-editor, Selma

K. Sonntag, enriched by discussions with Apoorva Lal, and further fine-tuned thanks to welcome and probing suggestions made by Erin Guntly, our tireless copyeditor. Needless to say, all remaining errors, misrepresentations and infelicities remain my own.

References

Bialystok, Ellen. 2011. 'Reshaping the Mind: The Benefits of Bilingualism', *Canadian Journal of Experimental Psychology/Revue canadienne de psychologie experimentale* 65 (4): 229–35.

van Driem, George. 1994. 'Language Policy in Bhutan', in *Bhutan: Aspects of Culture and Development*, ed. by Michael Aris and Michael Hutt (Gartmore: Kiscadale Publications), pp. 87–105.

Garcia, Nuria. 2015. 'State Tradition, Language, and Education Policies in France', in *State Traditions and Language Regimes*, ed. by Linda Cardinal and Selma K. Sonntag (Montreal: McGill-Queens University Press), pp. 219–36.

Groff, Cynthia. 2018. 'Language Policy and Language Ideology: Ecological Perspectives on Language and Education in the Himalayan Foothills'. *Anthropology & Education Quarterly* 49 (1): 3–20.

Hutt, Michael. 2003. *Unbecoming Citizens: Culture, Nationhood, and the Flight of Refugees from Bhutan* (Delhi: Oxford University Press).

Noonan, Michael. 1996. 'The Fall and Rise and Fall of the Chantyal Language', *Southwest Journal of Linguistics* 15 (1–2): 121–35.

Ojha, Anup. 2017. 'Nepal Bhasa as Official Language in Metropolis', *The Kathmandu Post* (22 June), https://kathmandupost.ekantipur.com/printedition/news/2017-06-22/nepal-bhasa-as-official-language-in-metropolis.html

Shneiderman, Sara. 2015. *Rituals of Ethnicity Rituals of Ethnicity: Thangmi Identities Between Nepal and India* (Philadelphia: University of Pennsylvania Press).

Turin, Mark. 2014. 'Mother Tongues and Language Competence: The Shifting Politics of Linguistic Belonging in the Himalayas', in *Facing Globalization in the Himalayas: Belonging and the Politics of the Self: Governance, Conflict, and Civic Action*, ed. by G. Toffin and J. Pfaff-Czarnecka, Vol. 5 (Dehli: Sage Publications), pp. 371–96.

Turin, Mark. 2013. 'Globalization Helps Preserve Endangered Languages' YaleGlobal Online, https://yaleglobal.yale.edu/content/globalization-helps-preserve-endangered-languages

Turin, Mark. 2007. Linguistic Diversity and the Preservation of Endangered Languages: A Case Study from Nepal. *Talking Points* 4 (07) (Kathmandu: International Centre for Integrated Mountain Development (ICIMOD)), http://www.digitalhimalaya.com/projectteam/turin/downloads/Talking_Points.pdf

Urciuoli, Bonnie. 1995. 'Language and Borders', *Annual Review of Anthropology* 24: 525–46.

Weinreich, Matthias. 2010. 'Language Shift in Northern Pakistan: The Case of Domaakí and Pashto', *Iran & the Caucasus* 14 (1): 43–56.

List of Tables and Figures

Introduction

Fig. 0.1	Map of the Himalaya region: areas discussed in this volume highlighted in blue. Created by Meredith Reba, CC BY.	1

Chapter 1

Table 1.1	Changes in the meaning of Hor over time.	25
Fig. 1.1	Map of Tibet with cultural regions and prefectures. Created by the authors, CC BY.	21

Chapter 3

Table 3.1	List of mother-tongue textbooks used in the Jana Kalyan Higher Secondary School (JKHSS). Published jointly by the (JKHSS), the United Mission to Nepal (UMN) and the government of Nepal.	87
Fig. 3.1	Mother-tongue textbooks in Tharu and Awadi. Photograph supplied by the author with the consent of the textbook publishers, CC BY.	88
Fig. 3.2	Math textbook, lesson 5, page 5. Photograph supplied by the author with the consent of the textbook publishers, CC BY.	89

Fig. 3.3	Class 2 Tharu textbook, lesson 10, page 33. Photograph supplied by the author with the consent of the textbook publishers, CC BY.	91
Fig. 3.4	Class 2 Awadhi textbook, lesson 3, page 68. Photograph supplied by the author with the consent of the textbook publishers, CC BY.	92
Fig. 3.5	Class 2 Awadhi textbook, lesson 16, page 54. Photograph supplied by the author with the consent of the textbook publishers, CC BY.	96
Fig. 3.6	Class 2 Awadhi textbook, lesson 3 page 66. Photograph supplied by the author with the consent of the textbook publishers, CC BY.	97
Fig. 3.7	Class II social studies textbook, lesson 2, page 40, written in Tharu, Awadhi and Nepali, using Devanagari script. Photograph supplied by the author with the consent of the textbook publishers, CC BY.	99

Chapter 4

Fig. 4.1	Tichurong Valley. Photograph provided by the author, CC BY.	111
Fig. 4.2	Tarang in the upper right; Tarakot in the lower left; Tupatara is to the right of Tarang out of the picture. November 2008. Photo courtesy of the author, CC BY.	114

Chapter 5

Fig. 5.1	Map of Chone County as situated within Amdo, within China. Adapted from Kolås and Thowsen (2005: 2), CC BY-NC-ND.	141

Index

adult literacy 37, 42
Ahom 11, 57
Ahom Kingdom 66, 69
   decline 65
   expansion 63
   labor 59
   language shift 64
   literary language 62
Ahom (language) 6, 8, 10, 51, 58, 61, 63–64, 66–70, 74
   written scripts 56, 60
Amdo region 21, 26–27, 140
Amdo Tibetan (language) 142, 153
Anderson, Benedict 49
Assam 52, 75, 165
Assamese 75
Awadhi 79, 81, 83, 87, 100, 102

Ban Ok Publik Muang Tai 73
Bengali 71
Bhattarai, Baburam 101
Bodo movement 73
Brahmaputra Valley 57, 59–60, 72
British colonial language policy 71
British rule in India 70
Buddhism 38, 54–55, 61, 64, 120
buranji 61, 64, 66, 69, 72

Chaudhury, Sheshram 98
China (PRC) 21, 25, 112, 137, 148, 150, 154–155, 159, 165
Chinese (language) 137, 145
Chone. *See* Chone (language)
Chone (language) 130, 158–159
   Shépa oral tradition 158

Chone region, Tibet 137, 159
   Amdo Tibetan (language) 150
   Chinese (language) 152
Chone Tibetans 137, 144
colonialism 71

Devanagari script 99–100
dialect 94, 137, 144
Dolpa district 112
Dunai, Nepal 114, 123, 127

education policy 102
   English-medium 115, 119, 123, 126, 129
Eighth Schedule (India) 70

Gansu Province 137
Gellner, Ernst 49
Gergyal Pedma 34

hierarchy 70
Hobsbawm, Eric 49
Hor, meaning of 29
Horpa 22, 29, 31, 40, 44

India 52, 57, 68–69, 75, 94–95, 114, 120, 126–127, 165, 169, 172–173
indigenous people 41, 117, 171
intergenerational transmission 131

Jones, William 68

Kaike (language) 110, 127, 130
   dictionary 122
Kaike (people). *See* Tarali
Kamarupa 59
Kanlho Tibetan Autonomous Prefecture (TAP) 137, 145

Kapilbastu 79–80, 83
Kathmandu 114, 123, 127
Khams (language) 142
Khams (region) 26, 142, 146

language 67
  and education 84
  and state 49
  attitudes towards 90, 94, 101, 128, 130, 156–157
  authority 105
  competence 93
  definition 41, 94, 98
  displacement 69
  ethnic identity 109, 130, 145
  identity 38, 146
  preservation 158
  recognition 20
  standardization 67, 145
  'standard' language 30, 41, 94, 98, 139, 153, 157
language contact 20, 40, 53, 57, 60–62, 66, 75, 85, 105, 119, 121, 138, 163, 173
  migration 110, 127, 142, 168, 173
  vertical and horizontal politics 20
language identity 49, 57, 67, 72
language ideology 39
language loss 20, 156
language maintenance 109
language policy 137
  China (PRC) 155
  education 32, 82, 104, 106, 128, 145, 153, 158, 172–173
  Nepal 82
  official language 84
  standard script 100
language politics 41, 70–71
  historical-institutional approach 50
language prestige 39
language regime 50–51, 53–55, 58, 61, 63, 66–71, 73–74, 165
language shift 20, 43, 51, 68, 143, 149, 152, 156, 163, 174
language standardization 137

linguistic assimilation 137
linguistic authority 80–81, 85, 105
linguistic diversity 83, 159
linguistic hegemony 137, 140, 156
linguistic hierarchy 138, 146
linguistic homogeneity 50
linguistic homogenization 70
linguistic hygiene. *See* verbal hygiene
linguistic nationalism 49–50
linguistic purism 157
linguistic vitality 109, 122
literacy 154
literary development 80, 95

Magar (people) 117
mandala state 57
mother tongue education 79–80
Mother Tongue Textbook Guidelines (Nepal) 102
muang 53, 57, 73
Mughals 63
multilingual education 106, 128
  textbooks 79
multilingualism 40, 42, 66, 73–75, 83, 85, 122, 128, 164, 174

nation-state model 70
Neo-Vaishnavism 64–67
Nepal 165, 174
  Constitution (1990) 82
  National Language Policy Commission 93
  National Language Policy Recommendations Commission 85
  School Sector Reform Plan 82
Nepali 106, 131, 173

Old Tibetan 31
orthography 93

padi state. *See* mandala state
Pali Buddhism 61
Pedma Trashi (Pad ma bkra shis) 33
Pöke (language) 119
politics of language 20

Pollock, Sheldon 52
power dynamics 121
power hierarchies 40
Putonghua. *See* Chinese (language)

rTa'u (language) 43
  attitudes toward 23, 37
  writing 39
rTa'u area 37

Saikia, Yasmin 57
Sanskrit 61
Scott, James 52
Shertan 34
States Reorganization Act (India) 70
state tradition 63–64, 66–67
Surma Valley 72
surzhik 97

Tai-Ahom identity movement 73
Tai-Kadai (language) 51, 58, 62, 66, 72, 74, 165
Taozhou Chinese dialect 144
Tarai region 80
Tarali 110, 114–115, 131
Tarali diaspora 122
textbook creation 103
textbook localization 90
Thailand 53
Tharu (language) 80, 106

Tibet 20, 43, 110, 116, 122, 126, 138, 145, 159, 169
  language contact 20
Tibetan (language) 23, 40, 116, 145, 159, 165
  attitudes toward 36
  literacy 37
Tichurong Valley 114, 125, 128
traditional ecological knowledge (TEK) 128
Tripathy, Bikram 102

United Nations Declaration on the Rights of Indigenous People 104
Universal Declaration of Human Rights 104

verbal hygiene 32

WeChat 38
Wolters, Oliver 53
writing 39
  competence 93
  textbooks 90
written script 56, 101

Yarru village 144
yarsagumba 112

Zomia 52, 56, 58, 69

This book need not end here...

Share

All our books — including the one you have just read — are free to access online so that students, researchers and members of the public who can't afford a printed edition will have access to the same ideas. This title will be accessed online by hundreds of readers each month across the globe: why not share the link so that someone you know is one of them?

This book and additional content is available at:
https://doi.org/10.11647/OBP.0169

Customise

Personalise your copy of this book or design new books using OBP and third-party material. Take chapters or whole books from our published list and make a special edition, a new anthology or an illuminating coursepack. Each customised edition will be produced as a paperback and a downloadable PDF.

Find out more at:
https://www.openbookpublishers.com/section/59/1

Like Open Book Publishers

Follow @OpenBookPublish

Read more at the Open Book Publishers BLOG

You may also be interested in:

Long Narrative Songs from the Mongghul of Northeast Tibet
Texts in Mongghul, Chinese, and English

By Li Dechun (李得春, Limusishiden) and Gerald Roche

https://doi.org/10.11647/OBP.0124

Searching for Sharing
Heritage and Multimedia in Africa

Edited by Daniela Merolla and Mark Turin

https://doi.org/10.11647/OBP.0111

Mobilities, Boundaries, and Travelling Ideas
Rethinking Translocality Beyond Central Asia and the Caucasus

Edited by Manja Stephan-Emmrich and Philipp Schröder

https://doi.org/10.11647/OBP.0114

Remote Capture
Digitising Documentary Heritage in Challenging Locations

Edited by Jody Butterworth, Andrew Pearson, Patrick Sutherland and Adam Farquhar

https://doi.org/10.11647/OBP.0138

www.ingramcontent.com/pod-product-compliance
Lightning Source LLC
Chambersburg PA
CBHW042043240426
43667CB00048B/2973